ArtTalk: Instructor's Guide and Teacher Resource Book

Rosalind Ragans

GLENCOE

Macmillan/McGraw-Hill

Lake Forest, Illinois
Columbus, Ohio
Mission Hills, California
Peoria, Illinois

14.64
Net

Send all inquiries to:
GLENCOE DIVISION
Macmillan/McGraw-Hill
15319 Chatsworth Street
P.O. Box 9609
Mission Hills, CA 91346-9609

ISBN 0-02-677070-9

Printed in the United States of America.

7 8 9 10 11 12 13 14 15   VER   99 98 97 96 95 94 93 92 91

Table of Contents

PART ONE

General Teaching and Planning Information

The following pages contain general information on such topics as grading, safety, and classroom management, to aid you in your overall teaching efforts. Also included in this section are lists, charts, and plans that will help you plan and organize your course.

ARTTALK AND ART EDUCATION

ArtTalk is designed to teach the four components of art education: production, criticism, history, and aesthetics. In *ArtTalk* these components are not treated separately but are integrated throughout. Students do not have to sacrifice the joy of production to acquire the knowledge of criticism, history, and aesthetics.

The four components could be thought of as four students. They all deserve equal attention, but sometimes one needs or demands more attention than the others.

Some children are a joy.
Some children are puzzles.
Some are complex.
Some are strange and new.

Art production is a joy. Almost everyone likes to manipulate art media.

Art Criticism is a puzzle-solving procedure.

Art history is complex. It relates to every aspect of the history of people.

Aesthetics is a strange new mystery. As teachers, we have been dealing with it, but we just didn't know its name.

Art Criticism

Art criticism is introduced in Chapter 2. The method is sequential. First, students are encouraged to look at art in terms of their personal experience. Then, the four steps in criticism are followed systematically. Judgment is postponed until every facet of the work has been explored.

Theories of judging art are also discussed in this chapter. They are presented in their simplest form. Advanced students may wish to explore them in more detail on their own.

In Parts Two and Three of *ArtTalk*, art criticism is used to help sum up all that students have learned in each chapter. In Chapter 5, "Line," for example, the students are asked to use all that they've learned about line during the analysis step of the Chapter 5 art criticism activity. Then, in Chapter 6, the student is asked to recall what was learned about line as well as all the new concepts introduced in Chapter 6. By the time students complete the final chapters, they are well equipped to analyze a work of art based on all of the elements and principles used.

The critical steps followed in the art criticism process are similar to those used in the scientific method. During the first two steps, description and analysis, students are asked to collect data objectively. During the third step, interpretation, students speculate about the meaning of the work based on the data collected. Meanings such as love, peace, loneliness, or the confusion of city life may be uncovered. During the fourth step, judgment, the student offers conclusions about the work.

Aesthetics

Aesthetics is the branch of philosophy concerned with the fine arts. In the past, aesthetics was defined as the study of beauty because the creation of beauty was thought to be the purpose of art. Today, in our more complex society, the purpose of art has also become more complex. The purpose of art is now expressive communication. A work of art may still be beautiful if that suits the artist. But art may also be disturbing and intentionally ugly. See, for example, Figure 8–16 on page 184, *Into The World There Came a Soul Named Ida* by Ivan Albright.

When a discussion about one work of art moves to a discussion about art in general, you have moved from the area of art criticism to aesthetics. For example, when your students compare the expressive qualities of music or poetry to painting they have moved into the realm of aesthetics. For students to be able to transfer what they have learned from a single work of art to art in general is a long neglected, but very important aspect of art education. For this reason *ArtTalk* stresses aesthetics in the text reading as well as through activities.

Art History

ArtTalk is not an art history book, yet there is no way a serious study of art can be begun without learning at least some art history. The evolution of different styles is more easily understood when considered in historical context. Throughout the text, works of art are used to illustrate specific concepts and, therefore, the works are not presented in their chronological order. The overview in Chapter 3 helps students relate better to the illustrations. Many captions as well as text references also give historical information.

Time line activity sheets are included in this guide. Suggestions for their use can be found in the material for Chapter 3. Biographical information about artists whose works have been featured in the art criticism sections also provides historical perspective. An effort has been made to include works of art from every period in history, but most works are from the twentieth century. They were selected for their ability to illustrate art concepts and to stimulate student interest.

Art Production

ArtTalk offers a variety of activities that help students develop and practice their skills. The sections labeled "Developing Your Skills" and "Something Extra" put into practice chapter concepts.

"Developing Your Skills" activities are planned for completion during one or two class periods. You may choose among different kinds of activities those most suitable to your teaching situation. Some activities require drawing. Others, based on cutting, pasting, and arranging, can be carried out successfully by students with limited drawing skills. The skill activities may also be given as homework assignments.

The "Something Extra" sections include in-depth problems requiring research, computers, or cameras. It was the author's intention that each student would choose only one or two "Extras" during the length of the course.

At the end of each chapter in Parts Two and Three several "Imagine and Create" activities are offered. These media problems are typical of those traditionally thought of as art projects, except that here students must recall aesthetic concepts and then apply these concepts to the creation of works of art. The students must consciously use the concepts, and they must analyze their works along with you to be sure they understand, use, and remember concepts correctly.

The end products of the "Imagine and Create" activities are not nearly as important as the concepts involved. If students tend to make the products only for the joy of manipulating media and do not consciously apply the concepts to achieve expressive effects, they are not benefiting from the course. Take time to evaluate each project according to its expressive qualities. A group critique is best, but if you have students who cannot handle peer criticism, talk to them privately. Either way, every student should be challenged to think about what was accomplished.

These activities require several class periods to complete, and there are many ways that they can be used. You may want to ask all of the students to work on the same problem at the same time. Or you may not have time for any at all. During the field testing of this material, several teachers allowed gifted students to move through the chapters at their own pace and complete more than one media problem on their own. This gave the teacher more time to work with students who needed more instruction.

GENERAL TEACHING SUGGESTIONS

Following are suggestions on general topics related to teaching art and using *ArtTalk*.

Preparing to Teach

In today's world of accountability, the "free spirit" style of teaching is no longer acceptable. If you truly believe that art is an important part of the curriculum, you must be willing to defend the content of your subject. You must be able to show parents, administrators, and fellow teachers that studying art is more than media manipulation— "messing around" with paint and "playing" with clay.

The keys to an art program that promotes significant and measurable learning are the development of clear goals and detailed plans to meet them, and the ability to give specific instructions to students so that they can implement the plans.

To set goals, you must get to know your students. Only you, the teacher, can decide what they are able to learn. You must know exactly what you want your students to know, to write, and to create. In *ArtTalk*, you will find general objectives at the beginning of each chapter that tell the students what they will learn in that chapter. But as you prepare to teach specific groups of young people, you must write more specific goals designed to meet the needs of each class.

Next, you must plan how your students will acquire concepts, skills, and appreciations. If you are a beginning teacher, you will quickly realize that the more carefullly you plan daily classes, the easier it will be to teach. If you are an experienced teacher, you already realize the importance of planning.

After setting goals and formulating plans, you need to tell your students exactly what you expect them to know and to do. You should tell them the objectives of each learning experience, explain the criteria by which you will grade their work, and evaluate their performance accordingly. Give your students specific instructions so they can see measurable progress in their work.

This guide contains a great deal of material that will assist you in developing goals, plans, and instructions. You will find course outlines for various time frames, lists of textbook activities according to type, and a scope and sequence chart in this part of the guide. In Part Two you will find chapter-by-chapter lesson plans in which each chapter is divided into units for teaching. For each unit, the following material is provided:

- Purposes
- Learning outcomes
- Teaching strategies
- Additional suggestions for teaching concepts

Whatever the goals, time frame, and ability levels of your students, you should find sufficient information to plan your course.

Classroom Activities and Environment

The following information relates to some general activities that the author has found to be valuable in her teaching experience. You may or may not choose to implement all of these activities in your course. Also included in this section are some tips on maintaining a classroom environment conducive to optimum student results.

NOTEBOOKS

Since *ArtTalk* is designed to be used in a disciplined-based art education course, the students should create their written work as carefully as their art products. Written activities help students develop their knowledge and skills.

Teachers who have field-tested this material have found that it is best to have each student keep a loose-leaf notebook in addition to a portfolio. The notebook is convenient for collecting vocabulary lists, study sheets, tests, the time lines, and other handouts that may be reproduced from this guide, as well as any other written work. You may also want the students to keep the "Developing Your Skills" activities in the notebook. Some teachers have found it convenient to have a three-hole punch in the room for the students' use.

There are study sheets for each chapter in Part Three of this guide which are intended to help students find important ideas as they read the text. If the students fill out the study sheets as they read, correct them as they discuss the material in class, and place them in their notebooks, they will have a guide to help them study for tests.

VOCABULARY ACTIVITIES

At the beginning of each chapter, there is a list of words to learn. Each word on that list is defined in the Glossary in the back of the text. The students should look up those words in the Glossary and write the definitions in their notebooks. On the review page for each chapter, there is a creative exercise for applying definitions as they relate to works of art reproduced in the chapter. These review questions force students to think about the meaning of the terms and require a much higher level of learning than simple recall.

Since reading is now being emphasized in every subject, there is no reason to limit vocabulary exercises to the words at the beginning of each chapter. The Glossary is extensive and can be used for many different word games.

PORTFOLIOS

Each student should have a simple portfolio in which to store his or her art products. A folder-like portfolio may be made by scoring and folding a sheet of poster board in half, punching holes on the three open sides, lacing strings through the holes, and tying them so that the artworks do not slip out. A more durable portfolio can be made with heavy cardboard and duct tape and covered with fabric.

To identify portfolios by class, assign a different color for each group's portfolios. It is easiest to store these portfolios vertically. If they are stored horizontally, one on top of the other, they must all be moved to reach one on the bottom of the stack. If one portfolio per child is more than your art room can accommodate, assign partners or teams of three or four to share a portfolio.

RESEARCH

In the lists of activities, there are several research problems. Academically gifted students could prepare written reports from the results of their research. Students who are able to read but have difficulty expressing themselves in written form could make audio or video tapes in place of written reports. The subject of art should be presented at an appropriate academic level but should not be threatening to students with learning disabilities.

DISCUSSIONS

Research demonstrates that teachers tend to dominate discussions. When leading class discussions, be careful that the discussion does not become a monologue. Don't be afraid of silence. Give the students time to think.

You must also watch out for the bright, verbal student who loves to talk. That student will have all the right answers, and it is easy to fall into the trap of thinking that everyone knows the answer to your question when, in truth, only this type of student does.

One technique that some teachers use to get all the students to participate in discussions is to assign a question by calling out a name from the roll. You might reserve one section of your roll book for the purpose of recording names of students who answer these questions.

DISCUSSION CENTER

Because the art room must be used for noisy production activities, the last thing many planners consider is the need for an area where quiet activities take place—films, slide presentations, lectures, and discussions. This space is not wasted. It can also serve as a reading/study center where books and prints are available.

You must work out a system for organizing the placement of students in a discussion area. It is hard to space young people around the room at tables and still keep their attention during a lengthy discussion. Even though you must crowd students together or ask them to move chairs from workstations to a discussion area, some provision must be made so that they can gather, facing the teacher.

Although placing students in close proximity might cause disturbances at first, in time you can exercise control since you have eye contact with them. Once students are accustomed to the idea that explanation precedes hands-on activities, the discussions move more smoothly.

Remember that this area, though crowded, must be comfortable because you may want to spend an entire class period in group discussion. Some teachers have bleacher-like benches built and arrange them so that one-quarter of the room becomes the discussion center. The benches face a demonstration area, which can be as simple as a low table and bulletin boards on the wall. Sometimes an area of carpeting is used in one corner of the room for the discussion center. Be innovative in designing this space.

ROOM ENVIRONMENT

Remember, even though art is a messy subject, the art room should not look messy. If you establish a well-organized, attractive environment from the start, the students will help you maintain it. But if you begin the year in chaos, the room will stay that way.

Since visual environment is an important consideration in art education, the art room itself should be aesthetically pleasing—orderly and interesting.

Even if you have no control over the wall color or carpeting in the room, organization will enhance the aesthetics of the environment. Organize your supplies and label shelves where they should be stored. The students should learn where to find certain materials that they use frequently and should be expected to return them to their proper places at the end of the work period.

Give credit in some way for the job of cleaning up. Some teachers have found it useful to appoint one person per week to oversee the return of materials to storage places and then give a grade to that person based on the room's degree of neatness. The monitor does not have to put all of the supplies away, but he or she should supervise the cleanup while you are conferring with students. The cleanup monitor is only responsible for putting away materials that he or she does not catch before the other students leave the room. If the students have assigned seats, the monitor can find and list the names of those who did not help clean up.

Making the art room interesting is as important as keeping it orderly. There are several inexpensive ways to make your room visually stimulating.

Try to keep a variety of live plants in your room. Not only will they enhance the visual environment, but they will also be useful during drawing activities. Select plants that are hardy, but try to find some with different leaf shapes and sizes. If your room has no windows, invest in a grow light.

Collect dried plant material and arrange it around the room. Set up a display corner, and change it to match the seasons.

Visit garage sales. An item that might seem like junk can be a treasure in a still-life arrangement.

Instead of keeping an odd assortment of cardboard boxes on your shelves, invest a little money in decorative adhesive papers to cover them, or paint all the boxes in some pleasing color scheme.

Buy some inexpensive fabric and cover the bulletin boards with it. Most fabrics don't fade, and none fade as quickly as paper.

COLLECTING MAGAZINES AND NEWSPAPERS

You will need a supply of newspapers for covering tables during messy activities. Also, in this course there are several perception activities that require the students to find pictures in magazines and newspapers. Whether you are teaching in an inner city school or an affluent private school, you will need to provide these. Even if students have access to magazines and newspapers at home, parents usually do not want them cut up. The following suggestions will help you collect them.

Save the magazine sections of newspapers, the colored advertisement sections, and even the comics.

Speak to librarians. School and public libraries save periodicals for a certain amount of time, but eventually they must be discarded.

Ask teachers to donate magazines that they no longer wish to save. Also check at your hairdresser's, your doctor's, and any other place where you see magazines in abundance.

Find out which teachers use newspapers in class activities and ask for old copies.

Safety in the Art Room

Many artists, both students and teachers, come into daily contact with dangerous, possibly deadly materials. The unfortunate truth is that many art supplies contain high levels of chemicals, such as hexane, lead, toluene, and asbestos, and many art teachers are unaware of the danger that these substances pose, both to their students and to themselves. In fact, the danger to art teachers, who are often exposed to toxins for several hours a day for many years, is often greater than to the students. Therefore, it is esssential that all art teachers become aware of the potential hazards in using art materials.

Many art supplies contain materials that can cause acute illness (that is, a severe sudden illness that can be caused by a single exposure to a toxic substance and result in permanent disability or death). Long-term exposure to materials in many other art supplies can cause chronic illness (which develops gradually after repeated exposure) or cancer. Other chemicals in art supplies are sensitizers, causing allergies, particularly in children. Lead, for example, is acutely toxic and can be found in such commonly used supplies as stencil paint, oil paint, some acrylics, gessos, ceramic glazes, copper enamels, and automotive paint in spray cans. Many highly toxic hydrocarbon-based solvents, including methyl hydrate (methyl alcohol), are used in school art programs. Other widely used art materials, such as preservatives, formaldehyde, epoxy glues, and dichromates, can contain dangerous chemicals like cadmium, nickel, silica, and pesticides.

There are three ways in which such chemicals can enter the body: absorption, inhalation, and ingestion. They can be absorbed through the skin from cuts or scrapes, resulting in burns or rashes, or into the bloodstream, moving to and damaging other parts of the body. Chemical irritants can be inhaled, causing lung problems like bronchitis and emphysema. Inhaling small particles, like the free silica in clay dust, can cause pulmonary fibrosis or asthma. Chemicals can be ingested through touching the mouth with the hands or fingers while working with supplies or unconsciously placing tools like paint brushes in or near the mouth. Since hazardous substances can easily enter the body, it is extremely important that art teachers make sure that materials used in their programs are safe and are used safely.

LABELING

Labeling can provide information on any potentially dangerous art supplies, but teachers need to be aware of what various labels mean. The label *non-toxic*, for example, does not guarantee a product's safety. According to federal regulations, toxicity means that a single exposure can be fatal to adults. The effect on children, who are more likely to be harmed by dangerous substances, is not considered in this definition. Also, the chance of developing chronic or long-term illnesses is not addressed by the legal definition of toxicity. Repeated exposure to non-toxic materials is not always safe. Many dangerous substances, such as asbestos, can legally be defined as non-toxic. Also, some art supplies, particularly those manufactured by small or foreign companies, may be improperly labeled as *non-toxic*.

Not all products whose labels provide chemical components, but have no warnings or list no information at all, are safe to use. Since manufacturers are not required to disclose ingredients, products without this information or warnings are potentially hazardous.

For more complete information on the presence of hazardous substances in art supplies, teachers may request a Material Safety Data Sheet (OSHA Form 20) from the manufacturer. This sheet provides information on potential health and fire hazards, a list of chemicals that might react dangerously with the product, and a list of all ingredients for which industrial standards exist. The manufacturer should supply this sheet on request, and a local public health official or poison control center technician can help interpret the information.

Art teachers can also take advantage of voluntary labeling standards developed by the art materials industry. The

MEETS PERFORMANCE STANDARDS

Saftey labels approved by the Art and Craft Materials Institute (ACMI).

Art and Craft Materials Institute (ACMI) administers a voluntary testing and labeling program that helps to insure the safety of those who work with art materials. This system uses the labels *CP*, *AP*, and *HL*. GL Figure 1

CP (Certified Product) and AP (Approved Product) labels are used mainly on products designed for younger children, while HL (Health Label) is used on products intended for older children and adults. Products labelled CP, AP, or HL (Non-Toxic) are certified in a program of toxicological evaluation by a medical expert to contain no materials in sufficient quantities to be toxic or injurious to humans or to cause acute or chronic health problems. Products labeled CP, in addition, meet specific requirements of material, workmanship, working qualities, and color. HL (Cautions Required) means that the product is certified to be properly labeled in a program of toxicological evaluation by a medical expert. The Art and Craft Materials Institute makes available a list of institute-certified products. For a copy, or for more information on the institute's certification program, write to:

The Art and Craft Materials Institute
715 Boylston St.
Boston, MA 02116

SAFETY RULES

There are certain guidelines to be followed in selecting art supplies to be used in the classroom. Perhaps the most important is to know what the materials are made of and what potential hazards exist. If a material is improperly labeled, or if adequate information cannot be obtained about it, don't use it. The following rules are also helpful:

• Be sure that all materials used by younger students (ages 12 and under) have the CP or AP label and that materials used by older children and adults are marked HL.

• Don't use acids, alkalies, bleaches, or any product that will stain skin or clothing.

• Don't use aerosol cans because the spray can injure lungs.

• Use dust-producing materials (such as pastels, clays, plasters, chalks, powdered tempera, pigments, dyes, and instant papier-mâché, except the premixed cellulose type) with care in a well-ventilated area (or better yet, don't use them at all).

• Don't use solvents (including lacquers, paint thinners, turpentines, shellacs, solvent-based inks, rubber cement, and permanent markers) in the art room.

• Don't use found or donated materials unless the ingredients are known.

• Don't use old materials. Many art supplies formerly contained highly dangerous substances, such as arsenic, or raw lead compounds, or high levels of asbestos. Older solvents may contain chloroform or carbon tetrachloride.

Working conditions in the art room also affect safety. A disorderly, confused art room leads to unsafe conditions, particularly when there are many people working close to each other. Controlling the buildup of litter and dust, insuring that tools are in good condition, and keeping workspace reasonably organized, not only help prevent common accidents but also make it easier to recognize and eliminate other hazards. An orderly art room is absolutely essential to the students' and teacher's safety.

Following the above measures will provide a safe and healthy art environment. However, some students who, for one reason or another, run a higher risk of injury will need special precautions. It's a good idea to identify these high risk students at the beginning of each school term by sending questionnaires to parents and checking school records. Teachers are urged to plan programs with these children's limitations in mind.

The safety of children with some physical impairment must also be considered. Visually impaired children, for example, tend to get closer (sometimes within one or two inches) to the work in order to see and are thus more likely to inhale fumes or dust. Also, they are less likely to notice spills. Some activities which create noise, such as hammering or using machinery, may be unsuitable for the hearing impaired. Asthmatics already have difficulties in breathing and should not be exposed to dust or fumes. Students with motor impairments may manipulate materials with their feet or mouths, making accidental ingestion or absorption more likely and cleanup more difficult.

Students who are mentally impaired may have trouble understanding rules for art room safety and may require extra supervision. Some students with emotional disturbances might deliberately abuse art supplies. Students who are taking medication or undergoing chemotherapy should be medically evaluated for possible interactions between their medication and art materials.

More information on safety in the art environment is available from The Center for Occupational Hazards, a national nonprofit clearinghouse for research and information on health hazards in art. For more information, or to subscribe to their newsletter, which covers a variety of topics on art safety, write to:

The Center for Occupational Safety
5 Beekman St.
New York, NY 10038

Evaluation and Grades

Grading is disliked equally by students and teachers, but it is the way the teacher reports to the parents and the administration about student achievement. For now, art teachers must work within this system. The following are suggestions to help the beginning teacher.

TESTING

Many schools require written tests as well as performance grades. Although written tests should be only one part of the total evaluation of art student performance, the art teacher should approach testing as creatively as possible. Below are some guidelines to follow if you want to use test items other than those included in this guide.
1. Always build some success into each test. Place a few simple items at the beginning of the test that everyone will be able to answer. The positive reinforcement received from answering the first questions correctly may overcome students' fear of tests.
2. The test items should span a range of cognitive levels instead of being limited to the recall of facts. The following list gives examples related to visual art for each level described by Benjamin S. Bloom and others in *The Taxonomy of Educational Objectives: Handbook 1: Cognitive Domain* (White Plains, NY: Longman, Inc., 1977).
   - Knowledge: This level requires the recall of facts, terminology, dates, events, or titles of artworks. It also involves the recall of simple processes such as cleaning a brush, mixing colors, and classifying works according to style. The highest level of knowledge required in the course is knowledge of universals and abstractions.
   - Comprehension: In visual art this level includes copying, diagramming, explaining, and summarizing, and predicting outcomes.
   - Application: This level relates to the proper use of material. It can be tested by asking students to describe how to make a glue print or what four steps must be followed to join clay.
   - Analysis: An example of this level of cognitive learning is the analysis step in art criticism. Analysis can deal with the students' work as well as reproductions of masterworks.
   - Synthesis: At this level students display their ability to use a combination of concepts or elements to solve a visual problem. This creative level can be tested by asking students to produce designs expressing a particular emotion. Synthesis is much more open-ended than the previous levels. In art, it is usually tested in an art production activity rather than by a verbal problem.
   - Evaluation: The evaluation level in the course involves the fourth step in art criticism. It requires judging and giving reasons for the judgment.

   By using various cognitive levels in designing tests, you will be able to distinguish among the achievement levels of students.
3. Keep the reading level of tests low so that you are testing art knowledge and not reading ability. Make your tests as visual as possible, using drawings and reproductions. For example, you can test knowledge of color theory in several ways that do not require reading. Put three reproductions on a bulletin board, number each work, and ask the students which one contains cool colors. This question is a better test of the student's understanding of cool colors than asking them to name these colors. Ask the students to describe how to change the value of a hue, to use paint to mix a light value of a hue, or to find a magazine picture showing a light value of a specific hue.

   You could also display several reproductions identified with numbers and ask the students to recognize different color concepts by listing which reproduction uses high intensity colors, which shows a large area with a light value of red, or which uses a split-complement color scheme.
4. Essay tests require high level thinking in which students must reorganize knowledge. Be sure to make expectations for the answers clear for these tests. For example, ask for at least *three* reasons, at least *four* works of art using a technique, or *similarities and differences* between two artists' works. Ask essay questions about the students' work as well as masterworks. For example, after the class has finished an "Imagine and Create" activity, students could be asked to use art criticism to evaluate their design.

OTHER EVALUATION METHODS

The following suggestions are based on classroom practices of experienced teachers. Not all of them are appropriate for every situation. Try the ones you think will work for you.

1. Daily participation grades: As the class works, quickly give each student a check in your roll book for satisfactory participation, a check-plus for exceptional work, a check-minus for below average participation, and a minus or zero for inadequate work.
2. Anecdotal records: At the end of the day, take a few minutes to record any outstanding student behavior, either positive or negative.
3. Daily journals: Have students record what they have done in class each day. These journals may be part of the students' notebooks. At the end of the grading period, they will help you remember what students have accomplished. The entries in the journals do not have to be elaborate. For example, they might be as simple as "I helped Joe mix colors to make a color wheel," or "Continued working on my expressive painting."
4. Performance criteria for creative work: Grading criteria should be planned and explained to students before they start an activity. One way to grade an artwork is to assign percentages out of a total of one hundred to each item in the evaluation checklist in the text (plus others you want to add). As an example, below are percentages assigned to criteria for the yarn painting activity in the text:

10%	1.	Planned a design with large, simple shapes.
10%	2.	Used sets of parallel yarn strands.
5%	3.	Used lines running in different directions to fill in the different shapes.
5%	4.	Used a variety of yarn colors and textures.
5%	5.	Left no cardboard visible between the yarn strands.
10%	6.	Attached the yarn firmly to the cardboard.
10%	7.	Covered the work area, followed proper cleanup procedures, and stored the work in progress on a flat surface.
10%	8.	Prepared the yarn painting for display.
5%	9.	Identified the finished work by writing name and class clearly on the back of the work. (Beginning teachers may not realize how important it is to train students to identify their artwork.)
10%	10.	Displayed general craftsmanship.
10%	11.	Used creative thinking.
10%	12.	Showed aesthetic quality.

Although the subjective aspect of grading art cannot be eliminated, it can be reduced by using performance criteria. You might decide to give A's for exceeding objectives, B's for meeting all of them, C's for completing a certain number, and so on.

5. Written evaluations: When you grade major works, whether they are verbal or visual, take the time to write evaluations of strengths and weaknesses.

Finally, remember that students' talent should not influence evaluation. Each student should be graded on his or her specific achievements. A student with little natural ability who struggles to draw a still life should be recognized for his or her effort. However, a talented student who does not finish the assignment or turns in careless work should not be given a high grade. (At the same time, don't penalize the gifted student for being able to produce work in little time.) Since most art classes are a good place to practice mainstreaming, they will often contain students with a wide range of abilities. Tailor your expectations to fit the different levels of your students' capabilities.

Advocacy and Art on Display

The fact that the *ArtTalk* program is different from the old product-oriented style of teaching does not mean that art teachers can ignore the responsibility of exhibiting students' work. The products resulting from this approach may look different, but they are still worthy of display. Art must be seen to be appreciated. In addition, exhibiting students' artwork is an important part of promoting your art program.

The following are teacher-tested ideas for displaying artwork both within the school and throughout the community and creating support for the program.

- Use bulletin boards and display cases in halls at school as concept teaching boards. You could display projects from a "Developing Your Skills" activity with the title "Art Concepts." Type a brief explanation of the activity and mount it to accompany the display. You would be surprised at how many people will take the time to read the explanation of the concept that is illustrated.
- Have a "principal's choice" work selected each year by a panel of judges, frame it, and place it on permanent display in the office. In a few years you will have an interesting collection.
- Buy some inexpensive frames at a discount store sale, and get permission to hang students' work in high-traffic areas around the school building, such as offices, the lunchroom, the teachers' lounge, the library, and entrance halls. These pieces should be products of "Imagine and Create" activities that students have had time to carefully plan and finish. These artworks can be changed at least three times a year.
- Hold an exhibit at the end of each semester or the end of the year. Send out invitations, have a guest book, and invite honored guests. Take photos and send them to the local newspaper.
- Contact local banks, other businesses, and government offices to display framed pieces. Volunteer to have your students paint store windows for special occasions.
- Hold an exhibit at the local mall.
- Encourage your students to participate in community art festivals and exhibits. If necessary, transport their works yourself.
- Create public art to make people notice your program. Paint a mural on the walls around a construction site, make relief tiles and mount them on a wall, stitch some banners, or weave wall hangings.
- Join and become active in the local art association. It can be a valuable source of contacts, information, and possible funding for special programs.
- Get a local art association or an art-related business to sponsor your class. Its members or employees could not only donate money but also help you collect

found items such as magazine pictures and fabric scraps for projects, hang artworks for shows, or go with your class on a weekend trip to a museum.

• Organize a parents' support group. Even if you don't hold meetings, send out newsletters. Although everyone is busy, some parents will be interested enough in art education to volunteer help with extras for your class.

• Speak to any community group that will listen about your art program: the PTA, garden clubs, civic groups. Teach the adults what you are teaching the students. Take along slides of the students' works. You might even get the students involved by having them tape a narrative to accompany the slides, explaining how and why they created their artworks.

STUDENT ACTIVITIES IN ARTTALK

Following are lists of the student activities in *ArtTalk*. If the organization of your course differs from the Element-and-Principles organization of *ArtTalk*, these lists may help you locate activities within the text for your specific purposes.

The activities have been divided into three major categories: *Art Production*, *Perception*, and *Research*. The Art Production activities have been further divided into the different types of production, such as painting, drawing, and sculpture.

In these lists the "Developing Your Skills" activities and the "Something Extra" activities are designated by titles, which do not appear in the text. They are also designated by number. The first digit of the number indicates the chapter; the second digit, or letter, indicates the specific activity within that chapter. Thus, *10–12* refers to "Developing Your Skills" activity 12 in Chapter 10. The "Imagine and Create" activities are designated by title only. Page numbers are given for all of the activities.

Art Production Activities

CERAMICS

Textured Clay Wind Chimes, 194
Clay Coil Pot, 234
Special Occasion Calender, 338

COLLAGE

collecting and organizing fabrics and papers decorated with lines, 5–E, 70
perspective collage, 6–21, 118
geometric creature, 6–23, 124
free-form creature, 6–24, 124
color wheel, 7–4, 142
organizing texture rubbings into a design, 8–4, 178
dream landscape, 8–6, 180

fabric collage, 8–8, 181
letter collage, 9–10, 218
creating faces: one in proportion, one distorted, 11–15, 293
two scenes: one in realistic scale, one in unrealistic scale, 11–6, 280
unified window display, 12–13, 330
Tissue and Found Paper Collage, 334
Mixed Media Combining Visual and Verbal Symbols, 336

DESIGN

using geometric and free-form shapes in designs, 6–4, 98
expanding a shape with negative space, 6–8, 102
one object from different points of view, 6–16, 109
active and static designs, 6–26, 124
values and intensities of one hue, 7–8, 148
chart to illustrate simultaneous contrast, 7–9, 154
catagorizing textures, 8–7, 181
symmetrical design, 10–5, 248
using informal balance, 10–12, 257
creative rhythmic designs, 9–7, 216
creating designs with strong contrast, 12–3, 311
creating subtle contrast, 12–4, 311
creating focal points, 12–8, 319
using unifying devices, 12–12, 330
organizing a bulletin board, 12–B, 311

SCULPTURE

paper sculpture, 6–5, 100
    creating three-dimensional geometric forms, 6–6, 100
free-standing, three-dimensional design from found objects, 6–12, 106
cardboard relief, 6–13, 106
curled paper relief: flowing rhythm, 9–16, 223
Contour Wire Sculpture, p. 85
Foil Relief, p. 89
Plaster Sculpture, 127
Soft Sculpture, 129
Three-dimensional Amusement Park Ride, 166
Modular Sculpture, 231
Round Plaster Relief, 265
Modern Spirit Mask, 296
Life Size Papier-Mache' Figure in Environment, 298
Life Size Soft Sculpture, 300

COMPUTER GRAPHICS

drawing line types, 5–D, 67
color schemes, 7–D, 155
design motif and rhythm, 9–D, 216
Drawing With a Computer, 132

FIBER ARTS

Yarn Painting, 82
Texture Stitchery, 197
Weaving, 200
Fabric Medallion, 263

Research Activities

BIBLIOGRAPHY

The following is an annotated listing of books dealing with various areas of art and art education. These books can provide valuable assistance to you and your students as you study and work in the visual arts.

Areas of Art

ARCHITECTURE

- Crouch, Dora P. *History of Architecture: Stonehenge to Skyscrapers.* New York: McGraw-Hill Book Co., 1985. Provides an analysis of architectural design in historical context.
- McAlester, Virginia and Lee. *A Field Guide to American Houses.* New York: Alfred A. Knopf, Inc., 1984. An informative guide to the various architectural styles in American houses from the seventeenth century to the present. Lavishly detailed and profusely illustrated.

COMPUTER GRAPHICS

- Jannel, Annabel, and Rocky Morton. *Creative Computer Graphics.* New York: Cambridge University Press, 1984. Explores the techniques used in creating computer graphic images and touches on modern computer graphic technology as well as a variety of applications.
- Lewell, John. *Computer Graphics: A Survey of Current Techniques and Applications.* New York: Van Nostrand Reinhold Co., Inc., 1985. An illustrated volume that provides an overview of computer graphics.
- Wilson, Mark. *Drawing with Computers.* New York: The Putnam Publishing Group, 1985. Describes the techniques of computer graphics, providing software and hardware information.

DESIGN

- Horn, George F. *Contemporary Posters: Design and Techniques.* Worcester, MA: Davis Pubns. Inc., 1976. Explains effective poster design, including uses of color and various reproductive techniques.
- Meilach, Dona Z., Jay Hinz, and Bill Hinz. *How to Create Your Own Designs: An Introduction to Color, Form and Composition.* New York: Doubleday and Co., Inc., 1975. An excellent introduction to the elements of design.
- Ocvirk, Otto, et al. *Art Fundamentals Theory and Practice.* 3rd ed. Dubuque, IA: William C. Brown, Pubs., 1975. A design resource book for teachers.

DRAWING

- Gatto, Joseph. *Drawing Media and Techniques.* Worcester, MA: Davis Pubns., Inc., 1986. Suggestions for using a wide variety of drawing media.
- James, Jane H. *Perspective Drawing.* Englewood Cliffs, NJ: Prentice-Hall, Inc., 1981. For students who want to know more about perspective.

- Sheaks, Barclay. *Drawing Figures and Faces.* Worcester, MA: Davis Pubns., Inc., 1986. A useful resource for students who wish to expand their drawing techniques.
- Sheppard, Joseph. *Anatomy: A Complete Guide for Artists.* New York: Watson-Guptill Pubns., Inc., 1975. A handbook of anatomy, including surface anatomy, with over 430 drawings in line and in tone.
- Wilson, Brent, Al Hurwitz, and Marjorie Wilson. *Teaching Drawing from Art.* Worcester, MA: Davis Pubns., Inc., 1986. Presents a unique approach to drawing. Masterworks of art are used to motivate drawing activities.

FIBER ARTS

Batik

- Meilach, Dona Z. *Contemporary Batik and Tie-Dye: Methods, Inspiration, Dyes.* New York: Crown Pubs., Inc., 1973. A detailed work for beginning and experienced artists with information on many different techniques and projects and a thorough treatment of dying.

Needlecraft

- Guild, Vera P. *Good Housekeeping New Complete Book of Needlecraft.* New York: Hearst Bks., 1971. Directions for a variety of needlecraft techniques.

Silk-screening

- Termini, Maria. *Silkscreening.* Englewood Cliffs, NJ: Prentice-Hall, Inc., 1978. Well-rounded work on the mechanics of silk-screening with good advice for the beginner.

Weaving

- Brown, Rachel. *The Weaving, Spinning, and Dying Book.* New York: Alfred A. Knopf, Inc., 1978. A good look at all phases of the weaving craft, including primitive and ethnic weaving.

FLORAL ARTS

- Cook, Hal. *Arranging: The Basics of Contemporary Floral Design.* New York: William Morrow & Co., Inc., 1985. A book which treats floral design as an art form. Extensively illustrated.

GENERAL CRAFTS

- Sprintzen, Alice. *Crafts: Contemporary Design and Technique.* Worcester, MA: Davis Pubns., Inc., 1986. An introduction to traditional and modern crafts, with instructions for beginners.
- Stribling, Mary Lou. *Crafts From North American Indian Art: Techniques, Designs and Contemporary Applications.* New York: Crown Pubs., Inc., 1975. Techniques and applications of many different crafts using a variety of materials.

JEWELRY

- Ferre, R. Duane. *How to Make Wire Jewelry.* Radnor, PA: Chilton Bk. Co., 1980. A good guide to beginning jewelry making using a variety of inexpensive and simple techniques.
- Meilach, Dona Z. *Ethnic Jewelry: Design and Inspiration for Collectors and Craftsmen.* New York: Crown Pubs., Inc., 1981. An overview of ethnic jewelry from around the world, made from a variety of materials.

PAINTING

- Mayer, Ralph. *The Artist's Handbook of Materials and Techniques, 4th ed.* New York: Viking-Penguin, Inc., 1981. An up-to-date reference.
- Porter, Al. *Expressive Watercolor Techniques.* Worcester, MA: Davis Pubns., Inc., 1982. A useful resource with valuable information on techniques and processes.
- Sheaks, Barclay. *Painting with Acrylics: From Start to Finish.* Worcester, MA: Davis Pubns., Inc., 1972. Information on techniques for teacher and student.

PAPER

- Betts, Victoria. *Exploring Papier-Mâché.* Worcester, MA: Davis Pubns., Inc., 1966. A classic technique book.
- Johnson, Pauline. *Creating with Paper.* Seattle: Univ. of Washington Pr., 1966. A variety of approaches to paper sculpture.
- Toale, Bernard, *The Art of Papermaking.* Worcester, MA: Davis Pubns., Inc., 1983. A source of ideas for additional texture experiences.

PHOTOGRAPHY

Film Making

- Eastman Kodak Co. *Movies and Slides without a Camera.* Rochester, NY: 1972. A creative approach to film making.
- Halas, John. *The Technique of Film Animation.* Woburn, MA: Focal Press, 1976. A look at the history and techniques of film animation.
- Laybourne, Kit. *The Animation Book: A Complete Guide to Animated FilmMaking—From Flip-Books to Sound Cartoons.* New York: Crown Pubs., Inc., 1979. An informative discussion of animation assuming no previous training.
- Linder, Carl. *Film Making: A Practical Guide.* Englewood Cliffs, NJ: Prentice-Hall, Inc., 1971. An interesting work that provides information for the amateur film maker.
- Piper, James. *Personal Film Making.* Englewood Cliffs, NJ: Prentice-Hall, Inc., 1975. An excellent introduction to "super-S" film making with step-by-step instructions on all phases of film.

Still Photography

- Craven, George M. *Object and Image*. 2nd ed. Englewood Cliffs, NJ: Prentice-Hall, Inc., 1982. An approach to photography as a creative medium.
- Feininger, Andreas. *The Complete Photographer*. Englewood Cliffs, NJ: Prentice-Hall, Inc., 1978. A good overview of basic photographic techniques.
- Feininger, Andreas. *Darkroom Techniques*. Englewood Cliffs, NJ: Prentice-Hall, Inc., 1974. An in-depth work covering the basic concepts of black and white development and printing.
- Patterson, Freeman. *Photography and the Art of Seeing*. New York: Van Nostrand Reinhold Co., Inc., 1979. Good advice on creative photography of particular interest to the beginning photographer.

Printmaking

- Ross, John and Clare Romane. *The Complete Relief Print*. New York: Free Press-Macmillan, 1974. A clear presentation of ideas and techniques for secondary students.

Sculpture

- Hall, Carolyn Vosburg. *Soft Sculpture*. Worcester, MA: Davis Pubns., Inc., 1981. Provides useful information for soft sculpture projects.
- Meilach, Dona Z. *Contemporary Art with Wood: Creative Techniques and Appreciation*. New York: Crown Pubs., Inc., 1968. Wood in art today including techniques of sculpture, selecting wood, and wood in architecture.
- Meilach, Dona Z. *Soft Sculpture and Other Soft Art Forms*. New York: Crown Pubs., Inc., 1974. A thorough book with useful information for soft sculpture projects.
- Meilach, Dona Z. and Melvin Meilach. *Box Art: Assemblage and Construction*. New York: Crown Pubs., Inc., 1975. Useful technique information.
- Morris, John. *Creative Metal Sculpture: A Step-By-Step Approach*. Encino, CA: Glence Publishing Co., 1971. Takes the novice metalworker through the process of creating various types of metal sculpture.

Art Education

- Clements, Claire B. and Robert D. Clements. *Art and Mainstreaming: Art Education for Exceptional Students in Regular School Classes*. Springfield, IL: Charles C. Thomas, Pub., 1983. Specific information and advice for dealing with a variety of disabled students.
- Dobbs, Stephen, ed. *Arts Education and Back to Basics*. Reston, VA: National Art Education Assn., 1979. A set of papers strongly defending the role of art in the school curriculum.
- Eisner, Elliot. *Educating Artistic Vision*. New York: Macmillan Publishing Co., Inc., 1972. An effective argument for aesthetics in the curriculum.

- Feldman, Edmund. *Becoming Human Through Art*. Englewood Cliffs, NJ: Prentice-Hall, Inc., 1970. An art education text that emphasizes aesthetics.
- Hurwitz, Al. *The Gifted and Talented in Art: A Guide to Program Planning*. Worcester, MA: Davis Pubns., Inc., 1983. A useful book for anyone dealing with talented art students.
- Hurwitz, Al. *Programs of Promise: Art in the Schools*. New York: Harcourt Brace Jovanovich, Inc., 1972. Exciting ideas for aesthetics education.
- Lowenfeld, Viktor and Lambert Brittain. *Creative and Mental Growth*. Rev. ed. New York: Macmillan Publishing Co., Inc., 1975. The classic art education text that still applies to the eighties.
- McFee, June and Rogena Degge. *Art, Culture and Environment*. Dubuque, IA: Kendall/Hunt Publishing Co., 1980. A different approach to art education.
- Michael, John A. *Art and Adolescence: Teaching Art at the Secondary Level*. New York: Teachers College Pr., 1983. An up-to-date approach to secondary art education.
- Qualley, Charles. *Safety in the Artroom*. Worcester, MA: Davis Pubns., Inc., 1986. A must for every art teacher.
- Wachowiak, Frank. *Emphasis Art*. 4th ed. New York: Harper & Row Pubs., Inc., 1985. Full of useful ideas for motivation and clear directions for creative activities.

Art History

- Armstrong, Tom, et al. *200 Years of American Sculpture*. Boston: David R. Godine, Pubs., Inc., 1976. An informative look at the evoluation of American sculpture.
- Barnicoat, John. *A Concise History of Posters 1870–1970*. New York: Oxford Univ. Pr., Inc., 1972. The importance of the poster, including its role in various artistic movements.
- Beaton, Cecil Walter Hardy and Gail Buckland. *The Magic Image: The Genius of Photography from 1839 to the Present Day*. Boston: Little, Brown and Co., Inc., 1975. An assortment of the work of over two hundred photographers since 1839, with biographical sketches.
- Broder, Patricia J. *American Indian Painting and Sculpture*. New York: Abbeville Pr., Inc., 1981. A good introduction to contemporary Indian art with excellent illustrations.
- Feldman, Edmund B. *Thinking About Art*. Englewood Cliffs, NJ: Prentice-Hall, Inc., 1985. Combines aesthetics, art criticism, and art history. For the academically gifted student.
- Gardner, Helen. *Art Through the Ages*. 7th ed. New York: Harcourt Brace Jovanovich, Inc., 1980. An art history resource book for teachers.
- Handlin, Oscar. *Statue of Liberty*. New York: W. W. Norton and Co., Inc., 1971. A history of the conception and building of the symbolic statue.
- Highwater, Jamake. *Arts of the American Indians: Leaves from the Sacred Tree*. New York: Harper and

Row Pubs., Inc., 1983. Provides an excellent view of the arts of North, South, and Central American Indians, with information on culture and history of native Americans.

- Hillier, Bevis. *The Style of the Century, 1900–1980*. New York: E. P. Dutton, 1983. A survey of style in art and industrial design from the turn of the century to the present with a look at the social, political, and economic situations that influenced each decade's sense of style.
- Janson, H. W. *History of Art for Young People*. 2nd ed. New York: Harry N. Abrams, Inc., 1981. Can be used for art history reports by academically advanced students.
- Johnson, Una E. *American Prints and Printmakers: A Chronicle of Over 400 Artists and Their Prints From 1900 to the Present*. New York: Doubleday and Co., Inc., 1980. A survey of artists involved in printmaking in this century.
- Lassiter, Barbara Babcock. *American Wilderness: The Hudson River School of Painting*. New York: Doubleday and Co., Inc., 1980. A history of this American realistic landscape school of painting.
- Lewinski, Jorge. *The Camera at War: A History of War Photography From 1848 to the Present Day*. New York: Simon and Schuster, A look at combat photographers, the problems they face and the work they produce.
- Sandler, Martin W. *The Story of American Photography: An Illustrated History for Young People*. Boston: Little, Brown and Co., 1975. A survey of American photographers and their work.
- Sayer, Chloe. *Crafts of Mexico*. New York: Doubleday and Co., Inc., 1977. An overview of Mexican crafts with good discussion of history and culture. Richly illustrated.
- Shadwell, Wendy J., et al. *American Printmaking, the First 150 Years*. Washington, DC: Smithsonian Institution Pr., 1969. A thorough retrospective on American printmaking.

Artists

- Adams, Ansel. *The Portfolios of Ansel Adams*. Boston: New York Graphic Society Bks., 1979. Adam's seven limited-edition portfolios in one volume. A definitive collection of his stunning photographic work.
- Bruzeau, Maurice. *Alexander Calder*. New York: Harry A. Abrams, Inc., 1979. A picture book of Calder's work.
- Feaver, William. *Masters of Caricature: From Hogarth and Gilray to Scarfe and Levine*. New York: Alfred E. Knopf, Inc., 1981. Brief biographical sketches of caricaturists of the last three centuries. Illustrated.
- Hoving, Thomas. *Two Worlds of Andrew Wyeth*. Boston: Houghton Mifflin Co., 1978. Includes many examples of Wyeth's work as well as a long interview.
- Levin, Gail. *Edward Hopper: The Art and the Artist*. New York: W. W. Norton and Co., Inc., 1980. A representative collection of Hopper's work, combined with text on Hopper's development and characteristic themes.
- Lisle, Laurie. *Portrait of an Artist: A Biography of Georgia O'Keeffe*. New York: Harper and Row Pubs., Inc., 1980. A fascinating account of O'Keeffe's life and work.
- Locher, J.L., ed. *The World of M.C. Escher*. New York: Harry N. Abrams, Inc., 1972. A catalog of the precise, visually intricate and often stunning work of the Dutch mathematician and artist.
- Rockwell, Norman. *Norman Rockwell: My Adventures As An Illustrator*. Indianapolis: The Curtis Publishing Co., 1979. Rockwell's own fascinating account of his life and career.
- Rubin, William, ed. *Pablo Picasso: A Retrospective*. Boston: New York Graphic Society Bks., 1980. The catalog of the huge Picasso retrospective at the Museum of Modern Art.
- Slatkins, Wendy. *Women Artists in History: From Antiquity to the 20th Century*. Englewood Cliffs, NJ: Prentice-Hall, Inc., 1985. An important reference since most art history books ignore the contribution of women artists.
- Snyder, Robert R. *Buckminster Fuller: An Autobiographical Monologue/Scenario*. New York: St. Martin's Pr., Inc., 1980. A thorough and personal depiction of Fuller's life and work.

The following books are from the Time-Life Library of Art, published by Time-Life Books, Alexandria, VA. They are excellent biographical sources, providing insight into the lives of the artists and their works, contemporaries, and times.

Brown, Dale. *The World of Valezquez (1599–1660)*. 1969.

Coughlan, Robert. *The World of Michelangelo (1475–1564)*. 1966.

Flexner, James Thomas. *The World of Winslow Homer (1836–1910)*. 1966.

Hals, William Harlan. *The World of Rodin (1840–1917)*. 1970.

Hirsch, Diana. *The World of Turner (1775–1851)*. 1969.

Koningsberger, Hans. *The World of Vermeer (1632–1675)*. 1967.

Leonard, Jonathan Norton. *The World of Gainesborough (1727–1788)*. 1970.

Prideaux, Tom. *The World of Whistler (1834–1903)*. 1970.

Russell, John. *The World of Matisse (1869–1954)*. 1969.

Schickel, Richard. *The World of Goya (1746–1828)*. 1968.

Wallace, Robert. *The World of Leonardo (1452–1519)*. 1966.

Wallace, Robert. *The World of Rembrandt (1606–1669)*. 1968.

Wallace, Robert. *The World of Van Gogh (1853–1890)*. 1969.

Wedgewood, C. V. *The World of Rubens (1577–1640)*. 1967.

Wertenbaker, Lael. *The World of Picasso (1881–)*. 1967.

Williams, Jay. *The World of Titian (c. 1488–1576)*. 1968.

ART SLIDE, FILMSTRIP, AND CASSETTE DISTRIBUTORS

Boston Museum of Fine Arts
Department of Photographic Services
Slide Library
465 Huntington Ave.
Boston, MA 02115

Educational Dimensions Corporation
Stamford, CT 06904

Metropolitan Museum of Art
255 Gracie Sta.
New York, NY 10028

Wilton Art Appreciation Programs
P. O. Box 302
Wilton, CT 06897

COLOR REPRODUCTION SUPPLIERS

Harry N. Abrams
100 E. 59th St.
New York, NY 10022

Art Education, Inc.
28 E. Erie St.
Blauvelt, NY 10913

Art Extension Press
Box 389
Westport, CT 06881

Associated American Artists
663 Fifth Ave.
New York, NY 10022

Catalda Fine Arts
12 W. 27th St.
New York, NY 10001

Imaginus, Inc.
R. R. 1, Box 552
Lee, MA 01238

Metropolitan Museum of Art
Book and Art Shop
Fifth Ave. and 82nd St.
New York, NY 10028

Museum of Modern Art
11 W. 53rd St.
New York, NY 10019

National Gallery of Art
Department of Extension Programs
Washington, DC 20565

New York Graphic Society
140 Greenwich Ave.
Greenwich, CT 06830

Oestreicher's Prints
43 W. 46th St.
New York, NY 10036

Penn Prints
31 W. 46th St.
New York, NY 10036

Konrad Prothmann
2378 Soper Ave.
Baldwin, NY 11510

Raymond and Raymond, Inc.
1071 Madison Ave.
New York, NY 10028

Reinhold Publishing Company
600 Summer St.
P. O. Box 1361
Stamford, CT 06904

Shorewood Reproductions
Department S
475 10th Ave.
New York, NY 10018

UNESCO Catalogues
Columbia University Press
562 W. 113th St.
New York, NY 10025

University Prints
21 East St.
Winchester, MA 01890

SCOPE AND SEQUENCE

The following chart shows the sequence of instruction in the art education components of aesthetics, art criticism, art history, and art production across the scope of *ArtTalk's* content. The numbers within the boxed areas of the chart are page numbers for pages containing information or activities related to the appropriate chapter and art component.

Chapter	Aesthetics	Art Criticism	Art History	Production
The Language of Art	3–5, 7–10, 11	5, 7–10, 11	11, 2	
Art Criticism and Aesthetic Judgment	13, 14, 18, 19, 22, 23	13–21, 23	12, 22, 23	
Art History	25–33, 35–45	35, 39, 41, 45	24–45	
Careers in Art	49, 51–55, 57	51, 56, 57	46, 48–55, 57	
Line	61–66, 78, 79, 81, 85, 86, 91, 93	61, 71–74, 90, 91, 93	60, 63, 68, 79, 80, 85, 86, 92, 93	64, 65, 67, 69, 70, 73, 75–78, 80–89
Shape, Form, Space	94–99, 101–108, 110, 111, 113–116, 118–125, 127, 129, 134, 137	95, 101, 105, 108, 110, 117, 123, 134, 135, 137	94, 97, 99, 103, 106, 110, 111, 114, 119–122, 129, 136, 137	98, 100, 102–104, 106, 109, 112, 118, 124–133
Color	138–157, 158, 159–163, 168, 171, 173	144, 145, 152, 154, 155, 158, 163, 170, 171, 173	138, 141, 146, 156, 157–163, 172, 173	139, 142, 143, 145–148, 154, 155, 158, 163–169
Texture	175–178, 180–184, 185, 186–192, 197, 204, 205, 207	177, 182, 188, 197, 199, 204, 205, 207	174, 183–189, 191, 206, 207	178–181, 190, 192–203
Rhythm and Movement	210, 211–215, 216, 217, 218, 219, 220–224, 225, 226–230, 239, 241	217, 220, 238, 239, 241	212, 216, 218, 227, 228, 240, 241	215–218, 220, 222, 223, 225, 229–237
Balance	242–261, 268, 269, 271	251, 257, 259, 260, 261, 268, 269, 271	242, 244, 245, 246, 247, 249, 250, 253, 254, 258, 259, 270, 271	248, 250, 257, 261–267
Proportion	272–293, 299, 300, 302, 303–307	277, 281, 282, 283, 287, 304, 305, 307	272, 274, 275, 276–279, 281, 282, 285, 288–291, 293, 299, 302, 306, 307	273, 277, 280, 281, 283, 284, 287, 293–303
Variety, Emphasis and Unity	308–331, 332, 333, 336, 337, 344, 345, 347	311, 315, 316, 317, 318, 319, 323–325, 328, 329, 332, 339, 344, 345, 347	308, 313, 320, 322, 327, 331, 333, 346, 347	311, 319, 330, 332, 334–343

SUGGESTED DAILY LESSON PLANS FOR USING *ARTTALK* IN VARIOUS TIME FRAMES

On the following pages you will find suggested daily lesson plans for using *ArtTalk* as the main text in four of the most common time sequences allocated for art.

Plan One was developed for the use of *ArtTalk* in three nine-week sessions, a format typically found in middle school programs where sixth, seventh, and eighth graders receive one quarter, or nine weeks, of art per year.

Plan Two was developed for two 18-week semesters of art taught in two consecutive years, either in middle or junior high schools.

Plan Three provides suggested lesson plans for using *ArtTalk* in a full-year, 36-week, course. Full-year courses are usually offered to eighth and ninth graders.

Plan Four shows how *ArtTalk* could be used as the basis for two full years of art offered in sequence.

The following plans outline the daily activities—they do not include explanations as to how the activities should be conducted in the classroom. The general and chapter-by-chapter teaching suggestions found elsewhere in this guide provide detailed information on how to do the individual activities listed in the four plans.

Many of the drawing and design skill activities must be allowed less time than they would receive in traditional art education programs because we are adding three major components—aesthetics, criticism, and history—to the production component. One way to save time is to work smaller. Another time-saver is to divide responsibilities. In assigning a problem in which students are asked to show one design using various color schemes, for example, you can save time by dividing the class into groups. You can then assign one color scheme to each group, put all the finished works on display, and ask the students to discuss the similarities and differences. When four choices are offered, it is assumed that the teacher may assign only one, or may divide the class and assign a different problem to each group.

Large blocks of time are allocated for the "Imagine and Create" activities because they are more complex than the "Developing Your Skills" activities and because you should place greater emphasis on the chapter concepts, skill development, and aesthetic quality when doing "Imagine and Create."

To repeat, all of the plans provide suggestions for organizing your teaching. It is assumed that the creative side of the art educator will take over as you teach your own course—that you will decide to spend more or less time with one concept, omit another, and so on, depending upon your particular goals and students.

Note: The numbers printed in bold type in the plans are page numbers from *ArtTalk*. The abbreviation "Ch" at the top of column 3 means *Chapter*; The numbers in that column indicate chapters in *ArtTalk*.

PLAN ONE: NINE WEEKS A YEAR FOR THREE YEARS

First Quarter

Wk	Da	Ch	Classwork	Homework
1	1	1	"Introduction to Part One;" Chapter Opening, **3**; "Elements and Principles" **4**; "The Media," **5**	Write diagnostic paragraphs; bring notebooks
	2		"The Work of Art,"**7**; "Purpose of *ArtTalk*," **9**; Organize notebooks	Assign selected questions from Chapter 1 Review, **11**
	3	2	Chapter opening, **13**; "Why Study Art Criticism," **14**; "How to Criticize a Work of Art," **15**	DYS 1 or 2
	4		"Analysis," **16**; Interpretation,**16**	DYS 3
	5		"Judgment," **18**	DYS 4
2	1		"Getting Started," **20**	Assign selected questions from Chapter 2 Review, **23**
	2	3	Chapter opening, **25**; Technique Tip, "Decoding a Credit Line," **28**; Assign report topics to small groups; Start time line in notebook	DYS 1; Read about assigned topic
	3		Work in small groups preparing reports	Make visuals for reports
	4		Share reports with class	
	5		(Continue)	Assign selected questions from Chapter 3 Review,**45**

(Continued on next page)

Wk	Da	Ch	Classwork	Homework
3	1	5	"Introduction to Part II," **59**; Chapter opening, **61**; "What is Line," **63**	DYS 1 or 2
	2		"Kinds of Lines," **66**; DYS 5	DYS 3 or 4
	3		"Line Variation," **67**; DYS 6	DYS 7 or 8
	4		"What Different Lines Express," **70**; DYS 9	Complete DYS 9
	5		"Contour Drawing," **74**, Technique Tip, **75**; Practice in class	
4	1	5	DYS 11	DYS 12
	2		"Gesture Drawing," **76**; DYS 13 or 14	
	3		"Calligraphic Drawing," **78**; Technique Tip, **78**, Technique Tip: Cleaning a Brush, **80**; DYS 15	
	4		Complete work with calligraphic drawing	
	5		"Line and Value,"**81**; DYS 17	Complete DYS 17
5	1		Art Criticism of *Cabinet Maker*, **91**; "About the Artist," **92**	Write personal interpretation and judgment of *Cabinet Maker*
	2		Test (Use Chapter 5 Review, **93**, or prepared test in guide)	
	3	6	Chapter opening, **95**; "Shapes," **96**; DYS 3	DYS 1 or 2
	4		"Forms," **98**; Technique Tip: Scoring Paper, **100**; DYS 5	
	5		"Space and Its Relationship to Shape and Form," **100**; DYS 9	Complete DYS 9
6	1		"Space in Three-Dimensional Art," **104**; Technique Tip: Viewing Frame	DYS 11
	2		"How You Perceive Shape, Form, and Space," **107**; DYS 14; "Point of View," **107**	
	3		DYS 15 or 16	Complete 15 or 16
	4		"How Artists Create Shapes and Forms,"**110**; Technique Tip: Shading, **112**	
	5		DYS 17	Complete DYS 17
7	1	6	"The Illusion of Depth," **114**; begin DYS 20 or 21	DYS 22
	2		Continue DYS 20 or 21	
	3		"What Different Spaces, Shapes, and Forms Express," **117**	Begin DYS 23 or 24
	4		Complete 23 or 24	
	5		Art criticism of *Dawn*, **135**; "About The Artist," **136**	Write personal interpretation and judgment

(Continued on next page)

First Quarter

Wk	Da	Ch	Classwork	Homework
8	1		Test C, (Use Chapter 6 Review, **137**, or prepared test from guide)	
	2		Select one or more "Imagine and Create" activities from Chapter 5 or 6	Write a report about one artist and write an art criticism of one of the artist's works
	3		(Continue)	
	4		(Continue)	
	5		(Continue)	
9	1		(Continue)	(Continue)
	2		(Continue)	(Continue)
	3		Mount finished projects	
	4		Class critique: turn in reports and notebooks	
	5		(Continue critique) **Note:** The "Imagine and Create" activities are placed at the end of the quarter as culminating, synthesizing activities. Since two of the total nine weeks are required for "Imagine and Create," grades for these activities should equal at least 20 percent of the total course grade.	

Second Quarter

Wk	Da	Ch	Classwork	Homework
1	1	2	Chapter 2 review, **23**	Bring in notebooks
	2	5	Chapter 5 review, **93**	Write vocabulary sentences
	3		Do art criticism of Figure 5–1, **58**	Write personal interpretation and judgment
	4	6	Chapter 6 review, **137**	Write vocabulary sentences
	5		Do art criticism of Figure 6–1, **94**	Write personal interpretation and judgment
2	1	7	Chapter opening, **139**; "How We See Color," **140**; "Hue," **142**; Begin DYS 3 or 4	DYS 1
	2		Continue DYS 3 or 4	
	3		"Value," **143**; Technique Tip: Mixing paint to change value, **145**	Start DYS 8
	4		DYS 5	Continue DYS 8
	5		"Intensity," **146**; DYS 6 (do only one primary color)	Complete DYS 8

(Continued on next page)

Wk	Da	Ch	Classwork	Homework
3	1		"Color Schemes," **148**	Make sketch for DYS 10
	2		DYS 10 (each student does only one color scheme)	
	3		"How Artists Use Color," **159**	Make sketch for DYS 13
	4		DYS 13	
	5		Art criticism of *The Red Studio*, **171**; "About The Artist," **172**	Write personal interpretation and judgment
4	1		Test (Chapter 7 review, **173**, or prepared test from guide)	
	2	8	Chapter opening, **175**; "How We Perceive Texture," **177**; Technique Tip: Rubbing, **179**	DYS 1 or 2
	3		DYS 4	Finish DYS 4
	4		"Texture and Value," **180**	DYS 7
	5		DYS 8	
5	1	8	Continue DYS 8	
	2		"How Artists Use Texture," **183**	DYS 12
	3		DYS 11	Continue DYS 12
	4		Art criticism of *Paul Revere*, **205**; "About the Artist," **206**	Write personal interpretation and judgment
	5		Test (Use Chapter 8 review, **207**, or prepared test from guide)	
6	1	9	"Introduction to Part III," **209**; Chapter opening, **211**; "How We Perceive Visual Rhythm," **213**	DYS 1, 2, 3 or 4
	2		"Repetition," **215**; DYS 7	DYS 5 or 6
	3		"Types of Rhythm," **217**; Technique Tip: Stamp Prints, **217**	Bring materials for DYS 8, 9 or 10
	4		DYS 8, 9, or 10	
	5		"Regular," **219**; DYS 11 (using same materials as in previous activity)	
7	1		"Alternating," **220**; DYS 12, 13, or 14 (using same materials as in previous activity)	
	2		"Flowing," **222**; DYS 16	DYS 15
	3		"Progressive," **224**; DYS 17 or 18	
	4		"How Artists Use Rhythm," **227**	DYS 20
	5		Art criticism of *The Starry Night*, **239**; "About the Artist," **240**	Write personal interpretation and judgment

(Continued on next page)

Second Quarter

Wk	Da	Ch	Classwork	Homework
8	1	9	Test (Chapter 9 Review, **241**, or prepared test from guide)	
	2	10	Chapter opening, **243**; "Visual Balance," **244**; "Formal Balance," **244**	DYS 1, 2, 3 or 4
	3		"Radial Balance," **248**; "Informal Balance," **251**; DYS 9, 10, 11, or 12	DYS 8
	4		"The Expressive Qualities of Balance," **257**; Finish DYS 9, 10, 11, or 12	DYS 13 or 14
	5		Art criticism of *Cow's Skull: Red, White, and Blue*, **269**, "About the Artist," **270**	Write personal interpretation and judgment
9	1		Test (Chapter 10 Review, **271**, or prepared test from guide)	
	2		Choose one "Imagine and Create" activity from Chapter 7, 8, or 9	Work on part of "Imagine and Create" at home
	3		(Continue)	
	4		(Continue)	
	5		Complete "Imagine and Create" activity **Note:** Since only four days are allowed for "Imagine and Create" in this quarter, the "Imagine and Create" grade should carry less weight than in the previous quarter. You may wish to eliminate some skill development activities to allow more time for "Imagine and Create."	

Third Quarter

Wk	Da	Ch	Classwork	Homework
1	1	2	Chapter 2 review, **23**	Bring back notebooks
	2	5	Chapter 5 review, **93**	Work on time line
	3	6	Chapter 6 review, **137**	(Continue)
	4	7	Chapter 7 review, **173**	Write art criticism Figure 7–1, **138**
	5	8	Chapter 8 review, **207**	Write art criticism Figure 8–1, **174**
2	1	9	Chapter 9 review, **241**	Write art criticism of Figure 9–1, **210**
	2	10	Chapter 10 review, **271**	Write art criticism of Figure 10–1, **242**
	3	4	Chapter opening, **47**; Assign report topics	Read about assigned topics
	4		Work in small groups to prepare reports	Make visuals for reports
	5		Share career reports	

(Continued on next page)

Third Quarter

Wk	Da	Ch	Classwork	Homework
3	1		Share career reports	
	2	11	Chapter opening, **273**; "Art and Math," **274**	DYS 1 or 2
	3		"Art and Math," **274**; DYS 3	DYS 4
	4		"Scale," **279**; DYS 6	DYS 5
	5		Complete DYS 6	DYS 7 or 8
4	1	11	"Drawing Human Proportions," **281**; "Figures," **282**; Technique Tip: Sighting, **284**	DYS 10 or 11
	2		DYS 9	
	3		DYS 12	
	4		(Continue)	
	5		"Heads and Faces," **285**	DYS 14
5	1		DYS 13	
	2		(Continue)	
	3		"How Artists Use Proportion and Distortion," **288**	DYS 16
	4		DYS 15	
	5		Art criticism of *The Family*, **305**, "About the Artist," **306**	Write personal interpretation and judgment
6	1		Test (Chapter 11 review, **307**, or prepared test from guide)	
	2	12	Chapter opening, **309**; "Variety," **310**; DYS 3 (only one or two elements)	DYS 1 or 2
	3		"Emphasis," **312**	DYS 7 or 9
	4		DYS 8 (only one design)	
	5		"Unity," **319**; "Creating Visual Unity," **320**	DYS 10
7	1		DYS 13	DYS 11
	2		Complete DYS 13	
	3		"How Artists Use Variety and Emphasis to Enhance Unity," **330**	DYS 14
	4		Art criticism of *The Gulf Stream*, **345**, "About the Artist," **346**	Write personal interpretation and judgment
	5		Test (Chapter 12 review, **347**, or prepared test from guide)	

(Continued on next page)

Wk	Da	Ch	Classwork	Homework
8	1	12	Select "Imagine and Create" activities from any chapter in *ArtTalk*	Work on project at home when possible
	2		(Continue)	
	3		(Continue)	
	4		(Continue)	
	5		(Continue) **Note:** Since two weeks are allowed for "Imagine and Create," the student may be able to complete two projects.	
9	1		"Imagine and Create"	Work on project at home when possible
	2		(Continue)	
	3		Prepare for display	
	4		Class critique	
	5		Class critique	

PLAN TWO: EIGHTEEN WEEKS PER YEAR FOR TWO YEARS

Semester One: Year One

Wk	Da	Ch	Classwork	Homework
1	1	1	"Introduction to Part One," **1**; Chapter opening, **3**; "Elements and Principles," **4**	Bring in notebooks, Write diagnostic paragraphs
	2		Diagnostic perception drawing: Still life; Organize notebooks	
	3		"The Media of Art," **5**; "the Work of Art," **7**; "Purpose of *ArtTalk*," **9**	Assign questions from Chapter 1 review, **11**
	4	2	Chapter opening, **13**; "Why Study Art Criticism," **14**; "How to Criticize a Work of Art," **15**	DYS 1, 2, 3, or 4
	5		"Getting Started," **20**; "About the Artist," **22** (Chapters 3 and 4 will be covered in depth during the second semester)	Assign questions from Chapter 2 review, **23**
2	1	3	Chapter opening, **25**; Begin using time line	
	2	5	"Introduction to Part II," **59**; Chapter opening, **61**; "What is Line," **63**	DYS 1 or 2
	3		"Kinds of Line," **66**; DYS 5; Line variation, **67**	DYS 3 or 4
	4		"What Different Lines Express," **70**; DYS 9	Complete DYS 9
	5		"Contour Drawing," **74**; Technique Tip, **75**	

(Continued on next page)

Wk	Da	Ch	Classwork	Homework
3	1		DYS 11	Do extra contour drawings
	2		DYS 12	
	3		"Gesture Drawing," 76; Technique Tip, 77; DYS 13 or 14	
	4		"Calligraphic Drawing," 78; Technique Tip, 78; Technique Tip: Cleaning a Brush, 80; DYS 15	Continue to add to time line
	5		Complete work with calligraphic drawing	
4	1	5	"Line and Value," 81; DYS 17	Complete DYS 17
	2		Select one "Imagine and Create" project	Work on "Imagine and Create" project
	3		(Continue)	Continue time line
	4		(Continue)	
	5		Complete project	
5	1		Class critique of "Imagine and Create" projects	
	2		Art criticism of *Cabinet Maker*, 91; "About the Artist," 92	Write personal interpretation and judgment
	3		Chapter 5 review, 93	Assign one review item
	4		Continue review	
	5		Test	
6	1	6	Chapter opening, 95; "Shapes," 96; DYS 3	DYS 1 or 2
	2		"Forms," 98; Technique Tip: Scoring Paper, 100; DYS 5	Continue time line
	3		Complete DYS 5	
	4		"Space and its Relationship to Shape and Form," 100; DYS 9	Complete DYS 9
	5		"Space in Three Dimensional Art," 104; Technique Tip: Viewing Frame, 104; DYS 12	DYS 11
7	1	6	Continue DYS 12	Continue time line
	2		"How You Perceive Shape, Form, and Space," 107; DYS 14; "Point of View," 107	
	3		DYS 15 or 16	Complete 15 or 16
	4		"How Artists Create Shapes and Forms," 110; Technique Tip: Shading, 112; DYS 17	
	5		DYS 18	DYS 19
8	1		"The Illusion of Depth," 114; begin DYS 20 or 21	DYS 22
	2		Continue DYS 20 or 21	Continue time line
	3		Complete DYS 20 or 21	
	4		"What Different Spaces, Shapes and Forms Express," 117	Begin DYS 23 or 24
	5		Complete 23 or 24	

(Continued on next page)

Wk	Da	Ch	Classwork	Homework
9	1		Select one "Imagine and Create" project	Continue time line
	2		Continue project	
	3		(Continue)	
	4		Complete project	
	5		Class critique of projects	
10	1		Art criticism of *Dawn*, 135; "About the Artists," 136	Write personal interpretation and judgment
	2		Chapter 6 review, 137	Assign one review item
	3		Continue review	
	4		Test	
	5	7	Chapter opening, 139; "How We See Color," 140; Hue, 142; Begin DYS 3 or 4	DYS 1
11	1	7	Continue DYS 3 or 4	Continue time line
	2		Complete DYS 3 or 4	Start DYS 8
	3		"Value," 143; Technique Tip: Mixing Paint, 145; Begin DYS 5	Continue DYS 8
	4		Continue DYS 5	(Continue)
	5		"Intensity," 146; Begin DYS 6	Complete DYS 8
12	1		Complete DYS 6	Make sketches for DYS 7
	2		Begin DYS 7	
	3		Complete DYS 7	Continue time line
	4		"Color Schemes," 148	DYS 9
	5		Continue color schemes	Make sketches for DYS 10
13	1		DYS 10	
	2		Continue DYS 10	Continue time line
	3		"Color in Pigments," 156; Technique Tip: Making Natural Earth Pigments, 158	
	4		Continue DYS 12	
	5		"How Artists Use Color," 159	Make sketches for DYS 13
14	1		DYS 13	
	2		Complete DYS 13; Select "Imagine and Create" project	Prepare for "Imagine and Create" project
	3		"Imagine and Create" project	
	4		Continue "Imagine and Create"	Continue time line
	5		Continue "Imagine and Create"	

(Continued on next page)

Semester One: Year One

Wk	Da	Ch	Classwork	Homework
15				
	1	7	Continue "Imagine and Create"	Continue time line
	2		Complete "Imagine and Create"; class critique	
	3		Art criticism of *The Red Studio*, **171**; "About the Artist," **172**	Write personal interpretation and judgment
	4		Chapter 7 review, **173**	Assign one review page problem
	5		Chapter 7 review	
16				
	1		Test from guide	
	2	8	Chapter opening, **175**; "How We Perceive Texture," **177**; Technique Tip: Rubbing, **179**	DYS 1 or 2
	3		DYS 4	Finish DYS 4
	4		"Texture and Value," **180**	DYS 7
	5		"How Artists Use Texture," **183**	DYS 12
17				
	1		Select one "Imagine and Create" project	Collect materials for "Imagine and Create"
	2		(Continue)	Continue time line
	3		(Continue)	
	4		(Continue)	
	5		Complete "Imagine and Create"; class critique of projects	
18				
	1		Art criticism of *Paul Revere*, **205**; "About the Artist," **206**	Assign one review problem
	2		Chapter 8 review, **207**	
	3		Chapter 8 review	
	4		Test; turn in notebooks	
	5		Catch-up and clean-up day	

Semester Two: Year Two

Wk	Da	Ch	Classwork	Homework
1				
	1	1	Chapter 1 review, **11**	Bring notebook
	2		Art criticism of Figure 1–1, 2; Organize notebooks	Write personal interpretation and judgment
	3	2	Chapter 2 review, **23**	
	4		Art criticism of Figure 2–1, 12	Write personal interpretation and judgment
	5	3	Chapter opening, **25**; Technique Tip: Decoding a Credit Line, **28**; Review purpose of time line	DYS 1; Continue adding to time line

(Continued on next page)

Wk	Da	Ch	Classwork	Homework
2	1		Organize class into small groups for reports. Assign one time period in Chapter 3 to each group. Groups read material together	Read about report topic
	2		Groups continue to prepare reports	Make visuals for reports
	3		Share reports with class	
	4		Continue reports	
	5		Chapter 3 review, **45**	Assign one review problem
3	1		Continue Chapter 3 review	
	2		Test from guide	
	3	4	Chapter opening, **47**; "Thinking About an Art Career," **48**; Divide class into small groups for reports on career fields	Read about report topic
	4		Groups read material together and prepare reports	Make visuals for reports
	5		Continue report preparations	
4	1	4	Share reports in class	
	2		Continue sharing reports	
	3		Chapter 4 review, **57**	Assign one review problem
	4		Continue review	
	5		Test	
5	1	5	Chapter 5 review, **93**	
	2		Do art criticism of Figure 5–1, **60**	Write personal interpretation and judgment
	3	6	Chapter 6 review, **137**	Continue time line
	4		Continue Chapter 6 review	
	5		Do art criticism of Figure 6–1, **94**	Write personal interpretation and judgment
6	1	7	Chapter 7 review, **173**	Continue time line
	2		(Continue)	
	3		Do art criticism of Figure 7–1, **138**	Write personal interpretation and judgment
	4	8	Chapter 8 review, **207**	
	5		Do art criticism of Figure 8–1, **174**	Write personal interpretation and judgment

(Continued on next page)

Wk	Da	Ch	Classwork	Homework
7	1	9	"Introduction to Part II," 209; Chapter opening, 211; "How We Perceive Visual Rhythm," 213	DYS 1, 2, 3 or 4
	2		"Repetition," 215; DYS 7	DYS 5 or 6
	3		"Types of Rhythm," 217; Technique Tip: Stamp Prints, 217	Bring material for 8, 9, or 10
	4		DYS 8, 9, or 10	Continue time line
	5		"Regular," 219; DYS 11	
8	1	9	"Alternating," 220; DYS 12, 13, or 14	Continue time line
	2		"Flowing," 222; DYS 16	DYS 15
	3		"Progressive," 224; DYS 17 or 18	Finish 17 or 18
	4		"How Artists Use Rhythm," 227	DYS 20
	5		Select one "Imagine and Create" project, begin	Collect materials for project
9	1		"Imagine and Create"	
	2		(Continue)	Continue time line
	3		Complete "Imagine and Create"	
	4		Art criticism of The Starry Night, 239; "About the Artist," 240	Write personal interpretation and judgment
	5		Chapter 9 review, 241	Assign one review problem
10	1		Test	
	2	10	Chapter opening, 243; "Visual Balance," 244; "Formal Balance," 244	DYS 1, 2, 3 or 4
	3		DYS 5	Complete DYS 5
	4		"Radial Balance," 248	DYS 8, 9, or 10
	5		"Informal Balance," 251; DYS 12 (Each student make only one design. Give out assignments so that all types are illustrated and shared)	DYS 11
11	1	10	"The Expressive Qualities of Balance," 257	DYS 13 or 14
	2		"Imagine and Create"	Collect materials for "Imagine and Create" project
	3		(Continue)	
	4		(Continue)	
	5		Class critique of finished products	
12	1		Art criticism of Cow's Skull: Red, White, and Blue, 269; "About the Artist," 270	Write personal interpretation and judgment
	2		Chapter 10 review, 271	Assign one review problem
	3		Test	
	4	11	Chapter opening, 273; "Art and Math," 274	DYS 1 or 2
	5		Continue "Art and Math"	DYS 3 or 4

(Continued on next page)

Wk	Da	Ch	Classwork	Homework
13	1		"Scale," 279; Begin DYS 6	DYS 5, 7 or 8
	2		Continue DYS 6	
	3		"Drawing Human Proportions," 281; "Figures," 282; Technique Tip: Sighting, 284	DYS 10, or 11
	4		DYS 9	Complete DYS 9
	5		DYS 12	
14	1	11	"Heads and Faces," 285	DYS 11
	2		DYS 13 or 14	
	3		"How Artists Use Proportion and Distortion," 288	DYS 16
	4		DYS 15	Complete DYS 15
	5		Technique Tip: Paper-Mâché, 294; Begin "Imagine and Create"	Collect materials for "Imagine and Create"
15	1		"Imagine and Create"	
	2		(Continue)	Work on time line
	3		Complete "Imagine and Create"	
	4		Art criticism of *The Family*, 305; "About the Artist," 306	Write personal interpretation and judgment
	5		Chapter 11 review, 307	Assign one review problem
16	1		Test	
	2	12	Chapter opening, 309; "Variety," 310	DYS 3 (only one element)
	3		"Emphasis," 312	DYS 7 or 9
	4		DYS 8 (do one design each)	
	5		"Unity," 319; "Creating Visual Unity," 320	DYS 11
17	1	12	"How Artists Use Variety and Emphasis to Enhance Unity," 330	DYS 14
	2		"Imagine and Create"	Continue time line
	3		(Continue)	
	4		(Continue)	
	5		(Continue)	
18	1		Class critique of finished projects	
	2		Art criticism of *The Gulf Stream*, 345; "About the Artist," 346	Write personal interpretation and judgment
	3		Chapter 12 review, 347	Assign one review problem
	4		Test	
	5		Catch-up and clean-up day	

(Continued on next page)

PLAN THREE: ONE YEAR, 36 WEEKS

Wk	Da	Ch	Classwork	Homework
1	1	1	"Introduction to Part I," **1**; Chapter opening **3**	Bring in notebook
	2		"Elements and Principles," **4**; "The Media of Art," **5**; Begin organizing notebook	Write diagnostic paragraph
	3		Diagnostic perception drawing: Still life	
	4		"The Work of Art," **7**; "The Purpose of *ArtTalk*," **9**	Diagnostic perception drawing: figure
	5		Chapter 1 review, **11**	Assign one problem from review page
2	1		Test	
	2	2	Chapter opening, **13**; "Why Study Art Criticism," **14**; "How to Criticize a Work of Art," **15**; "Step One: Description," **15**	DYS 1 or 2
	3		"Analysis," **16**; "Interpretation," **16**; "Judgment," **18**; "Theories of Judging Art," **18**; "Judging Functional Objects," **19**; "Judging Your Own Work," **19**	DYS 3 or 4
	4		"Art Criticism: Getting Started," **20**	Write personal interpretation of *Christina's World*
	5		"About the Artist," **22**; Chapter 2 review, **23**	Assign one problem from review page
3	1		Test from guide	
	2	3	Organize and begin time line; Chapter opening, **25**; "The Prehistoric and Ancient World," **26**; Technique Tip: Decoding a Credit Line, **28**; "The Middle Ages," **30**	DYS 1 or 2
3	3	3	"The Fifteenth Through the Eighteenth Centuries," **31**; "The Nineteenth Century," **33**	DYS 3, 4 or 5
	4		"The Beginning of the Twentieth Century," **35**	DYS 6
	5		"From the Fifties into the Future," **40**	DYS 7
4	1		"Art from Non-Western Cultures," **42**	DYS 8
	2		Chapter 3 Review, **45**	Assign one problem from review page
	3		Test	
	4	4	Chapter opening, **47**; "Thinking about an Art Career," **48**	DYS 1
	5		"Career Fields," **49**; Divide class into small groups and assign one career field to each group	Study assignment
5	1		Work in small groups preparing reports	Make visuals for reports
	2		Present reports to class (5 reports)	
	3		Continue reports (5 reports)	
	4		Continue (5 reports)	
	5		Chapter 4 review, **57**, or test	Assign one problem from review page

(Continued on next page)

PLAN THREE: ONE YEAR, 36 WEEKS

Wk	Da	Ch	Classwork	Homework
6	1	5	Introduction to Part II, **59**; Chapter opening, **61**; "What is Line," **63**	DYS 1 or 2, and 3 or 4
	2		"Kinds of Line," **66**; "Line Variations," **67**; DYS 6	DYS 5
	3		DYS 7	DYS 8
	4		"What Different Lines Express," **70**; Begin DYS 9 or 10	Complete DYS 9 or 10
	5		"Contour Drawing," **74**; Technique Tip: Contour Drawing, **75**; Practice blind contour	Work on time line
7	1		DYS 11	DYS 12
	2		"Gesture Drawing," **76**; Technique Tip, **77**; DYS 13 or 14	
	3		"Calligraphic Drawing," **78**; Technique Tip: Calligraphic Lines, **78**; Technique Tip: Cleaning a Paint Brush, **80**; DYS 15	Work on time line
	4		DYS 16	
	5		"Line and Value," **81**; DYS 17 or 18	Complete DYS 17 or 18
8	1		"Imagine and Create": choose one	Organize materials and make plans for "Imagine and Create" project
	2		(Continue)	
	3		(Continue)	Work on time line
	4		(Continue)	
	5		Class critique of completed works	
9	1	5	Art criticism of *Cabinet Maker,* **91**; "About the Artist," **92**	Write personal interpretation and judgment
	2		Chapter 5 review, **93**	Assign one review problem
	3		Test	
	4	6	Chapter opening, **95**; "Shapes," **96**	DYS 1, 2
	5		DYS 3 or 4	Work on time line
10	1		"Forms," **98**; Technique Tip: Scoring Paper, **100**; DYS 5 or 6	DYS 7
	2		"Space and Its Relationship to Shape and Form," **101**; DYS 8	
	3		Technique Tip: Viewing Frame, **104**; DYS 9 or 10	Complete DYS 9 or 10
	4		"Space in Three-Dimensional Art," **104**; DYS 12 or 13	DYS 11
	5		Complete DYS 12 or 13	

(Continued on next page)

PLAN THREE: ONE YEAR, 36 WEEKS

Wk	Da	Ch	Classwork	Homework
11	1		"How You Perceive Shape, Form, and Space," 107; DYS 14	DYS 15 or 16
	2		"How Artists Create Shapes and Forms in Space," 110; Technique Tip: Shading, 112; DYS 17	
	3		DYS 18	DYS 19
	4		Complete DYS 18	Complete DYS 19
	5		"The Illusion of Depth," 114	
12	1	6	Continue "Illusion of Depth"	DYS 22
	2		DYS 20 or 21	
	3		Continue DYS 20 or 21	Work on time line
	4		"What Different Shapes, Spaces, and Forms Express," 119	Begin DYS 23, 24, 25 or 26
	5		Complete DYS 23, 24, 25 or 26	
13	1		"Imagine and Create" choose one	Prepare plans and materials for "Imagine and Create"
	2		(Continue)	
	3		(Continue)	
	4		Complete "Imagine and Create"; Class critique	
	5		Art criticism of *Dawn*, 135; "About the Artist," 136	Write personal interpretation and judgment
14	1		Chapter 6 review, 137	Assign one review problem
	2		Test	
	3	7	Chapter opening, 139; DYS 2 (rough sketch)	DYS 1 or Finish DYS 2
	4		"How We See Color," 140	Make sketches for DYS 3 or collect materials for DYS 4
	5		Complete DYS 3 or 4	
15	1	7	"Value," 143; Technique Tip: Mixing Paint to Change Values, 145; Begin DYS 5	Work on time line
	2		Complete DYS 5	Begin DYS 8
	3		"Intensity," 146; Begin DYS 6	(Continue)
	4		Complete DYS 6	Make sketches for DYS 7
	5		DYS 7	
16	1		Complete DYS 7	Continue time line
	2		"Color Schemes," 148	DYS 9
	3		Continue "Color Schemes"; Begin DYS 10	Continue DYS 9
	4		DYS 10	Complete DYS 9
	5		Complete DYS 10	

(Continued on next page)

PLAN THREE: ONE YEAR, 36 WEEKS

Wk	Da	Ch	Classwork	Homework
17	1		"Color in Pigments," 156; Technique Tip: Making Natural Earth Pigments, 158	Continue time line
	2		DYS 11 or 12	
	3		"How Artists Use Color," 159;	Make sketches for DYS 13
	4		Continue "How Artists Use Color;" Begin DYS 13	
	5		Complete DYS 13	Collect materials and make plans for "Imagine and Create" activity
18	1	7	"Imagine and Create"	Work on time line
	2		(Continue)	
	3		(Continue)	
	4		Complete "Imagine and Create"	
	5		Class critique of finished products	
19	1		Art criticism of *The Red Studio*, 171; "About the Artist, 172	Write personal interpretation and judgment
	2		Chapter 7 review, 173	Assign one review problem
	3		Test	
	4	8	Chapter opening, 175; "How We Perceive Texture," 177	DYS 1, 2 or 3
	5		Technique Tip: Rubbings, 179; DYS 4 or 5	Complete DYS 4 or 5
20	1		DYS 6	Work on time line
	2		DYS 6	
	3		"Texture and Value," 180	DYS 7
	4		DYS 8	DYS 9 or 10
	5		"How Artists Use Texture," 183	DYS 12
21	1	8	DYS 11	Collect materials and make plans for "Imagine and Create"
	2		"Imagine and Create"	Work on "Imagine and Create" problem at home when possible
	3		(Continue)	
	4		(Continue)	
	5		Class critique of finished projects	
22	1		Art criticism of *Paul Revere*, 205; "About the Artist," 206	Write personal interpretation and judgment
	2		Chapter 8 Review, 207	Assign one problem from review
	3		Test	
	4	9	Introduction to Part III; Chapter opening; 211, "How We Perceive Visual Rhythm," 213	DYS 1, 2, 3, or 4
	5		"Repetition," 215	DYS 5, 6, or 7

(Continued on next page)

PLAN THREE: ONE YEAR, 36 WEEKS

Wk	Da	Ch	Classwork	Homework
23	1		"Types of Rythm," **217**; "Random," **217**; Technique Tip: Stamp Prints, **217**	Add to time line
	2		DYS 8, 9, or 10	
	3		"Regular Rhythm," **219**; DYS 11	Continue time line
	4		"Alternating," **220**; DYS 12, 13, or 14	
	5		"Flowing Rhythm," **222**; DYS 15 or 16	
24	1	9	"Progressive," **224**; "How Artists Use Rhythm," **227**	DYS 17, 18, or 19
	2		"Imagine and Create"	Work on "Imagine and Create" at home when possible
	3		(Continue)	
	4		(Continue)	Add to time line
	5		Class critique of finished products	
25	1		Art criticism of *The Starry Night*, **239**; "About the Artist," **240**	Write personal interpretation and judgment
	2		Chapter 9 review	Assign one review problem
	3		Test	
	4	10	Chapter opening, **243**; "Visual Balance," **244**; "Formal Balance," **244**	DYS 1, 2, 3 or 4
	5		DYS 5 or 6	DYS 7
26	1		Complete DYS 5 or 6	Add to time line
	2		"Radial Balance," **248**; DYS 10	DYS 8 or 9
	3		"Informal Balance," **251**; DYS 11 or 12	Complete DYS 11 or 12
	4		"The Expressive Qualities of Balance," **257**	DYS 13 or 14
	5		"Imagine and Create"	
27	1	10	"Imagine and Create"	Add to time line
	2		(Continue)	
	3		Class critique of finished products	
	4		Art criticism of *Cow's Skull: Red, White, and Blue*, **269**; "About the Artist," **270**	Write personal interpretation and judgment
	5		Chapter 10 review	Assign one review problem
28	1		Test	
	2	11	Chapter opening, **273**; "Art and Math," **274**	DYS 1, 2, 3 or 4
	3		"Scale," **279**; DYS 6	DYS 5, 7 or 8
	4		DYS 6	
	5		"Drawing Human Proportions," **281**; "Figures," **282**; Technique Tip: Sighting, **284**	DYS 10 or 11

(Continued on next page)

PLAN THREE: ONE YEAR, 36 WEEKS

Wk	Da	Ch	Classwork	Homework
29	1		DYS 9	Add to time line
	2		DYS 12	
	3		DYS 12	
	4		"Heads and Faces," 285	DYS 14
	5		DYS 13	
30	1	11	DYS 13	
	2		"How Artists Use Proportion and Distortion," 288	DYS 16
	3		DYS 15	Complete DYS 15
	4		Technique Tip: Paper-Mâché, 294	
	5		"Imagine and Create"	
31	1		Continue "Imagine and Create"	Add to time line
	2		(Continue)	
	3		(Continue)	
	4		Class critique	
	5		Art criticism of *The Family*, 305; "About the Artist," 306	Write personal interpretation and judgment
32	1		Chapter 11 review	Assign one review problem
	2		Test	
	3	12	Chapter opening, 309; "Variety," 310	DYS 1 or 2
	4		DYS 3	DYS 4, 5, or 6
	5		DYS 3	
33	1	12	"Emphasis," 312	DYS 7
	2		DYS 8	
	3		DYS 8	DYS 9
	4		"Unity," 319; "Creating Visual Unity," 320	DYS 10
	5		Continue "Creating Visual Unity"	DYS 11
34	1		DYS 12	Add to time line
	2		DYS 12	
	3		DYS 13	
	4		DYS 13	
	5		"How Artists Use Variety and Emphasis to Enhance Unity," 330	DYS 14

(Continued on next page)

PLAN THREE: ONE YEAR, 36 WEEKS

Wk	Da	Ch	Classwork	Homework
35	1		"Imagine and Create"	Add to time line
	2		(Continue)	
	3		(Continue)	
	4		(Continue)	
	5		Class critique	
36	1		Art criticism of *The Gulf Stream*, **345**; "About the Artist," **346**	Write personal interpretation and judgment
	2		Chapter 12 review	Assign one review problem
	3		Test; Turn in notebooks	
	4		Clean-up	
	5		Clean-up	

PLAN FOUR: TWO FULL YEARS

Year One

Wk	Da	Ch	Classwork	Homework
1	1	1	"Introduction to Part I," **1**; "Chapter opening," **3**	Bring in notebook
	2		"Elements and Principles, **4**; "The Media of Art," **5**; Begin organizing notebook	Write diagnostic paragraph
	3		Diagnostic perception drawing: Still life	
	4		"The Work of Art," **7**; "The Purpose of *ArtTalk*," **9**	
	5		Chapter review page	Write sentences for "Using the Language of Art"
2	1		Chapter 1 test	
	2		Diagnostic perception drawing: Figures	
	3	2	Chapter opening, **13**; "Why Study Art Criticism," **14**; "How to Criticize a Work of Art," **15**; "Description," **15**	DYS 1 or 2
	4		"Analysis," **16**; "Interpretation," **16**	DYS 3
	5		"Judgment," **18**; "Theories of Judging Art," **18**; "Judging Functional Objects," **19**; "Judging Your Own Work," **19**	DYS 4

(Continued on next page)

Wk	Da	Ch	Classwork	Homework
3	1	2	"Art Criticism: Getting Started," 20	
	2		Continue art criticism "About the Artist," 22	Write personal interpretation and judgment
	3		Chapter review page, 23	Write sentences for "Using the Language of Art"
	4		Chapter test	
	5	3	Chapter opening, 25; Organize and begin time line	
4	1	3	"Prehistoric and Ancient Worlds," 25; Technique Tip: Decoding a Credit Line," 28	DYS 1
	2		"The Middle Ages," 30	DYS 2
	3		"The Fifteenth Through the Eighteenth Centuries," 31	DYS 3 or 4
	4		"The Nineteenth Century," 33	
	5		Continue "The Nineteenth Century"	DYS 5
5	1		"The Beginning of the Twentieth Century," 35	
	2		(Continue)	DYS 6
	3		"From the Fifties into the Future," 46	
	4		(Continue)	DYS 7
	5		"Art from Non-Western Culture," 42	DYS 8
6	1		Chapter review page, 45	Write sentences for "Using the Language of Art"
	2		(Continue)	
	3		Chapter test	
	4	4	Chapter opening, 47; "Thinking About an Art Career," 48	DYS 1
	5		"Career Fields," 49	
7	1		Continue "Career Fields"	DYS 2, 3, or 4
	2		(Continue)	
	3		(Continue)	
	4		Chapter review, 57	Write sentences for "Using the Language of Art"
	5		Continue review	
8	1	4	Test	
	2	5	"Introduction to Part II," 59; Chapter opening, 61	DYS 1 or 2
	3		"What is Line," 63	DYS 3 or 4
	4		"Kinds of Line," 66	Add to time line
	5		(Continue); DYS 5	

(Continued on next page)

Wk	Da	Ch	Classwork	Homework
9				
	1		"Line Variations," 67; DYS 6	
	2		DYS 7	DYS 8
	3		"What Different Lines Express," 70	
	4		DYS 9 or 10	Add to time line
	5		Complete DYS 9 or 10	
10				
	1		"Contour Drawing," 74; Technique Tip, 75	Add to time line
	2		DYS 11	
	3		DYS 11	
	4		DYS 12	
	5		DYS 12	
11				
	1		"Gesture Drawing," 76; Technique Tip, 77; DYS 13	
	2		DYS 14	
	3		"Calligraphic Drawing," 78; Technique Tip: Calligraphic Lines, 78; Technique Tip: Cleaning a Paint Brush, 80	
	4		DYS 15	
	5		DYS 16	
12				
	1	5	"Line and Value," 81; DYS 17	Add to time line
	2		DYS 17	
	3		DYS 18	
	4		"Imagine and Create"	
	5		(Continue)	
13				
	1		Continue "Imagine and Create"	Add to time line
	2		(Continue)	
	3		(Continue)	
	4		(Continue)	
	5		(Continue)	
14				
	1		Continue "Imagine and Create"	Add to time line
	2		(Continue)	
	3		(Continue)	
	4		Class critique of finished products	
	5		Continue critique	

(Continued on next page)

Wk	Da	Ch	Classwork	Homework
15	1		Art criticism of *Cabinet Maker*, **91**	Add to time line
	2		(Continue); Write a personal interpretation and judgment of *Cabinet Maker*	
	3		"About the Artist," **92**	
	4		Chapter 5 review, **93**	Write sentences for "Using the Language of Art"
	5		Continue review	
16	1	5	Chapter test	
	2	6	Chapter opening, **95**; "Shapes," **96**	DYS 1 or 2
	3		DYS 3	
	4		DYS 4	Complete DYS 4
	5		"Forms," **98**; Technique Tip: Scoring Paper **100**; DYS 5 or 6	
17	1		Continue DYS 5 or 6	
	2		DYS 7	
	3		"Space and Its Relationship to Shape and Form," **101**; DYS 8	
	4		DYS 9	Complete DYS 9
	5		Technique Tip: Viewing Frame, **104**; DYS 10	Complete DYS 10
18	1		"Space in Three-Dimensional Art," **104**	DYS 11
	2		DYS 12 or 13	
	3		Complete DYS 12 or 13	
	4		"How You Perceive Shape, Form, and Space," **107**; DYS 14	DYS 16
	5		DYS 15	
19	1		"How Artists Create Shape and Forms in Space," **110**; Technique Tip: Shading, **112**	Add to time line
	2		DYS 17	
	3		DYS 18	
	4		DYS 19	
	5		"The Illusion of Depth," **114**	DYS 22
20	1	6	DYS 20 or 21	Add to time line
	2		(Continue)	
	3		Finish	
	4		"What Different Spaces, Shapes, and Forms Express," **119**	
	5		DYS 23, 24, 25, or 26	

(Continued on next page)

Wk	Da	Ch	Classwork	Homework
21	1		Continue DYS 23, 24, 25, 26	Add to time line
	2		(Continue)	
	3		"Imagine and Create"	
	4		(Continue)	
	5		(Continue)	
22	1		Continue "Imagine and Create"	Add to time line
	2		(Continue)	
	3		(Continue)	
	4		(Continue)	
	5		Class critique of finished projects	
23	1		Art criticism of *Dawn*, **134**	Write a personal interpretation and judgment
	2		"About the Artist," **135**	
	3		Chapter 6 review	Write sentences for "Using the Language of Art"
	4		Continue review	
	5		Chapter test	
24	1	7	Chapter opening, **139**; DYS 2	DYS 1
	2		"How We See Color," **140**; "Hue," **142**	
	3		DYS 3 or 4	
	4		Complete DYS 3 or 4	
	5		"Value," **143**; Technique Tip: Mixing Paint to Change Value," **145**; Begin DYS 5	
25	1		DYS 5	
	2		"Intensity," **146**; Begin DYS 6	Add to time line
	3		DYS 6	
	4		DYS 7 or 8	
	5		DYS 7 or 8	
26	1		"Color Schemes," **148**	DYS 9
	2		Continue "Color Schemes," begin DYS 10	
	3		DYS 10	
	4		(Continue)	
	5		Complete DYS 10	

(Continued on next page)

Wk	Da	Ch	Classwork	Homework
27	1		"Color in Pigments," **156**; Technique Tip: Making Natural Earth Pigments, **158**	DYS 12
	2		DYS 11	
	3		Continue DYS 11	
	4		(Continue)	
	5		(Continue)	
28	1	7	"How Artists Use Color," **159**	Add to time line
	2		DYS 13	
	3		DYS 13	
	4		DYS 13	
	5		"Imagine and Create"	
29	1		"Imagine and Create"	Add to time line
	2		(Continue)	
	3		(Continue)	
	4		(Continue)	
	5		(Continue)	
30	1		"Imagine and Create"	
	2		(Continue)	
	3		Class critique of finished products	
	4		Art criticism of *The Red Studio*, **171**	Write personal interpretation and judgment
	5		"About the Artist," **172**	
31	1		Chapter 7 review	Write sentences for "Using the Language of Art"
	2		Continue review	
	3		Chapter test	
	4	8	Chapter opening, **175**; "How We Perceive Texture," **177**	DYS 1, 2, or 3
	5		Technique Tip: Rubbing, **179**; DYS 4 or 5	
32	1	8	DYS 6	
	2		DYS 6	
	3		"Texture and Value," **180**	DYS 7
	4		DYS 8	
	5		DYS 9 or 10	Complete DYS 9 or 10

(Continued on next page)

Year One

Wk	Da	Ch	Classwork	Homework
33				
	1		"How Artists Use Texture," 183	DYS 12
	2		DYS 11	Continue DYS 12
	3		"Imagine and Create"	
	4		(Continue)	
	5		(Continue)	
34				
	1		"Imagine and Create"	
	2		(Continue)	
	3		(Continue)	
	4		(Continue)	
	5		(Continue)	
35				
	1		"Imagine and Create"	
	2		(Continue)	
	3		(Continue)	
	4		Class critique of finished products	
	5		Continue critique	
36				
	1	8	Art criticism of *Paul Revere*, 205	Write personal interpretation and judgment
	2		"About the Artist," 206	
	3		Chapter 8 review	Write sentences for "Using the Language of Art"
	4		Chapter test; Turn in notebooks	
	5		Clean-up day	

Year Two

Wk	Da	Ch	Classwork	Homework
1				
	1	1	Review page Chapter 1, 11	Bring notebooks
	2		Art criticism of Figure 1–1, 2	Write personal interpretation and judgment
	3	2	Review page, 23	
	4		Art criticism of Figure 2–1, 12	Write personal interpretation and judgment
	5		Review Chapter 3 content	

(Continued on next page)

Wk	Da	Ch	Classwork	Homework
2	1		Continue Chapter 3 start using time line	
	2		(Continue)	
	3		Chapter 3 review page, **45**	
	4		Chapter 4 review page, **57**	
	5		(Continue)	
3	1	5	Review Chapter 5; DYS 11 or 12	Write 4 steps of art criticism of Figure 5–1
	2		(Continue); DYS 13 or 14	
	3		(Continue); DYS 15 or 16	
	4		Chapter review page, **93**	
	5		(Continue)	
4	1	6	Review Chapter 6; DYS 9 or 10	Write 4 steps of art criticism of Figure 6–1
	2		(Continue); DYS 12 or 13	
	3		(Continue); DYS 18, 21, or 22	
	4		Chapter review	
	5		(Continue)	
5	1	7	Review Chapter 7; DYS 3 or 4	Write 4 steps of art criticism of Figure 7–1
	2		(Continue)	
	3		(Continue); DYS 5 or 6	
	4		Chapter review page	
	5		(Continue)	
6	1	8	Review Chapter 8; DYS 4	Write 4 steps of art criticism of Figure 8–1
	2		(Continue); DYS 5	
	3		(Continue); DYS 12	
	4		Chapter review page, **207**	
	5		(Continue)	
7	1	9	Introduction to Part III, **209**; Chapter opening, **211**	DYS 1 or 2
	2		"How We Perceive Visual Rhythm," **213**	DYS 3 or 4
	3		"Repetition," **215**	DYS 5 or 6
	4		DYS 7	
	5		"Types of Rhythm," **217**; "Random," **217**; Technique Tip: Stamp Prints, **217**	Bring in stamp making materials

(Continued on next page)

Year Two

Wk	Da	Ch	Classwork	Homework
8				Add to time line
	1		DYS 8, 9, or 10	
	2		(Continue)	
	3		"Regular," **219**; DYS 11	
	4		Continue DYS 11	
	5		"Alternating," **220**; DYS 12, 13 or 14	
9				
	1		Continue DYS 12, 13 or 14	
	2		"Flowing," **222**; DYS 16	DYS 15
	3		Continue DYS 16	
	4		Continue DYS 16	
	5		"Progressive," **224**; DYS 17 or 18	
10				
	1		Continue DYS 17 or 18	
	2		DYS 19	
	3		DYS 19	
	4		"How Artists Use Rhythm," **227**	Begin DYS 20
	5		DYS 20	
11				
	1	9	"Imagine and Create"	Add to time line
	2		(Continue)	
	3		(Continue)	
	4		(Continue)	
	5		(Continue)	
12				
	1		"Imagine and Create"	Add to time line
	2			
	3			
	4			
	5		Class critique of finished products	
13				
	1		Art criticism of *The Starry Night*	Write personal interpretation and judgment
	2		"About the Artist," **240**	
	3		Chapter 9 review, **241**	Write sentences for "Using the Language of Art"
	4		Continue review	
	5		Chapter test	

(Continued on next page)

Wk	Da	Ch	Classwork	Homework
14	1		Chapter opening, **243**	DYS 1 or 2
	2		"Visual Balance," **244**; "Formal Balance," **244**	DYS 3
	3		DYS 5	DYS 4
	4		DYS 6	DYS 7
	5		Continue DYS 6	
15	1	10	"Radial," **248**	DYS 8
	2		DYS 10	DYS 9
	3		"Informal Balance," **251**	
	4		DYS 11	
	5		DYS 11	
16	1		DYS 12	
	2		(Continue)	
	3		(Continue)	
	4		"Expressive Qualities of Balance," **257**	DYS 14
	5		"Expressive Qualities of Balance," DYS 13	
17	1		"Imagine and Create"	Add to time line
	2		(Continue)	
	3		(Continue)	
	4		(Continue)	
	5		(Continue)	
18	1		"Imagine and Create"	Add to time line
	2		(Continue)	
	3		(Continue)	
	4		(Continue)	
	5		Class critique of finished projects	
19	1		Art criticism of *Cow's Skull: Red, White, and Blue*, **269**	Write personal interpretation and judgment
	2		"About the Artist," **270**	
	3		Chapter review, **271**	Write sentences for "Using the Language of Art"
	4		Continue review	
	5		Chapter test	

(Continued on next page)

Wk	Da	Ch	Classwork	Homework
20	1	11	Chapter opening, **273**	DYS 1 or 2
	2		"Art and Math," **274**	DYS 4
	3		"Art and Math"; DYS 3	
	4		"Scale," **279**; DYS 5	DYS 7 or 8
	5		"Scale"; DYS 6	
21	1		Continue DYS 6	
	2		Continue DYS 6	
	3		Technique Tip: Sighting, "Drawing Human Proportions," **281**; "Figures," **282**	DYS 10 or 11
	4		DYS 9	
	5		DYS 9	
22	1		DYS 12	Add to time line
	2		DYS 12	
	3		DYS 12	
	4		"Heads and Faces," **285**	
	5		DYS 13	DYS 14
23	1		DYS 13	
	2		DYS 13	
	3		DYS 13	
	4		"How Artists Use Proportion and Distortion," **288**; DYS 15	DYS 16; DYS 17
	5		DYS 15	Finish DYS 15
24	1		Technique Tip: Paper-Mâché, **294**	Add to time line
	2		"Imagine and Create"	
	3		(Continue)	
	4		(Continue)	
	5		(Continue)	
25	1		"Imagine and Create"	Add to time line
	2		(Continue)	
	3		(Continue)	
	4		(Continue)	
	5		Class critique of finished projects	

(Continued on next page)

Wk	Da	Ch	Classwork	Homework
26	1	11	Art criticism of *The Family*, **305**	Write personal interpretation and judgment
	2		"About the Artist," **306**	
	3		Chapter 11 review	Write sentences for "Using the Language of Art"
	4		Continue review	
	5		Chapter test	
27	1	12	Chapter opening, **309**	DYS 1 or 2
	2		"Variety," **310**	DYS 5 or 6
	3		DYS 3	
	4		DYS 3	
	5		DYS 4	
28	1		"Emphasis," **312**	DYS 7
	2		DYS 8	
	3		DYS 8	DYS 9
	4		DYS 8	
	5		DYS 8	
29	1		"Unity," **319**; "Creating Visual Unity," **320**	DYS 10
	2		(Continue)	
	3		DYS 12	DYS 11
	4		DYS 12	
	5		DYS 12	
30	1	12	DYS 13	Add to time line
	2		DYS 13	
	3		DYS 13	
	4		"How Artists Use Variety and Emphasis to Enhance Unity," **330**	DYS 14
	5		(Continue)	
31	1		"Imagine and Create"	Add to time line
	2		(Continue)	
	3		(Continue)	
	4		(Continue)	
	5		(Continue)	

(Continued on next page)

Wk	Da	Ch	Classwork	Homework
32				
	1		"Imagine and Create"	
	2		(Continue)	
	3		(Continue)	
	4		(Continue)	
	5		(Continue)	
33				
	1		"Imagine and Create"	
	2		(Continue)	
	3		(Continue)	
	4		(Continue)	
	5		(Continue)	
34				
	1		"Imagine and Create"	
	2		(Continue)	
	3		(Continue)	
	4		Class critique of finished products	
	5		Continue critique	
35				
	1		Art criticism of *The Gulf Stream*, **345**	Write personal interpretation and judgment
	2		"About the Artist," **346**	
	3		Chapter review page	Write sentences for "Using the Language of Art"
	4		Continue review	
	5		Chapter test	
36				
	1		Each student write art criticism of one of his or her own works from "Imagine and Create"	
	2		Select one functional object and write an art criticism study of it	
	3		(Continue)	
	4		Clean-up	
	5		Clean-up	

(Continued on next page)

PART TWO

Chapter Lesson Plans

On the following pages you will find lesson plan information for each of the twelve chapters in **ArtTalk**. The information is organized according to the main headings in the text. Included for each main heading, and for the chapter introduction, are *Purpose Statements*, *Learning Outcomes*, and *Teaching Strategies*. In many cases you will also find *Additional Activities*. Following this information are the answers to the Chapter Review questions, the Study Question worksheets, and the Chapter Tests.

DRAWING WITH A COMPUTER

Drawing with a Computer

The artworks for the Imagine and Create project on pages 132 and 133 were created on a MacIntosh computer, using MacPaint software and a Laser Writer printer. You and your students can, of course, create similar artwork using many other combinations of computer hardware and software.

Where do you start if you have had no experience with computers and know little about them? First, if you are like many people, you must overcome your anxieties regarding the new technology. You need to find a computer, have someone show you how to turn it on, and simply "play" with it. You will soon become fascinated with the creative, artistic possibilities offered by this new medium.

Your second step will depend on whether or not any hardware (the computer itself and related equipment) is available to you in your school, and, if so, what kind of hardware. If your school can provide you, for example, with Apple IIe's, then you will want to make sure you buy software (sets of instructions for specific purposes) that works on that computer. In almost all cases, information on the software package will tell you what kind of hardware is needed to run the software.

It may be that no computers are available to you in your school, but the school will purchase computers for use in the art curriculum. In this situation you may want to experiment with various software packages before choosing your computer. Once you know which software you would like to use, have your school purchase the hardware that will run that software.

A great deal of very good, "user friendly" software for art and graphic production is available. Some of the more frequently used drawing and painting software in school classrooms are Mousepaint, Dazzle Draw, PIXIT, Blazing Paddles, and Art Studio. Check with agencies, such as your state education department, and your local school or library for more information. The periodical section in your library should contain several computer and consumer journals and magazines, in which you'll find lists and reviews of software for the different computers.

All of the commercially available software comes with user manuals (often called *documentation*) that explain how to use the software. Many of the directions will actually appear on the screen. By reading the manual and following the directions on the screen, you and your students can quickly learn how to make art with that particular software. Of course, the more you use the software, the more accomplished you, and they, will become.

Chapter 1: The Language of Art

INTRODUCING THE CHAPTER

Purpose

To introduce students to the idea that there is a language of art

Learning Outcomes

After completing this section students will be able to explain the meaning of the "language of art."

Teaching Strategies

Motion pictures, TV shows, and even popular music have aesthetic qualities that reach out to the audience. In the same way, visual art can communicate.

Ask if students have heard about the plaque attached to Pioneer 10 or the gold record sent along on Voyager 2. The first plaque was a last-minute idea dreamed up by Carl Sagan, his wife, and another couple. People all over the world raised such a fuss over what sights and sounds from earth should be carried out into space that a committee had to be formed to decide on the content.

THE ELEMENTS AND PRINCIPLES

Purpose

To familiarize students with terms and general concepts

Learning Outcomes

After completing this section students will be able to name the elements and principles.

Teaching Strategy

All elements and principles will be explained in much greater detail in Parts Two and Three. At this point simply have students memorize the names.

THE MEDIA OF ART

Purpose

To introduce media and differentiate them from art forms

Learning Outcomes

After completing this section students will be able to explain what is meant by media.

Teaching Strategies

Have students write a definition of *medium* and *media*. Also have them list examples.

THE WORK OF ART

Purpose

To help students understand that no two artists will interpret the same subject in the same way

Learning Outcomes

After completing this section students will be able to explain what is meant by subject, form, and content.

Teaching Strategies

Although many artists may begin with the same subject, each will bring a different background and a different style to the interpretation. That interpretation, as perceived by the viewer and understood in terms of the viewer's own personal experiences, becomes the content or meaning of the work. That meaning is like a metaphor; the work of art represents something more than just the subject of the work. A painting of a woman holding a child may stand for "motherhood," "loneliness," or "strength." The meaning of the work depends upon the way the artist has manipulated the elements using the principles and on the emotions and knowledge the viewer brings to a study of the work.

After reviewing the three works in Figure 1–7, ask the students to list their similarities and differences. Ask them to decide which works have the most in common and which have the least. Ask them to create a new, emotional title, such as "Celebration," for each work.

THE PURPOSE OF ARTTALK

Purpose

To help students understand why the study of art is worthwhile

Learning Outcomes

After completing this section students will understand the purpose of *ArtTalk*.

Teaching Strategies

Ask the students to look at all the illustrations in Chapter 1. Ask them to choose their favorite. Encourage them to discuss their preferences and to give reasons for them.

The students will probably be reluctant to give their opinions at first because they will feel unsure of themselves. Explain that *ArtTalk* will help them become more comfortable with all kinds of works. They may not like them all, and they are not expected to like everything, but they should not be afraid to say what they think.

Additional Activities

While the students are becoming acquainted with the text, you may want to use the time to get to know your students. School records can tell you a great deal about academic performance, reading abilities, and so on, but these records are not always true indicators of artistic potential. Also, with all of your other responsibilities, you may not be able to check school records before the first week of classes. Therefore, the following are offered as suggestions for getting to know the students in your classes in other ways.

Some students may feel insecure about trying these activities. Assure them that these assignments will not be graded and are intended for diagnostic purposes only. You will use the information you collect to discover what they need to learn.

1. Set up a large still life arrangement of odd objects, such as kitchen utensils, pots and pans, a bicycle wheel, hub caps, an old fashioned typewriter, stuffed toys, old posters, fabrics with bright colors, store mannequins dressed in strange outfits, big plants, stuffed animals, and animal bones. Whatever you choose, do not select a vase with pretty flowers. Pretty things inhibit the students. Then ask students to draw the arrangement.

The quality of the student's work should be a fair indicator of his or her drawing ability. Don't be impressed by quantity. Some very talented students work slowly and meticulously. Look for quality of line, accuracy in proportions, relationship of one object to the next, size of negative space, overlapping, and detail.

To rate these drawings objectively, use a scale of 1 to 5. Let 1 be the lowest rating, standing for undeveloped perception, objects floating on the picture plane, thoughtlessly made lines, inaccurately drawn shapes, and so on. Let 5 be the highest rating. Set up three stacks—ones, fives, and those in between. You can be more discriminating if needed later on.

2. Ask one or more students to dress up in wild costumes, the sillier the better. Then ask the class to draw the models. The crazier the costumes the less inhibited students will feel. Use these figure drawings as another indicator of previous training and natural drawing ability. The results may be anything from stick figures to mature work. Again, the easiest way to rate these is on an objective scale from one to five, separating the works into three piles.

3. One quick way to ascertain your students' ability to handle the academic material in the text is to ask them to write something for you. Some topics you might use are, "My definition of art," "My previous experiences with art," "My visit to an art galley or art show," "Why I signed up for an art class," and so on.

Just a few sentences will tell you a great deal about each student's verbal ability.

There are also several games and activities you can use to sharpen students' perceptions. The games can be used throughout the course.

1. Display for a few seconds a tray containing five or more objects. Then place the tray out of sight and ask the students to list or draw the objects on the tray. Repeat the activity increasing the number of objects and their complexity. Give the students more time to study the tray. As students' perceptive abilities grow over the duration of the course, decrease the amount of time for viewing the items. To make the game more interesting, assign different students the job of bringing in the objects, and challenge them to stump the class. You can even give the game a name like "Stump the Artists," and give points to those who get all of the items right.

2. Another perception-sharpening activity is to ask the class to write a paragraph describing a familiar object or area. For example, one day you might ask for a description of the main entrance to the school. Challenge them to remember outlines, shapes, forms, spaces, colors, and textures. Ask some of the students to read their descriptions aloud, then display a Polaroid photo of the entrance to learn what was forgotten. Choose very specific areas such as the lunchroom serving area, the principal's desk, the flagpole area, or the checkout desk in the media center. These are places students see every day but may never really look at.

3. Another game is a variation of the stunt pulled on law students to prove that witnesses are not accurate. Ask another teacher or staff member to interrupt your class while you are holding a discussion. Ask the students to excuse you; talk to the visitor for about one minute. Then, after the visitor leaves the room, ask the class to write a description of the visitor, or draw a sketch, indicating such things as hair style, clothing, shoes, any objects carried, any distinguishing features, and so on. Then call the person back into the room so that the students can compare their descriptions or sketches with the live model.

4. This game proves that no two people think exactly the same way. Give every student a sheet of paper exactly the same size, and be sure that each student has access to a box of crayons or markers in a variety of colors. Make sure that each student's paper cannot be seen by other students. Ask students to do the following: draw a straight, red line near the top of the paper; then, draw a blue, "S" curve that crosses the straight line; next, draw a green zigzag line beginning at one end of the curve; draw a violet curve that starts at the red line and finishes on the left side of the paper; and so on. . . . There will be many different results to these directions. When you are finished, have the students place their works on display so that they can see the variety.

ANSWERS

Chapter 1 Review: Talking about Art

USING THE LANGUAGE OF ART

Answers will vary according to the artworks selected. The answers should show, however, that students understand the meanings of the terms as given in Chapter 1 and in the text Glossary. You may wish to require that students include the artist and title for each work cited. If so, titles should be underlined.

LEARNING THE ART ELEMENTS AND PRINCIPLES

1. The language of art.
2. Visual symbols other than words.
3. Line, shape and form, space, value, color, and texture.
4. Rhythm, balance, proportion, variety, emphasis, and unity.
5. Answers will vary, but all will be found in the section entitled "The Purpose of *ArtTalk*." (a) to help you understand many different kinds of artworks, (b) to understand why you like certain artworks, (c) to understand why an artist does certain things and what he or she is trying to accomplish, (d) to help you learn the language of art, (e) to help you develop your skills of observing and thinking about what you observe, (f) to help you better express your ideas and feelings through your own works, (g) to help you be better able to understand your visual environment and the feelings and ideas of others, and (h) to help you learn more about your own feelings and ideas.
6. Skills of observing and thinking about what you observe.
7. Content.

INCREASING YOUR ART AWARENESS

1. The subject matter (the part of a work of art that the viewer can easily recognize) is a young woman.
2. The subject is an Ancient Greek vase. The vase has a function, whereas the artwork shown in Figure 1–2 does not. The subject of a work of art that has a function, such as a chair, is the chair itself.
3. Subject and content.
4. Answers will vary.
5. Answers will vary. The most obvious choice for comparison is Marisol's *The Family* (Figure 11–45).

UNDERSTANDING ART CULTURE AND HERITAGE

1. *Young Hunter with Dog.* 5th Century B.C.
2. *Saint George and The Dragon* and *Young Woman in Netherlandish Dress.*
3. The British defending the Rock of Gibraltar from the Spaniards in 1781.
4. The artist had to depend on someone else's description of the scene. Actually, he learned of it from an eyewitness account.
5. Answers will vary.

JUDGING THE QUALITY OF ART

Answers will vary.

LEARNING MORE ABOUT ART

Answers will vary.

Study Question Worksheet

1. Visual images that represent something else.
2. Elements of art.
3. Principles of design.
4. The material used to make a work of art.
5. Media
6. Subject, form, and content.
7. You do not need language to understand it.
8. Line, shape, form, space, value, color, and texture.
9. Rhythm, balance, proportion, variety, emphasis, and unity.
10. Sculpture; marble.
11. The house.
12. Painting.
13. The content.
14. Understand architecture better; choose clothes or hairstyles differently.
15. The dislike of technology.

Chapter Test

1. B
2. A
3. A
4. B
5. A
6. C
7. A
8. B
9. C
10. A
11. E
12. B
13. C
14. D
15. B
16. A
17. A
18. D
19. E
20. B
21. subject
22. medium
23. symbol
24. content
25. form

Chapter 2: Art Criticism and Aesthetic Judgment

WHY STUDY ART CRITICISM?

Purpose

To explain the importance of art criticism

Learning Outcomes

After completing this section, students will be able to
- name several benefits of art criticism and explain its purpose.
- define art criticism and aesthetic judgment.

Teaching Strategies

After discussing the reading in class, have students write their own definitions of *art criticism* and *aesthetic judgment*. Also have them list the benefits of studying art criticism.

HOW TO CRITICIZE A WORK OF ART

Purpose

To introduce students to the sequential procedures of art criticism

Learning Outcomes

After completing this section students will be able to
- begin to criticize works themselves.
- explain three theories of art.
- know what to look for when judging functional objects.

Teaching Strategies

It would be best if you discussed the four steps in criticism carefully with the class before you let them study *Christina's World*. To save time you might assign "Developing Your Skills" 1, 2, and 3 to three different groups. Then each group can present its results to the other members of the class.

In discussing the four steps of art criticism be sure to point out the procedures for each step. Emphasize the objectivity required for steps one and two.

Be very sure that the students understand that step three, interpretation, is much more than story telling. In the study of literature students must interpret and generalize from the given data. This process is also required in art if they are to perceive more than superficial qualities. During step three, each student must go beyond story telling to generalize, to find the metaphor or allegory in the work. To say that Figure 2–6, *The Blue Wall*, is about two boys by a wall is not enough. To understand the work, the student must study the relationship between the two boys. Ask them to notice that even though the boys look away from each other as if they are angry or frightened, their bodies touch ever so slightly. Ask the students what the touching means. To understand, they must see the touching and sense the relationship between the boys.

Because they are authority figures, teachers tend to talk more than they listen. While teaching about interpretation, however, it is very important that you not impose your own interpretation upon the students. Both you and they may confront the same visual facts, but you bring experiences and values to your interpretation that may vary greatly from theirs. This does not mean that you should totally avoid sharing your ideas with them, but you must respect their opinions. As long as a student's interpretation is backed up by visual facts, it is valid, even if you disagree with it philosophically or morally.

For example, when conducting an art criticism session with high school seniors in 1969, this author was surprised when students interpreted Mary Cassatt's *The Bath* as standing for the loneliness of someone separated from family. This interpretation didn't make sense until the author realized that those students were facing the draft and Vietnam. On another occasion, students studying Picasso's *Guernica* saw the theme as a protest against nuclear energy. This seemed unfounded until the author realized that there is a lightbulb in the center of an eye in the top center of the composition. Coincidentally, the discussion was held on the Monday after the Three Mile Island nuclear accident.

Interpretation is the most important step in art criticism, and it is the most difficult to accomplish. At first, students will want to tell stories about the subject matter. Later, if they do dig deeply into their emotions to uncover the metaphor in the work, they may be embarrassed to share their feelings. Making interpretive statements requires courage. Be sensitive to their feelings as they venture to make generalizations about each work. In the beginning you may even want to let them write their interpretations and turn them in while covering the other steps as a group.

When students approach *Christina's World*, ask them to stop and list everything they see in the picture. You may have them work separately, or, because this is their first critical attempt, you might like to have them do it as a group. One student can write the class's findings on the board or on chart paper. Then when they begin interpretation, you can keep referring back to the clues collected. Generalizations should be backed up by visual facts collected during the first two stages.

For extra practice or as homework, you might ask the students to apply the four steps of art criticism to Figure 2–1, Mary Cassatt's *The Bath*.

Keep in mind that as students begin to make their own artworks in Chapter 5, they can apply the four steps of art criticism to the result. This will help them become more independent. It will also acquaint them with the process of using objective procedures to criticize their works rather than subjective, often self-deprecatory procedures.

Additional Activities

1. A successful method for getting students to participate in critical activities is peer teaching. Divide the class up into small groups. Balance each group with students both below- and above-average academically. Groups of from three to five are a good size. Give each group one large print or one full page illustration from the text to study.

Ask each group to select a secretary to keep notes as they go through the critical procedure. Ask them to discuss the work together. Then, at the end of the class period, give each group a few minutes to report their findings to the class. The group can elect a representative speaker, or each person might report on a different part of the study.

Another version of this activity is to use role playing. Pretend the activity is a scientific study. For example, each group could pretend to be explorers from another galaxy who are trying to understand from artworks something about the civilizations on this planet. In this case, use realistic works that show the interaction of people, such as Moore's *Family Group*, Homer's *Hound and Hunter*, Rembrandt's *Portrait of a Lady with an Ostrich-Feather Fan*, or Benton's *I Got a Girl on Sourwood Mountain*.

Be sure that at the beginning of each report each group gives the name of the artist, the title of the work, the medium used, and the size.

Here, too, the group can discuss the first two steps together. Then each member of the group can write his or her interpretation and judgment.

2. To help the students understand the practical applications of art criticism, you might bring some functional objects to class, such as cookware, a chair, eating utensils, a hammer, a shoe, a typewriter, a coffee cup, or a drinking glass. Then ask the students to criticize the object. As they begin interpretation, remind them that they must consider how the object works. This means that they must try it out. At the judgment stage they must make two decisions: Is the object aesthetically pleasing? Does it function properly? It does not matter if a typewriter is beautiful if you can't write a letter on it.

3. You might take the class to a furniture store on a field trip. Perhaps a store representative could speak to the class and explain how to recognize the quality of something like a sofa. Ask each student to select a chair that looks good and then criticize it. Before the trip, set up some criteria for interpretation and judgment. When discussing shape and form consider the inner structure of the object. They should look for quality construction as well as aesthetic quality. Beauty is more than skin deep. An added advantage to this activity is that it helps students become better consumers.

4. Another very practical application of art criticism is in analyzing advertisements. For example, a cigarette ad may have few words, but the visual image sends a strong message. Ask students to use the critical method to "read"

the visual messages sent by magazine and television advertisements to see what they are really communicating. With magazine ads, block out the words. With TV, turn off the sound and interpret scenes and body language. For TV commercials, ask students to write a description of what they saw and new dialogue based on their interpretations. When they get to the judgment step, you might ask them to draw conclusions about the importance of the visual image in advertising. Is there a difference between the visual and verbal messages?

5. Brainstorm with the class to come up with new applications for critical analysis.

ANSWERS

Chapter 2 Review: Talking about Art

USING THE LANGUAGE OF ART

Answers will vary according to the artworks selected. The answers should show, however, that students understand the meanings of the terms as given in Chapter 2 and in the text Glossary. You may wish to require that students include the artist and title for each work cited. If so, titles should be underlined.

LEARNING THE ART ELEMENTS AND PRINCIPLES

1. The courage to speak your mind and make sound aesthetic judgments.
2. Description, analysis, interpretation, judgment.
3. Analysis.
4. Judgment.
5. Description.
6. Interpretation.
7. Height, width, and depth.
8. How the object works when it is used.

IINCREASING YOUR ART AWARENESS

1. Answers will vary.
2. Imitationalism.
3. Answers will vary. One possible choice is Figure 2–4, which is realistic, well organized, and emotional.
4. Answers will vary. The best answer may be emotionalism because of the strong feelings that the figure conveys.
5. Answers may vary but most students will probably agree that 2–6 is more emotional and that 2–7 is more lifelike.
6. Answers will vary. They have been judged a success. They are both beautiful and useful.

UNDERSTANDING ART CULTURE AND HERITAGE

1. Answers will vary.
2. Steinlen lived from 1859 to 1923. Students should guess dates within the adult years of Steinlen's life.
3. Mary Cassatt, Margareta Haverman, and Marianne Brandt

4. Théophile-Alexander Steinlen, *Winter: Cat on a Cushion*
5. Sir Jacob Epstein, *The Visitation*, 1926, bronze, 66 × 19 × 17 1/2".

JUDGING THE QUALITY OF ART

Answers will vary.

LEARNING MORE ABOUT ART

Answers will vary.

Study Question Worksheet

1. The skill of judging a work of art.
2. The reasons why we find a work of art beautiful or satisfying.
3. The theory that says art should speak to us through our emotions and create a mood.
4. Description—What do I see?
   Analysis—How is the work organized?
   Interpretation—What is happening? What is the artist trying to say?
   Judgment—What do I think of the work?
5. Helps you organize your thoughts, base sound judgments on observation, and worry less about what other people think.

6. People have different life experiences.
7. The elements and principles.
8. The theory that art should imitate real life.
9. You try to find hidden messages.
10. To explain the personal meaning of art.
11. You might miss something important or interesting.
12. You must consider how they work.
13. Description (could accept Analysis also).
14. People.
15. Watercolor and egg tempera.

Chapter Test

1. aesthetic
2. description
3. analysis
4. interpretation
5. judgment
6. interpretation
7. judgment
8. formalism
9. imitationalism
10. emotionalism
11. analysis
12. functional (accept such words as *useful* and *working*)
13. art criticism
14. description
15. analysis
16. objective
17. imitationalism
18. Wyeth
19. imitationalism
20. Christina or "the girl"

Chapter 3: Art History

Purpose

- To make students aware of their artistic heritage
- To help them see the relationship between world events and the creation of art.

Learning Outcomes

After completing this chapter the student will be able to
- decode the credit lines that accompany the reproductions in the text.
- place on a timeline the periods of art discussed in the text and/or make a statement concerning each period.
- research and write a paper on one or more of the periods of art discussed in the text.
- understand how historical events influence artists' works.

Teaching Strategies

When testing students on the information in this chapter, an open-book test is preferred. The primary focus of this course is not art history. To ask young, beginning students to recall an excessive number of names and dates is unreasonable.

If you don't wish to spend a lot of time on art history, you can divide the class into groups of two or three and assign different time periods to each group. The groups then would study only that period in the text and report on it to the class. To make the reports more interesting, they can be spaced throughout the year. Encourage the speakers to use as many visual aids as they can, and to use the school media center and the local library. Suggest that they use large prints of artworks if they are available; the library is a good source of either prints or oversize art books. Your media center might have equipment with which the students can make slides from books to use in the report. Slides ensure that everyone in the class can see the works being discussed. Dressing up in costumes, role playing, or presenting a dramatization can also make a report more fun for everybody.

A good choice for a dramatization is one event from the artist's life. Dramatizations make stronger impressions than straight reports. For example, a debate on style between Impressionists and Post-Impressionists would be interesting, especially if the students took on the roles of real characters, such as Monet, Renoir, Cezanne, or van Gogh.

Students usually know much more than they put in a report. Ask leading questions during the presentation if the report seems too dry or lacking in depth.

To be sure that the audience pays attention, let the students who give the reports create their own tests. Check the questions before using the test.

In this guide there are reproducible time line sheets, which students can keep in a loose-leaf notebook. On each time line page the vertical line represents time. The horizontal lines to the right of the time line represent major world events. The horizontal lines to the left of the time line should be filled in with the names of works of art that appear in the book. A few well known artworks not pictured in *ArtTalk*, but easily found in reference books, are listed to the left of the time line.

Notice that proportion of time span to line length is not in scale. Populations have grown; events of global importance have increased. As the twenty-first century is approached, more world events and works of art occur on the line. As a result, the first 30,000 years before Christ require about the same length on the time line as the last 25 years of the twentieth century. It may be helpful to keep in mind that the ancient city of Rome had a population comparable to that of an average American town today.

During the time this chapter is studied it is better for students to work with the time line sheets than regular study sheets. Using the time lines will help them grasp the relationship between art and world events.

Every effort was made to include a broad spectrum of works from all cultures and all periods of time, but since the major purpose of this book is to teach students the language of art rather than the history of art, some major works have had to be omitted. There are, for example, several monuments not included in the text that are named on the time lines. These are works, such as the Parthenon or the Great Wall of China, that the students will have seen in history books or can find pictured in encyclopedias.

If you have a copying machine with enlarging capability, you might make an enlargement of the major time line, laminate it, and display it somewhere in the room. Students might attach sketches of the masterpieces shown in the text in the proper spot on the time line. They might even add small prints of works that are not in the text or photocopy works from books, color the photocopies, and add the name of the artist and the title of the work. This kind of time line activity may be very casual, or you may wish to give points to students who bring in works to be placed on the line. If there is not enough room for all of the pieces at one place in time, strings of yarn can be attached to the photocopy and pictures arranged above or below the proper place with yarn leading to the proper place on the time line.

Additional Activities

1. To help students learn the names of artists and styles, look at the new materials appearing on the commercial scene every day. Check your supply catalogs.

2. Turn some extra prints found in magazines into puzzles. Dry mount the print on a strong backing, such as poster board or mat board. If you are going to make more than one puzzle, put each on a different color backing so that if the pieces get mixed up they can be separated by color. Laminate the work, if possible, to protect the surface. Then, using a sharp cutting blade, cut the print into

puzzle pieces. (Another way to distinguish between puzzles is to cut with different types of lines. Use vertical and horizontal lines for one puzzle, diagonals for another, and curves for another.) Since the main purpose of the puzzles is to familiarize students with artworks, don't make the pieces too small. Use a separate storage container for each puzzle. Puzzles help slower learners, but they may not be stimulating enough for brighter and/or older students. For them you might hold puzzle speed competitions. Teams of students can compete to see which team can assemble a puzzle the fastest.

3. Another spare time activity to familiarize students with artworks is using prints in card games. This will help them become familiar with the names of artists and the titles of works, as well as become familiar with the look of the works.

These card games will be fun for all students, but they will be especially helpful for slower learners.

Mount medium-size prints on poster board, leaving a small margin around the print. Cut the print in fourths. Print the name of the artist and the title in the margin of each section of the print. Laminate the sections to make them last longer. Using about 10 prints (40 sections), create a "deck" of cards with which the students can play a variation of "Go Fish." The students must ask for cards by artist and/or title. If you have many works by one artist, they must always use titles, but if you only have one print from each artist, they may use just artist. The students request the work by saying, "Do you have any Picassos?" After a player has collected all four sections of a print, that print must be placed on the table for all to see. This exposes all players and observers to the print. The more times the students hear the names repeated, and the more times they see the works of art, the more they learn. Use artists and works that you really think are worth learning about.

4. If you can find individual prints that are small enough, you might organize them into a time-period recognition game. For example, you might set up one deck with four Ancient Egyptian works, four Byzantine works, four Gothic, four Renaissance, four Tribal African, four Chinese, etc. At the beginning of the year you can use stick-on labels that identify the periods. Later you can remove the labels. Be careful that each set of four in a deck is distinctly different from every other set in that deck. For example, don't put a set of Japanese and a set of Chinese cards in one deck unless you are using labels.

For a more advanced game, organize the cards by style. In this deck you might include four Impressionist works, four Cubist works, four Surrealist works, and so on. Again, be very careful not to use two styles that might be confused, such as Non-Objective and Abstract Expressionist, or American Regionalist and English Landscape.

Sources for prints are listed in the bibliography section of this guide.

5. Another way to help students become more familiar with artists is to set aside one small bulletin board as an "Artist of the Week" board. The first week of school you yourself can provide the display. Later, responsibility for the bulletin board might be assigned to one student or a

team of students. There are several ways to plan displays. You might decide which artists you want to feature and assign the artist as you assign the group. Or you might have a list of artists you wish to include during the year, and allow each student or group to select one from your list. A third method might be to allow each student or group to freely choose an artist, as long as you reserve the right to approve the choice. This third method gives the students a chance to do a little research and include artists that appeal especially to them.

It would be best if you set up some guidelines for student displays. Grade the display according to the guidelines. Some of the criteria you might include are neat lettering, quantity of information, accuracy of information, creativity, and aesthetic quality. The minimum information would include artist's name, country, dates of birth and death, style, and titles of works displayed.

Answers

Chapter 3 Review: Talking About Art

USING THE LANGUAGE OF ART

Answers will vary according to the artworks selected. The answers should show, however, that students understand the meanings of the terms as given in Chapter 3 and in the text Glossary. You may wish to require that students include the artist and title for each work cited. If so, titles should be underlined.

LEARNING THE ART ELEMENTS AND PRINCIPLES

1. The distinct, identifying methods and features of a group of artists.
2. A combination of the behaviors and ideas of a group of people.
3. Answers will vary according to the credit line chosen. Answers should reflect an understanding of the information given in the Technique Tip entitled "Decoding a Credit Line" on page 28.
4. Perspective is a technique that creates the illusion of depth on a flat surface. An architect, Filippo Brunelleschi, developed it.
5. It is a name given to moving scuptures. As in Alexander Calder's work, the sculpture is a balanced arrangement that stays in motion.

INCREASING YOUR ART AWARENESS

1. Mannerism
2. Neoclassicism
3. Realism
4. Fauves
5. Futurists
6. *De Stijl*
7. Pop Art
8. Color Field Painting

UNDERSTANDING ART CULTURE AND HERITAGE

1. *Horses with Black Manes* (3–2)
   Coffin (Detail) (3–3)
   Discobulus (3–4)
   Seated Figure (3–27)
2. *Man of the Republic* (3–5)
3. 17th - Baroque.
   18th - Rococo.
   19th - Neoclassicism, Romanticism, Realism, Impressionism, Post-Impressionism.
   20th - German Expressionism, Abstract, Cubism, De Stijl, Dadaism, Futurism, Fauves, Surrealism, Ashcan, Regionalists, Mexican Muralists.
4. Answer will vary.
5. Raised the artist's rank; artists mingled with nobles.
6. The French Revolution brought an end to the Rococo style because the style mirrored the idle, useless life of the aristocracy and the Revolution caused the downfall of the aristocracy.
7. Neoclassicism, Romanticism, Realism, Impressionism, and Post-Impressionism.

JUDGING THE QUALITY OF ART

Answers will vary.

LEARNING MORE ABOUT ART

Answers will vary.

Activity 1: Study Question Worksheet

1. A combination of behavior and ideas that distinguish a people.
2. Distinct, identifying methods and features of a group of artists.
3. Cave paintings.
4. Religion.
5. Greece.
6. In the catacombs of Rome.
7. Greek, Roman, and Oriental.
8. 1,000 years.
9. The Age of Faith.
10. Romanesque.
11. Gothic.
12. Rebirth.
13. Bankers and merchants became powerful; artist mixed with nobles.
14. Creating the illusion of depth on a flat surface.
15. Oil painting.
16. Emotional scenes and distorted figures.
17. In the distance, space was opened to infinity.
18. For dramatic effects, creating bright spots and dark shadows.
19. Greek and Roman.
20. Coolness, rules, lack of emotion.
21. Political, social and moral issues; peasants and factory workers, everyday subjects.
22. Effects of sunlight and reflected light; melted solid forms and blurred colors; dabs of paint.

23. Cézanne, van Gogh, Gauguin.
24. Art that emphasizes structures and design.
25. Africa.
26. Mondrian.
27. Atomic theory.
28. Fantasy and anger.
29. Realistic details.
30. City scenes of tenements, crowded streets, and poor people.
31. Sculptures that move.
32. The beauty of America.
33. Architect. Form should follow function.
34. Mexican muralists.
35. Printmaking, weaving, fabrics, ceramics, jewelry, crafts.
36. Elements and principles as subject matter. Stresses emotion.
37. Everyday objects.
38. To create optical illusions.

39. Color field painting.
40. Hyper-realism and Super-realism.
41. Hinduism and Buddhism.
42. A calm, deep reflection about life.
43. Human figures in sculpture.
44. To link people to unseen forces.

Activities 2 and 3

Answers will vary.

Activity 4: Using the Credit Line

1. Judith Leyster.
2. *Self Portrait*.
3. 1635.
4. Oil on canvas.
5. Height 72.3 × width 65.3 cm (29 3/8 × 35 5/8 in.).
6. National Gallery of Art, Washington, D.C.
7. Mr. and Mrs. Robert Woods Bliss.
8. Answers will vary.

Activity 5: Time Line

	Dates A.D.	
Bayless, Thai Silk . . . , 12–15	1986	
Clements, Evening . . . , 10–25		
Garrison, *Long* . . . , 10–11		
Hansen, *Traveler* . . . , 3–20		
Hardin, *Blossoms*, 10–13	1984	Pioneer 10 leaves the solar system
Carrasco, *Glads* . . . , 9–8		
Garrison, *Georgia*, 12–34	1983	*Time* magazine names the microcomputer as its "man of the year"
Ragans, *Firebirds*, 9–32		
Aubin, *I Dreamed* . . . , 12–32	1982	
Dvorak, *Lizards*, 12–6		
Fish, *Raspberries* . . . , 8–14	1981	First reusable space vehicle, the shuttle, launched
Bak, *Interpene* . . . , 12–4	1980	Beginning of the Information Age
Bayless, *Family*, 11–41		
Bak, *Grand* . . . , 8–4		
Gordon, *Wall* . . . , 8–22	1978	
Pei, *East . . . Int*, 8–20		
Pei, *East . . . Ext*, 8–19		
deKooning, *Untitled*, 8–26	1977	
Jacquette, *East* . . . , 5–6	1976	
Johnson, *Pennzoil* . . . , 3–21		
Calder, *Untitled*, 3–17		
	1975	Microcomputers available for home use
	1973	Britain becomes member of Common Market
Tichich, *Body* . . . , 10–6	1970	
Aron, *Menorah* . . . , 8–25		
Bak, *Holocaust*, 7–3	1969	Neil Armstrong first man on the moon
Twiggs, *Blue* . . . , 2–6		
Dodd, *Night* . . . , 1–7C		
Fernandes, *Appollo* . . . , 1–7B		
Kingman, *Higher* . . . , 1–7A		
Albers, *Homage* . . . , 10–27	1966	Indira Ghandi first woman prime minister of India
Oldenburg, *Soft* . . . , 6–50		
Oldenburg, *Falling* . . . , 11–11	1965	U.S. enters Vietnam conflicts (1965–75)
Anuszkiewicz, *Iriden* . . . , 7–20		
Smith, *Cubi* . . . , 6–43		

Barnet, *Kiesler* . . . , 10–15	**1963**	
Poons, *Orange* . . . , 7-6		
Loewy, *Avanti* . . . , 4–5		
Lichtenstein, *Blam*, 12–27	**1962**	Silicon chips mass-produced
Marisol, *Family*, 11-45		
Segal, *Bus* . . . , 11–40		
Warhol, *Marilyn* . . . , 9–15		
Burchfield, *October* . . . , 9–2		
Glarner, *Relational* . . . , 7–22		
Nevelson, *Dawn*, 6–55		
Malevich, *Suprem* . . . , 12–16	**1961**	Berlin Wall erected
		Alan B. Shepherd first American astronaut in space
		Yuri A. Gagarin first person to orbit earth
Rodriges, *Black* . . . , 8–23	**1960**	Laser light developed
Arp, *Torso* . . . , 6–48		
Hepworth, *Figure* . . . , 6–16		
Soyer, *Farewell* . . . , 12–24	**1959**	Silicon chip invented
Nevelson, *Sky* . . . , 12–21	**1958**	
van der Rohe, *Seag* . . . , 9–14	**1957**	Kornberg grows DNA in a test tube
		Sputnik I launched by Soviets
Lawrence, *Cabinet* . . . , 5–50		
Hofmann, *Flowering* . . . , 3–19		
Saarinen, *Armchair*, 2–9		
Rothko, *Orange* . . . , 7–21	**1956**	
Corbusier, *Chapelle* . . . , 11–10	**1955**	Martin Luther King leads civil rights movement
Escher, *Relativity*, 6–13	**1953**	Jonas Salk's polio vaccine
Moore, *Draped*, 6–44	**1952**	
Gage, *New York* . . . , 4–3		
Hopper, *First* . . . , 10–16	**1951**	
Wright, *David*. . . , 1–8		
Matisse, *Beasts* . . . , 6–21	**1950**	Television era begins
		Korean conflict (1950–53)
Johnson, Johnson . . . , 6–42	**1949**	Communists establish People's Republic of China
		Germany divided into East and West
Johnson, Johnson . . . , 6–41		
Harrison, UN . . . , 6–15		
Lippold, *Variation* . . . , 5–18		
Giacometti, *City* . . . , 5–21	**1948**	Cold War begins between Russia and U.S.
Rouault, *Man* . . . , 5–17		
Wyeth, *Christina's* . . . , 2–10		
Moore, *Family* . . . , 1–9		
	1947	Transistor developed
	1946	ENIAC (first electronic computer) invented
		Republic of Italy established
Sutherland, *Thorn* . . . , 6–38	**1945**	Bombing of Hiroshima - end of World War II
		UN Charter goes into effect
Ernst, *Eye* . . . , 8–27	**1943**	Italy surrenders to Allies
Mondrian, *Broadway*. ., 7–36	**1942**	Atomic reactor developed
	1941	U.S. enters World War II (1941–45)
MacIver, *Hopscotch*, 11–3	**1940**	Italy sides with Germany in World War II
Tchelitchew, *Hide*. ., 7–1		
Calder, *Lobster*. ., 9–31	**1939**	World War II begins (1939–45)
Stella, *Brooklyn*. ., Pt 3		
Shahn, *Handball*, 6–12		
Wood, *New*. ., 3–16		
SA Indian, *Feather*. ., 8–24	**1938**	
Benton, *I Got*. ., 5–23		
Siqueiros, *Echo*. ., 12–11	**1937**	Photocopying invented

(Continued on next page)

1936	Spansh Civil War begins (1936–39)
1935	Fluorescent light invented
	The "Great Purge" in Russia
1933	Adoph Hitler comes to power
1931	
1930	
1929	Stock Market crash
1928	
1926	
1924	
1923	
1922	Stalin comes to power in Russia
1920	First radio station (KDKA, Pittsburgh)
	Mahatma Ghandi begins non-violent disobedience against British rule in India
	TV camera and receiver invented
1919	
1918	Leonard Bernstein, American music composer, born
1917	Communist Revolution in Russia - Lenin becomes dictator
1915	
1914	World War I begins (1914–18)
1913	Assembly line production first used
1912	Republic of China established
1911	Rutherford develops theory of atomic structure (England)
1910	
1909	
1908	
1906	San Francisco earthquake

Artworks	Year	Events
	1905	Albert Einstein develops theory of relativity
Picasso, *Frugal.* ., 11–29	1904	
Picasso, *Tragedy*, 7–37	1903	Wright Brothers' first flight at Kittyhawk, NC
	1902	Air conditioning invented
Fed/Nigeria, *Three.* ., 11–32B	1900	Aaron Copeland, American music composer, born
Wright, *Stained.* ., 10–18		
Seneca, *Corn.* ., 3–28		
Cezanne, *Le Chateau.* ., 3–12		
Homer, *Gulf.* ., 12–38	1899	
	1898	Spanish American War
		George Gershwin, American music composer (1898–1937)
Munch, *Shriek*, 11–28	1895	Marconi sends first radio waves through air
Monet, *Rouen* . ., 7–35	1894	
Monet, *Rouen* . . *Sun* . . , 7–34		
Sullivan, *Elevator* . . , 9–7	1893	
Toulouse . . *Monsieur* . . , 6–19		
Gauguin, *Fatata* . . , 7–33	1892	
Homer, *Hound* . . , 1–5		
Homer, *Sketch* . . , 1–4		
Steinlen, *Winter* . . , 2–3	1891	
Cassatt, *Bath*, 2–1		
Twachtman, *Waterfall*, 7–12	1890	
Sullivan, *Wainwright* . . , 3–18		
Van Gogh, *Self* . . , 9–49	1889	
Van Gogh, *Starry* . . , 9–48		
Van Gogh, *Cypresses*, 8–17		
Harnett, *Gems*, 6–23	1888	
Rodin, *Burghers* . . , 12–13	1886	
Curry, *Baptism* . . , 12–10		
Park, *Flax* . . , 11–24	1885	Gasoline automobile invented
	1884	First skyscraper built
	1883	Brooklyn Bridge built in New York
	1882	Igor Stravinsky, Russian music composer (1882–1971)
	1881	
Degas, *Little* . . , 8–21	1880	
Cezanne, *Houses* . . , 6–7		
Johns, *Map*, 12–17	1879	Incandescent light invented
	1878	Carl Sandburg, American poet (1878–1967)
Manet, *The Plum*, 3–10	1877	Phonograph invented
Renoir, *Young* . . , 8–15	1876	Telephone invented
Homer, *Breezing* . . , 2–4		
	1875	Maurice Ravel, French music composer (1875–1937)
	1874	Robert Frost, American poet (1874–1963)
	1873	Sergi Rachmaninov, Russian music composer (1873–1943)
	1871	Rome becomes capital of unified Italy
	1867	Typewriter invented
	1865	Rudyard Kipling, English author (1865–1936)
	1863	Emancipation Proclamation, U.S.
Whistler, *White* . . , 11–1	1862	Gregor Mendel develops laws of heredity
		Claude Debussy, French music composer (1862–1918)
Church, *Icebergs*, 12–8	1861	American Civil War (1861–65)
Irequois, *False* . . , 11–32C	1860	Internal combustion engine developed
Brown/Owen, *Bench*, 9–18		Gustav Mahler, Austrian music composer (1860–1911)
Daumier, *Advice* . . , 4–1		Maxwell's electromagnetic theory developed (Scotland)
Olmsted, *Central Park*, 4–8	1858	Darwin's theory of evolution developed (England)
		Great Britain takes control of India
		Giacomo Puccini, Italian music composer (1858–1924)

(Continued on next page)

(Continued on next page)

De Vinci, *Gineura* . . , 6–1	1474	
	1473	Nicholaus Copernicus, astronomer, develops theory of earth as a moving planet
Van der Weyden, *Portrait* . . , 11–4	1460	
	1455	
	1440	Gutenberg printing press invented in Germany
	1412	Joan of Arc rallies France to fight England
	1400	
	1368	Ming Dynasty (1368–1644)
	1350	Aztecs establish Mexico City
	1348	Black Death (plague) kills 50% of Europeans
	1337	Hundred Years War between France and England (1337–1453)
	1325	
Giotto, *Madonna* . . , 6–22	1320	
	1300	Renaissance begins in Italy
	1275	Marco Polo visits China (1275–92)
Reims, Cathedral . . , 3–6	1250	
	1231	Spanish Inquisition
	1225	
	1215	King John (England) signs Magna Carta
Italy, Bell Tower . . , 10–2	1174	
	1096	Crusades start
	1066	William the Conqueror, Duke of Normandy, invades England
	960	Sung Dynasty, China (960–1279)—source of magnetic compass, gun powder, movable type for printing
South India, *Figure* . . , 3–22	900	Toltec Empire in Mexico (900–1200)
	800	First Russian city-state, Kiev
	768	Emperor Charlemagne, Holy Roman Empire (768–884)
	618	T'ang Dynasty, Golden Age of China (618–909)—printing invented
	610	Mohammed preaches Islam
Sant' Apollinaire in Classe, Ravenna	549	
	500	Rise and fall of Buddhism (500-800); replaced by Hinduism in India
	478	Western Roman Empire ceases to exist
	400	Fall of Western Roman Empire (400–500)
	395	East and West Roman Empire split; beginning of Byzantine era
	387	Rome sacked by the Gauls
	325	Constantine recognizes Christianity
	324	Constantine rules Roman Empire (324–337)
	200	
Pantheon (118-125)	118	
	105	Paper invented during rule of Han Dynasty, China
SA, *Ornamental* . . , 11–32A	100	
	79	Mount Vesuvius eruption destroys Pompeii
Roman Colosseum (70-82)	70	
	B.C.	
	36	Anthony and Cleopatra married
	44	Caesar assassinated
Roman, *Man* . . , 3–5	50	
Greece, *Dancing* . . , 11–9		
	55	Caesar invades Britain (55–54)
Nike of Samothraco (Winged Victory)—Greek sculpture	190	
	220	Han Dynasty (220-207 B.C.)—beginning of Chinese empire
Great Wall of China, Chin Dynasty (221-206 B.C.)	221	

	280	Archimedes, Greek mathematician and inventor (280–212 B.C.)
	300	Euclid, Greek mathematician
	310	
Roman Aqueduct	312	
	331	Alexander the Great conquers the Persian Empire
Pan Painter, *Young . . ,* 1–3	400	
Parthenon (448–432 B.C.)	448	
Lancillotti, *Discus . . . ,* 3–4	450	
	510	
	550	
Babylonian, *Walking . . ,* 6–17	600	
	750	Homer writes *The Iliad* and *The Oddysey*
	753	Romulus and Remus found Rome (legend)
	900	
Mexico, Baby . . , 3–27	1000	Phoenician writing developed
	1006	King David's rule in Israel (1006–966 B.C.)
	1027	Chou Dynasty in China (1027–256 B.C.)
Temple of Karnak, Egypt	1280	
	1348	Tutankhamen is pharoh of Egypt (1348–39 B.C.)
	1400	Shang Dynasty (1400–1027 B.C.)—first dynasty recorded in China
	1500	Tribes of Israel go to Palestine
		Village life develops in Mexico
	1570	New kingdom of Egypt (1570–715 B.C.)
	1600	
Egyptian, *Figure . . ,* 6–37	1850	
	1890	
	1900	
Stonehenge, England	2000	
Egyptian, *Coffin,* 3–3	2050	
	2052	Middle Kingdom of Egypt (2052–1570 B.C.)
Ziggurat at Ur (Mesopotamian)	2100	
Egyptian pyramids at Gizeh	2500	
	2850	Old Kingdom of Egypt (2850–2052 B.C.)—hieroglyphics developed
	3000	Cuneiform writing developed in Middle East Indus Valley civilization in India Upper and lower kingdoms of Egypt united
	3500	Wheel invented
	4000	Mesopotamian civilization develops
		Copper smelting
	5000	Plow invented
	6000	First cities
	7000	Agriculture established
	7500	Jericho wall
Altamira, *Deer,* 7–29	15,000	
Cave painting, 3–2	15,000	
	30,000	

Chapter Test

1. D	9. F	17. D	25. C
2. A	10. G	18. H	26. G
3. E	11. E	19. I	27. E
4. B	12. A	20. J	28. F
5. C	13. F	21. A	29. J
6. H	14. B	22. D	30. I
7. C	15. G	23. B	
8. F	16. C	24. H	

Chapter 4: Careers in Art

Purpose

To acquaint students with opportunities for art careers in various fields

To help students think about whether they are suited to an art career

Learning Outcomes

After completing this chapter, students will be able to
- name fields in which an art career is possible.
- name some skills artists need.
- think meaningfully about their interest as they relate to an art career.

Teaching Strategies

This chapter does not have to be covered at any set time. If you like, you can wait until the end of the course. You can also use it as a resource chapter. You might divide the class into thirteen groups and assign one career field to each group. Throughout the course, these groups can be scheduled to present their reports to the class. Groups should check with you periodically so you can review their progress.

Encourage creativity in presentation of the reports. If you can, take the entire class to the school media center one day so the media specialist can review with them the procedures for using the *Reader's Guide to Periodicals*. They will find many current articles they can use to make the reports interesting.

Again, as with the art history reports, the group giving the report should be allowed to write an objective test. But, it cannot be emphasized enough, the teacher must check the test to see that it covers the material presented. Creating a test forces the report group to analyze their material more carefully.

There is a simple way to check students' understanding of the report. On the same day, give the class five minutes to write a description of the occupation reported on that day.

If you have a group of students who are interested in art and potential careers in art, it will not be difficult to interest them in this material. Even if your students are not talented and would not consider a career in the arts, they will be surprised at how many artists are involved in the world of work.

If you can bring in resource people during the time that careers are being studied, the material will be more meaningful. Even though you may know more about the subject than the resource person, students will be interested in listening to someone new. If you live in an urban area it will not be difficult to find people who work at some of these careers. Even the smallest newspaper in a rural area needs a layout person. The local TV station will also employ someone who fits one of the categories. Artists are also needed in industry. Other workers to consider are florists who can demonstrate flower arranging, a cosmetologist who can discuss make-up, or a hairstylist who can show how hair styles complement face shape. If you are near a college, there should be at least one instructor there involved in the arts.

If you cannot find any commercial artists, a local art hobbyist or craftsperson may substitute, as might an art college student home on vacation.

If there is a local artist in your area, a field trip to this person's studio can be exciting.

Many people associate art with relaxation and recreation. They think that artists live a carefree life and that anything associated with art is FUN. You, as an art teacher, know that this is far from the truth. There is joy in art, but it is no greater than the joy people get from creativity in other fields. While covering this chapter it is important to emphasize that work in the area of art is really work, sometimes very demanding work. But a job well done is rewarding in any field.

Additional Activities

1. (Graphic Design.) Select a variety of magazines. Choose them from different interest areas, such as high fashion, mechanics, photography, architecture, teen life, current events, health, sports, science, science fiction, TV, and so on. Compare such things as layout, illustrations, and advertising. What similarities and differences do you find?

2. (Graphic Design.) Look through newspapers for clothing advertisements. Collect ads from discount stores, department stores in the moderately priced range, and expensive, high-fashion stores. What conclusions can you draw about the look and layout of the ads from the three different types of stores?

3. (Illustration.) Collect newspaper editorial cartoons about a similar topic. Since you will probably have to do this at the library, you will have to photocopy the cartoons. Mount all of the cartoons on one large sheet of poster board. Describe their similarities and differences.

4. (Illustration.) Do some research at the library to find out about the Caldecott Award books. Ask the librarian to explain the award to you. Find some books that have won this award and take them to class. Explain the award to your class and show the books. How many do you and your classmates recognize?

5. (Computer Graphics.) If your school has a computer specialist, interview that person to learn about the graphic capabilities of the computers in your school. Ask a local computer store to give your class a demonstration on the graphic possibilities of computers.

6. (Television Graphics.) At home watch a few hours of TV. Watch for examples of graphic design. Keep a journal to record your observations. Remember, every time you see letters and words on the screen, a graphic designer had

to plan them. During a news report you may see drawings of courtroom scenes where photographers were not admitted. Make a note of the time and the type of graphic art observed.

7. (Industrial Design.) Think of one manufactured product you use every day, such as a hairdryer or a toothbrush. Study the object. Think of one thing you would do to make the product easier to use or more aesthetically pleasing. Either describe your idea in writing or make a sketch and label the changes you would make.

8. (Industrial Design.) Find out more about the accomplishments of Raymond Loewy. Prepare a report using visual aids and present it to the class.

9. (Fashion Design.) If fashion is your interest, do some research to find out what people wore long ago. Study at least three different historical periods that are widely separated, such as the Middle Ages, Colonial America, and Ancient China. Study the clothes of the ruling classes and compare them with the clothes of the peasants. Can you find any similarities among the three groups you chose, such as fabrics used?

10. (City Planning.) Imagine that you have been hired as a city planner to improve your town. If you live in a big city, limit the area to your own neighborhood. Prepare a survey to ask people what they like the most and what they like least about the town or neighborhood. Find out which building is considered the most important and which is considered the most attractive. Ask about traffic flow, stores, recreation, entertainment, health services, police protection, and water and sewerage. Add questions that interest you to the survey. Then carry out the survey. Talk to students at your school and adults who live in the area. Put all of your findings in graph or chart form. Compare adult and teen replies. Do the two groups agree or disagree on each item?

11. (Landscape Architecture.) Imagine that you are a landscape architect. What would you do to improve the appearance of your school campus? Make sketches to illustrate your ideas.

12. (Interior Design.) Imagine that you are an interior designer who has been asked to plan a student lounge for the school. Before you make your design, survey your friends to see what they would like in a lounge. Try to think of the lounge as a multipurpose area that could serve as space for a party, a meeting, art exhibits, and so on. What areas will you need to include? Be creative and let your imagination run free. Write a description and draw plans for your lounge.

13. (Display Design.) Make a list of some stores where you like to shop. From the displays in the windows and those inside of the store, can you guess which stores employ display designers? Indicate on your list which stores you think do and which do not. Give reasons for your guesses.

14. (Photography.) Look through your local newspaper. Notice the credit lines under the photographs. Some have come in over the wires, and they carry labels such as "UPI." Others have been taken locally. Notice the name of the photographer. Is there just one photographer working for the paper or can you find many different names on the credit lines? Does one person seem to specialize in one type of photography, such as sports? Write a brief description of your findings.

15. (Photography.) Ask a local photographer if you can come in for an interview. Plan your questions ahead of time. Find out about the photographer's education, training, experience, areas of interest, and so on.

16. (Animation.) Research the field of animation at the library. Find out how to make a flip book. Make one and show it to the class.

ANSWERS

Chapter 4 Review: Talking About Art

USING THE LANGUAGE OF ART

Answers will vary according to the artworks selected. The answers should show, however, that students understand the meanings of the terms as given in Chapter 4 and in the text Glossary. You may wish to require that students include the artist and title for each work cited. If so, titles should be underlined.

LEARNING THE ART ELEMENTS AND PRINCIPLES

1. Possible answers include the apprentice system, courses in high schools and post-secondary schools, vocational and professional art schools, and four- and five-year college programs.
2. *The Occupational Outlook Handbook.*
3. Possible answers include graphic design, industrial design, fashion design, architecture, city planning, landscape architecture, interior design, exhibit and display design, photography, art direction for the performing arts, animation, special effects design, and art education.
4. Editorial design and illustration, computer graphics, and television graphics.
5. A medical knowledge and ability to work with a variety of media.
6. Shape and color; package function.
7. An architect must know about building materials, ventilation, heating and cooling systems, plumbing, stairways, and elevators. He or she must be creative, be able to make accurate mechanical drawings, have a strong background in mathematics and drafting, and be able to deal with customers.
8. City planners are mainly concerned with the care and improvement of city environments. Some of the responsibilities of the city planner are land use, harbor development, city parks, shopping malls, and urban renewal projects.

INCREASING YOUR ART AWARENESS

1. Answers will vary. Possibilities include oil, canvas, wood, watercolor, paper, bronze, lithograph, tempera molded plastic, nickel silver, ebony, gesso panels, aluminum, steel, and ink.

2. The subject is the mother and her three children. One theme expressed in the photograph is that survival was difficult for migrant workers and their families during the Great Depression. Answers will vary as to differences between 4–9 and 1–9.
3. The subject is the young man conferring with the older man about whatever appears on the sheet of paper the older man is holding. An example of the content could be that a young artist can learn much from the advice of his elders. The form is oil paint on canvas.
4. Answers will vary. All three theories of judging art could be helpful in understanding this work.
5. Answers will vary, depending on local situation.
6. Answers will vary.

UNDERSTANDING ART CULTURE AND HERITAGE

1. Answers will vary.
2. Romanticism.
3. Editorial cartoonist.
4. Fifteenth century; printing press.

JUDGING THE QUALITY OF ART

Answers will vary.

LEARNING MORE ABOUT ART

Answers will vary.

Activity 1: Study Question Worksheet

1. They apprenticed themselves to master artists.
2. Art directors, illustrator, layout artist, photographer, printer.
3. Children's books, science fiction illustrations, medical illustration, cartoonist, fashion designer, technical illustration.
4. To make people think about current issues; to try to influence public opinion.
5. To entertain.
6. The products of industry, such as dinnerware, furniture, automobiles, and so on.
7. It must function efficiently to do the job for which it was designed; it must look like it can do the job for which it was intended; it must be visually pleasing.
8. To make every package unique and appealing.
9. A designer credited with many outstanding advances in industrial design. He is best known for his automotive designs, such as the 1953 Starlight Coupe and the Avanti, a luxury sportscar.
10. Coats, suits, dresses, hats, handbags, shoes, gloves, jewelry, and other apparel.
11. Sets fashion trends.
12. Function of the structure (what it will be used for); construction—the way a building is put together—materials and methods; aesthetic qualities—how a building looks and fits in with its environment.
13. Must be creative; must be able to make accurate mechanical drawings; must have a strong background in mathematics and drafting; must be able to deal with customers.
14. The care and improvement of the city environment.
15. Land use, zoning laws, harbor development, city parks, shopping malls, and urban renewal projects.
16. Outdoor areas around buildings, in playgrounds and parks, and along highways.
17. Flowers, plants, trees, shrubs, rivers, ponds, benches, signs, and lakes.
18. Interior spaces.
19. Trade shows, department stores, showrooms, art galleries, and museums.
20. To design merchandise displays that will attract customers into the store.
21. Computers, photocopiers, laser scanners, overhead projecters, and duplicating machines.
22. Art director, graphic designer, computer graphic designer, layout and paste-up artist, letterers, calligraphers, air brush artists, block engravers, sign painters, typographers.
23. Visual reporters; newspapers, magazines, or as freelance artists.
24. Fine arts photographer, photojournalist, fashion photographer, product and food photographer, architectural photographer, medical photographer.
25. Strong background in design with computer technology.
26. Any image can be drawn and colored; the design process is speeded up; designs can be stored, recalled, and revised; images can be transmitted along telephone lines.
27. To make all elements of the show fit together.
28. Scenic designer, costume designer, lighting designer, make-up artists, hair stylists.
29. Selection of a story; research the period of the story; develop the story by drawing storyboards; paint settings from the layout artists' sketches; draw major poses of each character; fill in the many other drawings required to complete each movement.
30. Still drawings that show the story's progress.
31. 24.
32. Come up through the ranks of designing theater sets or film backgrounds.
33. Elementary schools, middle schools, high schools, museums, colleges.
34. Help people with emotional and physical problems to change their behavior in a positive manner.

Activity 2: Art Careers Checklist

Answers will vary.

Chapter Test

1.	I	8.	N	15.	K
2.	H	9.	E	16.	animation
3.	A	10.	C	17.	storyboard
4.	J	11.	F	18.	apprentice
5.	B	12.	G	19.	layout
6.	D	13.	O	20.	politics
7.	L	14.	M		

Chapter 5: Line

INTRODUCING THE CHAPTER

Purpose

To help students become aware of line in the natural and manufactured environment

Learning Outcomes

After completing this section the student will demonstrate an awareness of line in the natural and manufactured environment by
- describing lines in the photographs in Figure 5–2.
- recalling and listing lines that are a part of everyday things.

Teaching Strategies

To help students become aware of the need for words that can define line types, ask one student to describe the lines in one of the photos in Figure 5–2 without naming anything in the photo. Then let the others try to guess which photo is being described.

Ask students to differentiate between natural and manufactured lines.

"Developing Your Skills" 1 emphasizes perception of the environment. Skill 2 requires the student to generalize about the concept of line. Either one may be done in class within a limited amount of time or assigned as homework.

Stimulate perception by playing a "spelling bee"-type game based on the skill activities. Divide the class into two teams. Each person must name and describe the location of a different line. Do not allow anyone to point. The others guess which line it is. Encourage the use of adjectives that help to identify the line in question.

A *Reminder:* Have your students save all of the drawings and designs they create for the "Developing Your Skills" activities throughout the text. These will be useful later as resource sketches for other works. They will also serve as evidence that students have progressed and made an effort during the course. Small works may have holes punched in them for placement in notebooks. Larger works should be kept in student portfolios.

WHAT IS LINE?

Purpose

- To help students understand line in terms of mathematics and art
- To differentiate between real and implied lines

Learning Outcomes

After completing this section, students will be able to
- define line in terms of drawing and geometry.

- describe line dimensions.
- describe how artists use line to control eye movement.
- describe the difference between real and implied lines and give specific examples of each.
- illustrate how line is a record of visual movement.

Teaching Strategies

Emphasize the concept of dimension as measurement.

To save time and/or help slower students with "Developing Your Skills" 3 and 4, photocopy a floor plan of the school or a map of the community. Skills 3 and 4 help students conceive of line as a path of visual movement. A map of the route to school will help them think of movement as linear.

Students should learn to make a ruler bridge to keep from smearing their work. The materials needed include one ruler, three nickels, and some masking tape.

1. Place the three nickels on the back of the ruler, spaced equally apart.

2. Tape each coin in place.

3. Place the ruler on the work, nickel-side down. The nickels will keep the ruler from touching the work and smearing it.

4. Hold the ruler bridge steady with your free hand while you make paintbrush or marker lines.

5. When you have drawn the line, lift the ruler carefully so you don't make a smear.

If you give your students prepared maps, they should spend time working on symbols to mark places on their route. If you do not give them prepared maps to work on, these activities will take a few hours; therefore, you might want to give one of them as a homework assignment. This type of map-making is called conceptual mapping. It does not require mathematical accuracy.

As mentioned before, the "Something Extra" activities are not intended for everyone. Either one in this section will take some time to carry out. Suggest that the student keep a record of lens openings and exposure times.

KINDS OF LINES

Purpose

To help students identify and describe line types

Learning Outcomes

After completing this section, students will be able to recognize, define, and illustrate vertical, horizontal, diagonal, curved, and zigzag lines.

Teaching Strategies

To help the students remember the names of the lines, you might use flash cards on which you have drawn the line types. Call the students by name, hold up a card, and ask them to name the lines.

Slower students could use these cards to coach each other. The student who is playing teacher might point to illustrations in the book while the others name the lines.

"Developing Your Skills" 5 serves two purposes. First, it helps students become more familiar with works of art in *ArtTalk*. After each student has made a diagram of one work in the book, put all the diagrams up on the board and let the students take turns guessing which is which. Before they begin guessing, ask them if any diagrams match. This will help their perception skills.

If you want to make the guessing game easier, limit them to one section of the text. Part One would be a good choice since they will not be studying the works in that section as thoroughly as those in the rest of the book.

LINE VARIATION

Purpose

To make students sensitive to the many different ways lines can be created and varied.

Learning Outcomes

After completing this section, students will be able to
- recognize, describe, and illustrate the five ways in which lines may vary.
- list at least four media and five tools that can be used to create lines.
- identify works of art in which the artists have used unusual methods to create line.
- use a variety of media and tools to create lines.
- use line to draw objects in the environment.

Teaching Strategies

Collect as many different media and tools as you can for students to experiment with in making lines. After they have experimented, challenge them to go home and find at least one different way to create a line. Ask them to bring the results to school the next day.

To encourage creative thinking, hold a brief brain-storming session to dream up ideas for unusual media and tools. Some media you might suggest to get them started are coffee and tea; tools might include twigs, fingers, day lily stems and yarn dipped in paint.

"Developing Your Skills" 6 can be achieved by every student successfully. Skills 7 and 8 require some expertise in perception drawing. If your students lack confidence in their ability to draw, you can help. Bring a bicycle into the room. When they complain that it is too hard to draw, agree with them. Then ask if anyone can draw a circle. Ask someone to point out the circles on the bike. Have them find vertical, horizontal, and diagonal lines on the bike.

Now challenge the students to forget that this thing is a bike and to think of it as a combination of lines. They can draw the bike by drawing the various lines of which it is

made. Demand silence and concentration. If necessary, help them draw the bike in the air. Do this over several times if necessary. Then, if they are still hesitant, explain that they are not cameras. If you wanted a photograph you would have asked them to bring in a camera.

After they have conquered their fears, you can ask them to do "Developing Your Skills" 7 or 8. Demonstrate how to use the sharp point of the pencil for thin lines and the side of the pencil for wide lines. As they draw, walk around the room and encourage them, but do not draw on their paper. Carry around a little pad and if you need to demonstrate something, draw on that.

WHAT DIFFERENT LINES EXPRESS

Purpose

To acquaint students with the expensive qualities of lines

Learning Outcomes

After completing this section students will be able to
- recognize, describe, and illustrate the expressive qualities of the five line types.
- define and differentiate between active and static lines.
- use lines to create expressive drawings.

Teaching Strategies

Ask students to find specific line types in the works of art throughout the text. Discuss how the line type affects the expressive quality of each work. To help the students grasp the idea of expressive line qualities, refer to the pull of gravity. Vertical lines are in balance with gravity. When you are standing upright, gravity is pulling through the center of your body. When you are horizontal, you are totally at rest. You are lying flat and gravity is pulling evenly on all parts of your body. However, anyone in a diagonal position must be supported. A diagonal looks as if it is falling or rising. It seems to be in motion.

If your students are not too inhibited, ask them to act out the line directions—to stand straight as a vertical, for example—and then ask them how they feel.

To emphasize the active quality of diagonals, ask some volunteers to play the "trust" game. One friend stands a few feet behind another. The student in front stands with arms tight against the sides and falls backward to be caught by the other. Ask the student who has fallen how it felt.

Get the students involved in creative dramatization. Ask one to move like a vertical, a diagonal, a curve, or a zigzag. If a horizontal could move, what would it look like?

"Developing Your Skills" 9 can be achieved successfully by every student. To help students understand skill 10 have them study the different lines used in the student example. Ask how the lines have affected the expressive quality of the work. Provide students with photographs of various buildings and discuss with them the lines of the buildings to help them get ideas. Do not let them copy the photos. Put the photos away before the students do any drawing.

CONTOUR DRAWING

Purpose

To teach a type of drawing that will help students develop more perceptive drawing skills

Learning Outcomes

After completing this section students will be able to
• define contour and blind contour drawing.
• make contour and blind contour drawings.

Teaching Strategies

Read the technique tip with the students. Go over the directions. Have them practice the two-pencil technique, which will really help. Be sure that they understand that whether they are making blind or regular contour drawings, the pencil must not leave the paper.

Additional Activities

1. Have partners sit across the table from each other and take turns making blind contour face drawings. Clarify ahead of time that this is an exercise in learning how to concentrate. These drawings will not look like the other person.

2. Set small still life arrangements around the room in various places so that every student can see one clearly. You might have to place one on each table. Limit the arrangements to three objects each. Try to include one plant in each arrangement. Ask the students to make contour drawings. First, have them point to the objects and draw them in the air. Get them to notice that the bottom of round things, like pots and cylinders, usually curve. Observe when they draw in the air that they are drawing on a flat picture plane and not in depth.

If students have trouble with this, try to get some pieces of glass to use as the picture plane. Prop up the glass and ask students to draw on it with crayons or markers. (Be sure to tape the edges of the glass so that no one is cut.)

GESTURE DRAWING

Purpose

To help students grasp the concept of a gesture as a position of the body

Learning Outcomes

After completing this section students will be able to
• identify and define gesture drawing.

• make quick gesture drawings that capture the position of a live model.

Teaching Strategies

The best way to help students understand gesture drawing is to demonstrate it for them. Have a model pose, point out the position to the students, and explain that you are going to draw only the position and not the details of the model. Before you draw, show them that you are observing the curve of the back or the diagonal line of one leg, etc. Then quickly demonstrate.

Have a second model pose, point out the different lines of the body, and then ask students to draw quickly. Give them 30 seconds. Most of them won't finish. Then show the students what you see and let them correct their sketches.

Challenge volunteer students to invent difficult poses that they can hold for thirty seconds. Have one student pose while you point out curves and directions in the position. Then let the model rest a moment before posing for the class to draw. Limit each pose to thirty seconds. Call out every five seconds so they maintain speed. If they begin to finish before thirty seconds, cut them down to 20, then 15.

There will always be a few in each class who are willing to pose. Don't force anyone who does not wish to pose to get up in front of the class.

All students will be successful with skills 13 and 14.

Additional Activities

1. Ask students to do gesture homework. Sketch a pet, an animal at the zoo, athletes practicing after school, children playing on a playground, etc.

2. Combine gesture and contour drawing. Have the students make a gesture drawing using chalk; then add contour lines with a marker color. Try watercolor gesture. When it dries add contour lines with markers. Ask the students to suggest other combinations of media.

3. Have the students make chalk gesture drawings from photographs of action figures from sports or fashion magazines. They should then put the photograph away and turn the gestures into a different scene of the student's choice. For example, the gestures of a basketball player could turn into those of a dancer. Make these sketches into finished works using oil pastels or paints.

CALLIGRAPHIC DRAWING

Purpose

To understand the relationship of calligraphic line to Oriental calligraphy

Learning Outcomes

After completing this section students will be able to
• define calligraphy.
• make drawings using calligraphic lines.

Bring in other examples of Oriental calligraphy. Read over the technique tip directions and study the photographs with the students to help them see how they can gain control over their brushes. This activity will be more successful if you have some nylon sable brushes for them to use. If your brushes will not come to some kind of a point, the lines made will not be very successful.

Watch the students as they try to make thin lines. Be sure that the brush is not loaded with water. Students must wipe off extra liquid to make the brush come to a point. An absorbent towel is useful. If the brush is loaded, press the wet brush gently against the towel to remove excess moisture without breaking the point.

Before working with brushes, be sure that you go over the correct way to clean a brush covered in the technique tip. The close-up photos show clearly what steps they must take to clean the brush properly.

LINE AND VALUE

Purpose

To explain value and relate value to line

Leaning Outcomes

After completing this section students will be able to
• define value as an element of art.
• define value in terms of line.
• use hatching and crosshatching and a variety of media to create a variety of values.

Teaching Strategies

Try to provide a variety of pencil hardnesses and a variety of pens for the students to experiment with. Even if you can only get a few of each kind, students can share them so that they can discover the effects they can create with different pens and pencils.

IMAGINE AND CREATE

The activities in the "Imagine and Create" section of each chapter are more complex than the "Developing Your Skills" activities. They require more time, and all involve fairly "messy" media. Depending upon your style of teaching, you may wish to have all the class do one problem together, or you may divide the students into groups and have several different media problems going on at the same time. As suggested earlier, you may wish to allow gifted students to move more quickly through the chapter and start the media problems on their own.

These "Imagine and Create" activities have been written so that gifted students will be able to follow directions with no problems. This procedure was tested in the classroom and found to be successful. But after the instructions have been read and before the activity is begun, you should

have a conference with any student who is going to work independently.

These activities are the "fun" things that have always been done in art classes, and they are the type that students look forward to. But it is not necessary that the class do one at the end of every chapter. In fact, they are not necessary at all if you do not have the time or supplies to carry them out.

As students make finished works, they will want to mat or mount them. In the reproducible section of this guide, following the Chapter 5 Test, are two extra technique tips on mounting and matting. You may copy these and distribute them when the students are ready to try both tasks.

ALTERNATE "IMAGINE AND CREATE" ACTIVITIES

1. *Make contour drawings of a still life arrangement.* Be sure to place the arrangement high on a counter or table so that it can be seen by everyone in the class. This may require that you rearrange the seating. Some students may need to lean on drawing boards or sit upon countertops or table tops so that they can see the arrangement. You will not have discipline problems if you insist upon quiet concentration while drawing is going on. Sometimes playing music on the radio helps students concentrate. The choice of music is up to you. Some prefer classic or easy-listening while others will want pop and rock. Be sure to get permission from your administrators before you bring a radio into the room.

2. *Make contour drawing of a figure dressed in an elaborate costume and sitting in an interesting setting.* For example, you could pose a girl wearing a long, old fashioned dress and large decorated hat in a rocking chair. Place a plant next to the chair. If you can find an old, over-stuffed chair, ask a model to drape himself or herself in it in a typical "teen-phone" position. Challenge different students to come up with costumes and poses, reminding them that the poses must be comfortable enough to hold for a long time.

One successful device for motivating students in posing for the class is to have birthday drawings. Stop everything for a student's birthday, and instead of cake or the usual junk food, hold a drawing party. The birthday person is the one who poses. One student can make a list of all the class birthdays for you, including students who are willing to pose but whose birthdays do not occur during the class term. Once more, it is important to remember that no student should be forced to pose.

ART CRITICISM

If you did not spend a significant amount of time on Chapter 2, go back to it and review the four steps in art criticism. Then, as suggested in the guide material for Chapter 2, there are several ways you may approach art criticism:

1. You can go through the first two steps with the class as a group and then let each individual write his or her own interpretation and judgment.

2. You can divide the class into small discussion groups to cover the first two steps and then have each individual write his or her own interpretation and judgment.

3. You can allow friends to team up as partners and write all four steps together.

4. You can assign art criticism as written homework. After you have collected and graded the papers, hand them back and call on students to share their interpretations.

ANSWERS

Chapter 5 Review: Talking About Art

USING THE LANGUAGE OF ART

Answers will vary according to the artworks selected. The answers should show, however, that students understand the meanings of the terms as given in Chapter 5 and in the text Glossary. You may wish to require that students include the artist and title for each work cited. If so, titles should be underlined.

LEARNING THE ART ELEMENTS AND PRINCIPLES

1. Vertical, horizontal, diagonal, curved, zigzag. Vertical, horizontal, and diagonal lines do not change direction. A curved line changes direction gradually. A zigzag line changes direction suddenly.
2. Length, width, texture, direction, and degree of curve.
3. Vertical lines because of their uplifting effect.
4. Gesture.
5. Calligraphic.
6. Number of lines, size of the spaces between the lines, media, and tools.

INCREASING YOUR ART AWARENESS

1. Answers will vary according to the photograph selected but should show that students can recognize the five main kinds of lines and the five major ways in which lines can vary.
2. Answers will vary according to the artwork selected but should show that students can recognize several different kinds of lines and several line variations in the artwork.
3. Answers will vary.
4. Figure 3–7.
5. Answers will vary. Two possible answers are Figure 5–22 (in which horizontal lines create a sense of calm) and Figure 5–23 (in which diagonal lines create a sense of excitement).

UNDERSTANDING ART CULTURE AND HERITAGE

1. Answers will vary. Three possible answers are Figures 5–3, 5–24, and any one of the works shown in 5–44.

2. *An Oriental Ruler Seated on the Throne* by Albrecht Dürer (Figure 5–1)
3. 16th—*Standing Youth with His Arm Raised (Seen from Behind)*
   17th—*Hollyhocks* (non-Western)
   18th—Bedroom from the Sagredo Palace
4. Alexander Calder.
5. *Midnight Ride of Paul Revere* by Grant Wood (Figure 5–3); *New Road* (Figure 3–16)

JUDGING THE QUALITY OF ART

Answers will vary.

LEARNING MORE ABOUT ART

Answers will vary.

Study Questions Worksheet

1. Answers will vary.
2. Answers will vary.
3. (a) a mark drawn by a person with a pointed, moving tool.
   (b) an infinite (never ending) series of dots.
4. Your eyes follow the direction the line is going.
5. The amount of space an object takes up in one direction.
6. Its length is so much greater than its width.
7. A series of points that the viewer's eyes automatically connects.
8. (a) implied.
   (b) real.
   (c) implied.
   (d) implied.
   (e) real.
9. (a) Peace, rest, stability, etc.
   (b) Stability, dignity, stiffness, etc.
   (c) Action, movement, tension, etc.
   (d) Calm activity, luxury.
   (e) Confusion, excitement, nervousness.
10. Lines that give the feeling of action or movement.
11. Lines that appear to be at rest, not rising or falling.
12. Active: curved, diagonal, and zigzagged. Static: horizontal and vertical.
13. (a) Lines that define edges and surfaces by creating a boundary separating one area from another.
    (b) Expressive movement.
    (c) Chinese for "beautiful writing."
    (d) How dark or light something is.
    (e) Using lines that cross each other for shading.
14. How much light a surface reflects.
15. Length, width, direction, texture, curvature.
16. Contours or boundaries of an object.
17. Feeling of motion.

Chapter Test

1. gesture
2. curved
3. line
4. vertical

5. zigzag
6. static
7. contour
8. calligraphy
9. crosshatching
10. value

11. blind contour
12. active
13. line
14. horizontal
15. implied

16. diagonal
17. line
18. eye
19. gouache
20. casein

Chapter 6: Shape, Form, and Space

INTRODUCING THE CHAPTER

Purpose

- To help students understand that shape, form, and space are closely related elements
- To make students aware that every object has a shape or form and that it exists in space

Learning Outcomes

After completing this section, students will be able to:
- classify shape, form, and space as three closely related elements of art.
- identify and describe the elements of shape, form, and space in the environment.

Teaching Strategies

The reading and sharing of descriptions of shapes, forms, and spaces observed in the environment will help students become aware of the need for definite terminology. At this point it is not important if the students confuse shape and form. The differences between them will be spelled out quite clearly over the next few sections.

"Developing Your Skills" 1 and 2 are very similar. You can choose whichever one is easier to carry out in your classroom. If you assign the skills as homework, you might allow students to choose one or the other.

SHAPES

Purpose

To introduce students to the definition of shape and the idea that shapes can be either geometric or free-form

Learning Outcomes

After completing this section students will be able to
- define shape.
- name the two dimensions of shape.
- explain and demonstrate how outline and area can be used to define shape.

- define silhouette.
- classify shapes as either geometric or free-form.
- recognize, identify, describe, and create the basic geometric shapes as well as name and create some of the more complex geometric shapes.
- recognize, identify, describe and create free-form shapes.
- draw the outlines of objects.

Teaching Strategies

To help students think about shapes that can be made without drawing outlines, hold a brain-storming session. You can stimulate their thinking by naming a few examples, such as spilled paint, pressing a hand in wet sand, shaping cookie dough with a cookie cutter, or cutting a shape with scissors.

A more dramatic way to get students' attention is to pour paint on a large sheet of paper on the floor and then, by lifting edges of the paper, change the paint's shape. A second device might be to "accidentally" spill water on the floor.

Help them see geometric shapes in the classroom, such as the rectangles made by walls, windows, the chalkboard, and doors; the circle made by the clock; and those patterns on their clothes. Ask a student to bring in a geometry text and look for examples of shapes in that. See if you can get some charts or other visual material from the math teacher.

It is important that they understand that although free-form shapes do not have specific names, such as "circle" or "square," they may have object names such as "tree" or "dog."

"Developing Your Skills" 3 must be carried out in class because the overhead projector is an important part of the activity.

Skill 3 requires some drawing ability. Skill 4 is a design problem that can be achieved successfully by all students.

Be sure to point out the difference between contour and outline. Contour drawings define all the lines on an object, the interior as well as the outlines. Outlines are like a fence around a shape—they define the area of a shape. In skill 3 they will be drawing pure outlines.

The activity will be more interesting if students place their own possessions on the projector. But, just to warm things up, you should have a few things handy to start the activity. For instance, you might place several different keys on the projector and then ask the students to describe verbally the differences in their outlines. They all know that you need different keys to open different locks, but have they ever thought about what makes each key different? Ask them to notice the different patterns of zigzag lines that create the outline of each key. You might also check with the industrial technology teacher to see if there are any charts that explain how the tumblers in a lock work. Or perhaps one of your students will know how a lock functions.

FORMS

Purpose

To help students understand the distinction between shape and form and to become aware of forms in the visual environment.

Learning Outcomes

After completing this section, students will be able to
• identify and define form.
• name the three dimensions of form.
• classify forms as geometric or free-form and give specific examples of each.
• name and give examples of the relationship between geometric shapes and forms.
• score both straight and curved folds in paper and use this technique to create a three-dimensional form from a two-dimensional shape.
• construct geometric forms.
• draw forms with contour lines, differentiating between geometric and free-form by the style of drawing.

Teaching Strategies

One concrete way to clarify the concept of three dimensions for slower learners is to use a cardboard box. Color each set of parallel lines on the box form with different colors. Label one set "length," the second set "width," and the third set "depth." Show them how length and width just outline a flat shape, but that when you add the dimension of depth the box takes up space.

Be sure to emphasize safety if you let students use sharp blades to score paper. If you use construction paper, the scoring can be done easily with the point of a pair of scissors. The purpose of scoring is to weaken the paper along one line and make it thinner so it will give when bent.

If you have never tried scoring before, do so before you work with the class. You need to discover how much of a curve you can score before it gets too tight to bend without wrinkling the rest of the paper. If you wish to make a semicircular curve, you will have to make a cut from the open side of the curve to that edge of the paper.

Students are always surprised that they can make curved forms from flat paper. "Developing Your Skills" 5 can be done successfully by all students after practice. Skill 6 has

two levels of complexity. It is very easy to model the forms from clay, but constructing them from paper is more difficult and takes a bit of ingenuity. For either method, be sure that the students measure the forms they make so that they are accurate. To make a base for a cylinder or cone, have the student trace a circle using a jar lid or other round object; the circle can also be drawn with a compass.

Skill 7 requires perception. Notice that it calls upon skills learned in Chapter 5—contour drawing and making calligraphic lines.

SPACE AND ITS RELATIONSHIP TO SHAPE AND FORM

Purpose

To help students understand space and its relationship to both two- and three-dimensional works of art

Learning Outcomes

After completing this section students will be able to
• identify, define and illustrate positive and negative space in both two- and three-dimensional works of art.
• identify and explain the figure/ground relationship in two-dimensional works.
• identify and explain ways that artists use positive and negative space in two-dimensional works.
• make and use a viewing frame to focus in on one aspect of the environment.
• experiment with negative space in a design by expanding a geometric shape.
• use color or pattern to emphasize the negative space in a still life drawing.
• use a viewing frame to draw the negative spaces in and around a complex object, such as a chair.
• name a minimum of five three-dimensional art forms.
• explain the importance of negative space in architecture and other three-dimensional art forms.
• identify and define relief sculpture, bas-relief, and high relief.
• list the various enclosed spaces he or she uses for one week and categorize them as either large spaces, shared spaces, or private spaces.
• create a free-standing sculpture.
• create a cardboard relief sculpture.

Teaching Strategies

It is important for students to realize that every bit of empty space around them is negative space. Someone in the class is bound to argue that this space is full of air, etc. You can explain that we are talking about visual space and, therefore, we are concerned only with things that can be seen.

Almost everyone has seen the figure/ground, vase/face design. You can have students create their own. Fold a small piece of paper in half. On one side of the fold have the students draw a profile with a pencil. It can be accurate or distorted. Go over the line of the profile with a dark crayon, pressing heavily to lay down a heavy layer of wax. Then fold the paper again and rub heavily over the area of the profile line to transfer it to the other half. Unfold the paper and go over the transferred line. Then have some students color in the center shape and others color in the two outside shapes. Display these so that the class can see how the different designs keep reversing as they look at them.

Ask students to look through the text for examples of two-dimensional works that (1) illustrate obvious distinctions between figure and ground, (2) make negative space as important as the positive, and (3) reverse the figure and ground. Examples of (1) will be easy to find. Some of the most obvious are Figures 3–9 (Rembrandt), 4–1 (Daumier), 4–9 (Lange), 6–22 (Giotto), 9–15 (Warhol), and 11–4 (Van der Weyden). Examples of (2) are Figures 9–48 (Van Gogh), 8–37 (Zorach), 9–32 (Ragans). Examples of (3) are Figures 7–1 (Tchelitchew), 10–27 (Albers), and 7–20 (Anuskiewicz).

An activity that will help students grasp the way the size and shape of negative space affect feelings involves another large cardboard box. You can usually get one from a furniture store that sells large appliances. Ask one student to sit inside the box. Then add as many students as will fit into the box without hurting anyone. After all the giggling is over, ask the first student to express the difference between the way he or she felt all alone in the box and the way he or she felt after the crowd came. Ask other students who participated in the experiment to choose one word that expresses the feeling of being packed closely together.

The viewing frame technique tip is important. Students will be asked to use a viewing frame many times during drawing activities. They do not have to hold the viewing frame all of the time while drawing. The purpose of the frame is to limit the field of vision and to help make decisions about which part of a larger area will be the subject. When students first begin drawing outside, the expanse of landscape may be overwhelming. The viewing frame helps students tame the visual environment.

"Developing Your Skills" 8 emphasizes the importance of negative space. Warn the students not to glue down any pieces until they are satisfied with the arrangement of shapes and space. Emphasize that the shapes will not change, but the negative space must vary, and that the negative space will control the final look of the design. All students should be able to complete this problem successfully.

Both skills 9 and 10 involve drawing. Skill 10 is more difficult than 9 to master. It requires that the students block out the usual clues for drawing and look at the shapes of the negative spaces.

To help students comprehend space in three-dimensional art, bring in a few examples of three-dimensional works if you can. In discussing three-dimensional art forms, ask the students to name specific objects that they have seen or used. Don't omit manufactured objects such as pots, dishes, vacuum cleaners, and so on.

In studying Figure 6–16 try to get the students to imagine what kind of a person this three-dimensional form represents. What human qualities does it express? Is it kind or cruel, etc?

If you are in a very modern building it may not have the relief work that is found in older buildings. In this case, center the discussion about relief on the things that are a part of the students' world, such as jewelry. Skill 11 may be assigned for homework, or it may be used for a class discussion. This is one of those activities that might be better carried out in small groups with one person acting as secretary, rather than with the entire class. Each group of about five might list enclosed spaces, categorize them, and then read the list to the class as a group. It will be interesting to see if all of the groups come up with similar or different reports.

Unless the students do skill 12 at home it will be wise to start collecting cardboard tubes and boxes about a week before they construct their forms. The paint is not necessary, but it enhances the forms.

Be sure that the students use heavy cardboard for skill 13. The layers will not show if they are made with thin poster board. Again, the surface decoration is not necessary, but if you want to put the works on display, a painted surface looks better. If they use aluminum foil to cover the relief, apply some glue to the sculpture. Then lay the foil lightly over the highest part of the relief. Start pressing it on in the center. As you get to the first ridge of the top layer, carefully press the foil around the vertical ridge. Then press out again. Each time you pull the foil down, be sure that it is pushed against the vertical wall so that you don't lose the shape of the relief.

HOW YOU PERCEIVE SHAPE, FORM, AND SPACE

Purpose

To help students comprehend how their eyes and brains work together when viewing depth

Learning Outcomes

After completing this section students will be able to
- demonstrate and explain how a person perceives depth.
- explain how and why point of view can change the shape or silhouette of a form.
- illustrate objects from different points of view.

Teaching Strategies

To help students understand that they have stereoscopic vision, try to bring in an example of stereography (3-D photography) and the special glasses required to merge the two pictures into one.

Check with your optician to see if there is anything like a "stereoptican," (an old-fashioned two image viewer) available to show your class.

If the students have not seen a 3-D movie, they will at least know about them. Try to get one of your students to explain how a 3-D illusion is created.

Have the students do "Developing Your Skills" 14 in class so that you can point out how it works. To take this activity further you might place several small objects on a table top. Ask one student to stand by the table with closed eyes. Then tell him/her to open just one eye and pick up an item that you name. Be sure to call on a student who does not object to being laughed at, since he/she will probably not be able to pick up the object.

You need to explain that people with one eye do adjust to the three-dimensional world. Somehow the brain learns that only one eye is operating and adapts. If a student is interested in the subject you might send him/her to an opthamologist to research the subject further.

The three views of the sculpture in Figure 6–18 dramatically illustrate how different views of one object can vary. Emphasize that this is one piece of work. Ask students to list adjectives that describe the mood of each view.

Using a slide or overhead projector, have students make hand shadows. Project the light onto a large piece of white paper. Have one student trace the silhouette on the paper while another "poses" the hand. To take this even farther, use a slide projector and trace the silhouettes of full length figures. This is a different activity than skill 3. There you were looking at the silhouettes of inanimate, fairly flat objects. Here you are silhouetting larger, changing forms. You are still using outlines, but you are concerned with the concept that one object can have many different silhouettes.

Be sure to emphasize that there are two ways that you can change your point of view: you can move or the object can move.

If students are having trouble with the changing table top, bring a safe ladder into the room and let them use a viewing frame to see how the shape changes as they move up and down. A simpler but less dramatic method is to bring in a rectangular solid similar to a table and hold it at different levels while students study it through viewing frames. The viewing frame is important because it acts as the picture plane. They can note how the angles of the edges of the table change in relationship to the edges of the viewing frame.

When students first look at the three views of a baseball glove in Figure 6–20, they won't think about the differences. But after they do contour drawings and trace over the outline with color, the drastic differences will become obvious. To make the differences even more dramatic, let the students cut out their three drawings and mount them on a sheet of dark construction paper.

"Developing Your Skills" 15 requires drawing skills. Skill 16 illustrates the same concept. It requires perception to find different silhouettes of a similar object. This is not as easy as it sounds. Very often students can see things when we point them out and show them how to see, but when we ask them to find examples of the same concept on their own, they cannot.

HOW ARTISTS CREATE SHAPES AND FORMS

Purpose

- To help students distinguish between natural and manufactured forms and between mass-produced and handmade forms
- To make students sensitive to the various methods and materials that artists use to create shapes and forms in works of art
- To help students perceive how artists create the illusions of form and depth in two-dimensional works of art
- To explain how to create the illusions of form and depth on a two-dimensional surface

Learning Outcomes

After completing this section students will be able to

- identify natural, manufactured, mass-produced, and handmade shapes and forms.
- describe the various methods and materials that artists use to create shapes and forms.
- explain how the illusion of angular or curved surfaces is created in two-dimensional works of art.
- illustrate hatching, crosshatching, blending, and stippling.
- experiment with various materials and techniques for shading curved and flat surfaces.
- set up and draw a still life arrangement of angular and curved objects and then create the illusion of form through shading.
- make a shaded drawing of his/her own face without drawing contours.
- define chiaroscuro, perspective, picture plane, foreground, background, and middleground.
- explain and illustrate the following perspective techniques: overlapping, size, placement, detail, color, and converging lines.
- explain and illustrate the use of vanishing points in one-point and two-point linear perspective.

Teaching Strategies

Students must understand the use of value in creating illusions of three-dimensional form. This is much more difficult for them to grasp than contour drawing. They have been drawing lines all of their lives, but they have not been as aware of values. After helping them become aware of the different values used in Figures 6–1, 6–22, 6–23, and 12–5, let them practice shading techniques without looking at real objects. Then ask them to try to see the relationships between the values they have created through experimentation and the values in the works of art just studied.

Try to set up a still life in the classroom as described in skill 18. Turn off as many of the overhead lights as you can, and place a strong spotlight on one side of the still life. Before they start to draw, talk them through an analysis of the values they perceive. Help them find the darkest and lightest areas. Help them see the difference between gradual changes of value on rounded forms, and jumps in value on angular surfaces. Insist that they use all of the values from white to black in their works. Many students try to stay in the safe gray areas of value and need to be pushed to go to black.

"Developing Your Skills" 19 will probably be easier to do as homework unless you can collect enough mirrors for the entire class. One way to control the lighting in your room is to turn off overhead lights and open the shades or blinds on one side of the room only. If you don't have windows, try to bring in enough lamps, which can be placed on one side of the room.

Notice that the skills 20–22 do not ask the student to draw with a ruler a complete perspective work with vanishing points. Skill 22 is really an exercise in perception rather than a creative exercise. Even in the "Imagine and Create" activity related to depth, the student is asked to use perception rather than measuring. Accurately measured linear perspective is not a subject of this course. It is not worth the necessary effort and time. It is, however, very important that students recognize and identify all the perspective techniques used to accomplish depth, of which linear perspective is only one. Not even linear perspective is always mathematical. Of course, if you have some students who would like to know more about it, there are many "how to" books in the libraries.

When discussing the six perspective techniques, be sure to have available large prints of realistic paintings, or use those in the book, so that students can identify the techniques and understand how artists created them. Make sure that the students can identify foreground, middleground, and background in these works.

To help them understand picture plane, bring in a rectangular piece of glass taped on the edges to prevent cuts. Have the students hold the glass perpendicular to the table and draw on the glass. The glass represents the surface of the painting. If you have windows in your room, several students at a time may draw what they see outside directly on the panes of glass. The windows can be cleaned afterward with any commercial household glass cleaner.

Besides recognizing the perspective techniques in works of art, you will want students to notice them in the environment. One effective method is a "treasure hunt." If you can take the class outside, do so. This activity will also work, however, in the art room. The first step is for you to find in the environment examples of overlapping, size, placement, and so on, that are easy to spot. Then set up a route for students to follow. You might put out footprints or a piece of yarn, or, if you have time, write creative clues. Put a large number at each stop on the route where a student must stand to see a particular example. Then prepare a treasure hunt sheet, with questions to be answered either verbally or visually, that must be filled out along the route. For example, one item might read: "While standing on number one, look at the tree and the bench. Which is overlapping the other?" Things

like size, detail, and color will be easy to find. For placement, you might put two colored squares on the floor, a red one close to the observation point and a blue one a minimum of ten feet away. Ask them to point to the red square and then point to the blue one. In this way they will see that things farther away are higher up on the picture plane. To help them see converging lines you will need a sidewalk or a hallway that is long enough. Ask them to put the paper down and point with both hands to both edges of the walk or floor. Then they should trace the lines of the walk until it ends or disappears on the horizon. Make sure they notice how their pointing fingers have almost come together and are almost at eye level. If you are using a hallway, have them point to where the ceiling meets the wall beside them. Then trace those lines until they reach the end. This time they will notice that their arms have lowered, but once more their fingers are almost touching and are almost at eye level.

Notice that skills 20, 21, and 22 are all different but can all be achieved by all students.

WHAT DIFFERENT SPACES, SHAPES, AND FORMS EXPRESS

Purpose

To help students comprehend the expressive qualities of shapes, forms, and spaces as they are used by artists

Learning Outcomes

After completing this section, students will be able to
- identify, explain, and illustrate the expressive qualities of outline and surface, density, openness, and activity and stability in works of art.
- identify hard-edge, opaque, and transparent shapes.

Teaching Strategies

This section is the heart of the chapter. Here the students learn to recognize the aesthetic qualities of shapes, forms, and space. Dramatization might help them grasp the expressive qualities.

Encourage students to think of examples from their environment to illustrate the concepts. Ask them to think of smooth objects they like to touch, of sharp angular things that they have learned to handle carefully. Now ask them to look through prints in the room or in the text to find examples of works that express each quality.

"Developing Your Skills" 23 through 26 are all design problems that can be achieved successfully by all students. Skill 27 is a verbal research problem. All students except those severely mentally disabled should be able to carry it out successfully.

Density and texture are often confused. This point will be discussed during the chapter on texture, but it is important that students realize now that hard and soft are properties of shape and form, while texture is a surface quality.

IMAGINE AND CREATE

All of the "Imagine and Create" activities are more complex than the other activities throughout the chapter.

Drawing an Outdoor Scene. Be certain that this scene is drawn from life. Do not let the students use photographs. Photos have already translated all three-dimensional forms into shapes and arranged them on a two-dimensional surface. While photos are useful as resource material for other activities, in this case they defeat the purpose.

Here you want the students to translate three-dimensional forms into two-dimensional shapes. Even if the drawing is limited to rooftops or the buildings around the schoolyard, it is important that students look at three-dimensional objects.

If necessary, change this assignment into a drawing of a scene inside the school building. Get permission to take students out of the art room to the media center, the industrial technology shop, the lunchroom, the office area, the home economics complex, the gym, the science lab, the auditorium, and so on.

Plaster Sculpture. If you have not worked with plaster before doing this activity, be sure that you practice all the procedures yourself so that you can help the students. Notice that for this activity it is necessary to wait until the plaster is almost ready to set up before you put it in the bag. If you put it in the bag while it is still watery, it takes too long to form and students will loose patience or you will be left with a bunch of flat glops!

An alternative to forming the plaster in plastic bags is to pour it into milk containers. Then, after it sets, challenge the students to transform the geometric solid into a freeform solid. Once more remind them to keep turning the form as they work so that all sides are equally interesting.

If you want to make the plaster a little softer and easier to carve, add an aggregate, such as zonolite, to it, but be careful to wear a mask when handling the material dry. The dust is hazardous.

If the plaster gets too hard to carve, wet it again by immersing it in water for a few minutes until it absorbs moisture. The length of time depends on many variables such as humidity.

Soft Sculpture. This activity will be easier if the students have access to a sewing machine.

Photogram. Remember that if you use this activity you must warn the students against leaning too close to the developing tray and inhaling ammonia fumes.

Drawing with a Computer. See page 53 for information to help you teach this activity.

ART CRITICISM

Notice that in this chapter during analysis students are asked to look back at the questions about line in Chapter 5. The art criticism activity in each chapter is cumulative. The student is always asked to build on the previous concepts before using new ones.

ANSWERS

Chapter 6 Review: Talking About Art
USING THE LANGUAGE OF ART

Answers will vary according to the artworks selected. The answers should show, however, that students understand the meanings of the terms as given in Chapter 6 and in the text Glossary. You may wish to require that students include the artist and title for each work cited. If so, titles should be underlined.

LEARNING THE ART ELEMENTS AND PRINCIPLES

1. Geometric and free-form; geometric.
2. Form has depth, but shape does not.
3. By the space around them.
4. Positive and negative.
5. Overlapping, size, placement, detail, color, converging lines.
6. Atmospheric and linear.

INCREASING YOUR ART AWARENESS

1. Answers will vary.
2. Answers will vary. You may wish to have students read their descriptions aloud in class to see how many students can recognize the object described. The elements of line, shape, form, and space should be important parts of the descriptions.
3. Both Giacometti's *City Square* (Figure 5–21) and Shahn's *Handball* (Figure 6–12) contain large negative spaces around positive areas. Both works express loneliness and isolation.
4. Figure 6–16 contains negative (free-form) space within positive space. Figure 6–16 expresses an open, inviting feeling and has an almost human-like appearance. Figure 6–40 seems to be dense, unyielding, and unemotional. Figure 6–48 expresses a relaxed, positive feeling. (answers, however, will vary.)
5. Figure 3–14; with shading to show changes in value.
6. Answers should reflect an understanding of the different types of lines (see Chapter 5), forms, and spaces and the various effects they create.

UNDERSTANDING ART CULTURE AND HERITAGE

1. Cézanne, *Houses in Provence* (Figure 6–7).
2. Figure 6–17: subject matter, lion; culture, Mesopotamian or Babylonian.
   Figure 6–37: subject matter, hippopotamus; culture, Egyptian.
3. Figure 5–21 is three dimensional and Figure 6–12 is two dimensional. In both the positive areas, the people, are separated by large areas of negative space. Both works express loneliness.
4. Figure 6–16 by Hepworth contains freeform negative space within the positive space. Figure 6–48 by Arp looks alive. Figure 6–40 by Brancusi seems mechanical and forbidding, and Figure 6–16 by Hapworth seems to represent the human spirit.

5. Figure 6–21 is flat; Figure 3–14 has more form and depth because of changes in value.
6. Figure 5–25, the Sagredo Palace, seems closed in while Figure 6–42 has open space. The lines and forms of the Johnson house are static, while those of the Sagredo Palace are curving and decorative.

JUDGING THE QUALITY OF ART

Answers will vary, but all should reflect an understanding of the perspective techniques discussed in this chapter.

LEARNING MORE ABOUT ART

Answers will vary.

Study Question Worksheet

1. A two-dimensional area that is defined in some way.
2. Objects having three-dimensions.
3. Natural shapes and forms - made by the forces of nature; manufactured shapes and forms - shapes or forms made by people.
4. A two-dimensional, shadow-like shape.
5. Precise shapes that can be described with mathematical formulas:

circle	trapezoid
square	pentagon
triangle	hexagon
oval	octagon
rectangle	
parallelogram	

6. Shapes that are irregular and uneven.
7. (a) cylinder and sphere.
   (b) cube.
   (c) cone or pyramid.
8. Snowflakes, the honeycomb, iron pyrite crystals (salt) sodium chloride, etc.
9. A technique for making neat, sharp folds in paper by cutting part of the way through the surface with scissors, knife, or other sharp instrument.
10. The arrangement of light and dark; developed by Italian Renaissance artists.
    Purpose: to create illusion of form.
11. The highlight is the area where the most light is reflected; usually small areas of white in a drawing.
12. (a) hatching - shading with parallel lines.
    (b) crosshatching - shading with parallel lines intersecting each other.
    (c) blending - shading through the smooth, gradual application of dark value.
    (d) stippling - shading with dots.
13. Shapes with clearly defined outlines; dense, forbidding.
14. Length, width, and depth.
15. Open shape - a shape that you can see into or through. It is inviting, such as an overstuffed arm chair. Closed shape-shapes that look solid and self-contained. They look forbidding, keep people out.
16. Active shape - look as if they are about to move.
    Static shapes - seem to be fixed in one place. A square, triangle, or rectangle would most likely look static unless it were resting on a corner, in which case it would appear to be more active. Diagonal forms are active.
17. The eyes see an object at slightly different angles. The brain causes these two separate and slightly different views to merge into one, resulting in a three-dimensional image.
18. (a) Relief sculpture - sculpture that projects from a flat plane into negative space.
    (b) Bas-relief (low relief) - when the positive forms in a relief sculpture projects slightly from the flat surface.
    (c) High relief - relief sculpture in which the positive forms project far out into the negative space.
19. An image in three dimensions created with a laser beam.
20. (a) Foreground - the space in a two-dimensional artwork which is closest to the picture plane and the viewer.
    (b) Middleground - the area in a two-dimensional artwork that is between the foreground and the background.
    (c) Background - the area in a two-dimensional artwork that represents the most distant space from the picture plane and the viewer.
21. (a) Overlapping - when one object covers part of a second object, the first seems to be closer.
    (b) Size - large objects appear to be closer to the viewer than small ones.
    (c) Placement - objects that are either high or low on the picture plane seem to be closer to the viewer than objects that are close to eye level.
    (d) Detail - objects with sharp edges and visable detail seem to be closer.
    (e) Color - brightly colored objects seem closer than dull colored shapes.
    (f) Converging lines (linear perspective) - parallel lines moving away seem to meet at a point on the horizon.
22. The place on the horizon where parallel lines seem to vanish or converge.
23. Air affects how we perceive objects in the distance.
24. The emptiness or area between, around, above, below, or within objects.
25. Positive areas are shapes and forms; negative space is the surrounding area.
26. The angle from which you see an object.
27. (a) Perfection idealism.
    (b) Protection, solidity.
    (c) Comfort, living things.
28. Many pieces put together; a three-dimensional collage.
29. Russia

Chapter Test

1. highlight
2. silhouette
3. natural

4. crosshatching
5. scoring
6. manufactured
7. blending
8. stippling
9. hatching
10. geometric
11. dimension
12. free-form

13. chiaroscuro
14. open
15. three
16. relief
17. static
18. linear
19. high relief
20. background
21. negative

22. vanishing point
23. middleground
24. perspective
25. hologram
26. positive
27. foreground
28. plane

29. D
30. F
31. A
32. G
33. E
34. C
35. B

Chapter 7: Color

INTRODUCING THE CHAPTER

Purpose

To introduce the element of color, its importance, and its complexity

Learning Outcomes

After completing this section students will be able to
• classify color as an element of art.
• describe and illustrate some ways that color communicates.
• conduct a survey concerning people's color preferences.

Teaching Strategies

Ask students to suggest ways that color communicates and to offer additional examples of the symbolic use of color.

You might start a good debate about the colorization of old black and white movies. Do students approve? How might the atmosphere of the films be affected?

If you know a photographer who uses black and white to create aesthetic (as opposed to journalistic) photographs, invite him/her to visit and explain working procedures.

"Developing Your Skills" 1 must be done as a homework assignment. The compilation of the survey, if done, requires the participation of the entire class.

An alternative to skill 1 would be an informal vote for favorite color in the classroom. Each student could write the name of a favorite color on a slip of paper, and the result of the vote can be compiled by a few students while the rest go on to another activity.

Skill 2 requires creative thinking regarding the symbolic qualities of color. The illustrations should be done quickly and should look more like cartoons than finished drawings.

HOW WE SEE COLOR

Purpose

• To help students understand the relationship between color and light
• To help students understand how people see color
• To explain the three properties of color: hue, value, and intensity

Learning Outcomes

After completing this section students will be able to
• explain the relationship between color and light.
• explain and/or illustrate how a person sees color and how that perception is dependent on light.
• define afterimage and explain how it occurs.
• identify the three properties of color.
• name the three primary hues and explain why they are unique.
• name the three secondary hues and tell which primary hues they are made from.
• name the six intermediate hues and tell which other hues must be mixed to make them.
• create a unique, twelve-color wheel containing the primary, secondary, and intermediate hues and paint it using only mixtures of primary hues.
• make a color-wheel collage.
• define value in relation to color.
• name and illustrate the three neutral colors and explain how people preceive them.
• define and illustrate tints and shades.
• identify and explain the expressive qualities of high-key and low-key colors.
• make a seven-step color value scale.
• identify and explain high- and low-intensity colors.
• identify complementary colors and explain what happens to a color when it is mixed with its complement.

- make a nine-step intensity scale for the three primary colors.
- demonstrate an understanding of the relationships among hue, value, and intensity.

Teaching Strategies

The most effective way to illustrate the relationship between light and color and to explain the spectrum is to use a prism. Every science lab has one you can borrow. If you cannot take the students outside, you can use the strong light from a slide projector to demonstrate the spectral colors. You will not always get all six colors evenly spaced as they are shown on charts. If you play with the prism and turn it slowly you can demonstrate how the color spread occurs.

If it's possible to darken the room completely, you can illustrate how colors change after the sun goes down. Otherwise, ask the students to observe the colors they see outside after sunset. This works best if first they make some color record of how a given hue looks in full sunlight. Next, they should make a second record of the same hue after the sun goes down. Students should then compare the two in a well-lit room.

One exciting activity you can do with afterimage is to draw an American flag and paint it with its opposite colors: green for red, orange for blue, and black for white. Have the students stare at the newly colored flag and then stare at the white wall. They will see the true colors of the flag in the afterimage. For slower learners you might duplicate a drawing of a flag and have them color it.

While discussing Figure 7-6, ask students to stare at one dot. After a few seconds the dot will begin moving no matter how they try to stop it. That will explain the relationship between the work and the image of musical notes that Larry Poons was trying to create. Of course no afterimage exercise will work unless the students make the effort to concentrate.

The facts about hue are extremely important. The students must know the primary hues and the order of the spectrum before they can control color. This information is as basic to working with color as simple addition is to mathematics.

"Developing Your Skills" 3 is a creative solution to a rather dull color-wheel exercise. The two student examples are evidence that this activity can be exciting. There is no limit to the kinds of objects that the students can use for their wheels.

An alternate activity for less creative students, which will help them memorize the order of the spectrum, is to make a picture of whatever they like using the colors of the spectrum in the correct order. The results can be anything from a scene with a rainbow in the sky to an eighteen-wheeler truck decorated with color stripes. Anything is acceptable, as long as the colors are in order.

Skill 4 encourages perceptive rather than creative skills. But the end result is still the same—memorization of the spectrum.

When discussing the absorptive power of black and the reflective power of white, explain to the students that in the days before air conditioning people wore more white in the summer to stay cooler.

Read the instructions in the technique tip before the students start mixing colors or there will be a lot of wasted paint. Notice that the student work included in that box is a transparent watercolor painting. Water was added to the colors to make them lighter.

The seven-step value scale in skill 5 is easier to make using opaque paints than with transparent watercolors. Some teachers prefer that students mix colors on the palette; others prefer that students mix paint on the paper until it looks just right.

Styrofoam trays, like the ones used to pack meat, make excellent mixing palettes. Sometimes store meat managers will sell some to you rather cheaply if you explain that they're for school. If you can't get them, try purchasing large styrofoam picnic plates. Of course, the students will wash and reuse them. If you want to save time, the cheapest paper plates can be used and disposed of after each work session. Some of the art supply catalogs sell plastic palettes with air-tight covers. If you students buy their own paints, these make excellent storage and work containers for saving acrylics.

Working with color intensities demands that students remember the order of the color wheel. They cannot remember opposites unless they remember what goes where. The colors of the spectrum are pure hues. Explaining the relationships of the complements to the three primaries clarifies the concept. If you start with red, you have blue and yellow left. They combine to make green, and green is the opposite, or complement, of red. This works even with intermediate colors. The opposite of blue-green is the opposite of blue (orange), plus the opposite of green (red) or red-orange.

Skill 6 works best with opaque colors, but it can also be done with transparent watercolors. The students must be careful to control the amount of water used so that the values are consistant.

Skill 7 is a creative application of low intensities. This problem does not need to be limited to trees. You can challenge students to invent other subject matter. When they are given choices, they become more interested in the product.

Skill 8 is a perception problem. They will soon discover that it is often difficult to distinquish between a low intensity and a dark value of the same hue.

COLOR SCHEMES

Purpose

To make students aware of the different schemes they can use to organize colors

Learning Outcomes

After completing this section students will be able to
- explain simultaneous contrast and give a specific example of how it works.
- identify and illustrate a monochromatic color scheme.

- identify and illustrate an analogous color scheme.
- identify and illustrate complementary color schemes.
- identify and illustrate a color triad color scheme.
- identify and illustrate a split complement color scheme.
- identify and illustrate warm and cool color schemes.
- explain the relationship of warm and cool colors to the illusion of advancement and recession in a two-dimensional work of art.
- make a chart to illustrate simultaneous contrast.
- tell the similarities and differences among various color schemes and select the best color scheme for a specific purpose.

Teaching Strategies

It is important that students understand that color schemes are not "rules," but simply methods for organizing colors for different effects.

The value of understanding color schemes is in knowing how they may be used for specific purposes. Discuss the attributes of various color schemes. Ask students to analyze colors such as the colors they are wearing, the colors they would like to use to decorate a room in their home, and the colors they would choose for a car. Would they choose the same color scheme for a family sedan as for a sports car? Would they wear the same colors to a formal prom as to a beach party? What kind of a color scheme would they use to paint a battle scene, a scene of children playing, or an old couple sitting together on a park bench? Name a color scheme and let the students suggest a scene that would be effective painted in those colors.

One variation of "Developing Your Skills" 9 that could be done quickly with the class would be to give everyone in the room a small square of the same piece of construction paper. Let each one take the square home and find a larger square of color on which to glue the small one. (You can dictate a specific size if you wish). Encourage the students to use different materials, such as construction paper, wrapping paper, fabric, paper towels, small pieces of wood, and leather for the larger square. When students bring the squares to class mounted on unique backgrounds, have them glue the squares onto a large sheet of poster board or cardboard. When the color collage is complete, ask them to write a few sentences describing unusual combinations within the collage. Or you could just ask them to discuss the different effects that have been achieved.

Another activity that will help students see the effects of different color schemes would be to have each student find one reproduction in *ArtTalk* that fits one of the color schemes described in this section. Make a rough sketch of the reproduction and then color it using oil pastels or crayons in a different color scheme.

Ask them if they have noticed that during one season a certain color scheme seems to be emphasized by fashion designers. Whether the clothes are high-fashion or mass-produced, there seems to be a dominant color scheme. Then, by the next year at the same time, the color scheme may be completely different. Ask the class to suggest reasons why this happens. Make this one of those open-ended discussions that the students can run. Sit back and moderate—don't dominate. Also, remember that men are as interested in what they wear as women. This kind of discussion is not for women only.

COLOR IN PIGMENTS

Purpose

To make students aware of the sources for color and how different vehicles affect the final look of the pigment.

Learning Outcomes

After completing this section students will be able to
- distinguish between the colors of pigment and the colors of light.
- explain the relationship between pigment and vehicle.
- explain the difference between paint and dye and tell how they relate to surfaces.
- explain how various vehicles and surfaces affect the colors people perceive.
- describe the difference between natural and synthetic pigments.
- explain the sources of natural pigments, cite three specific sources, and tell what color they produce.
- collect and grind three earth pigment colors and mix them with a vehicle to produce paint.
- use the natural pigment paints to paint a design.
- experiment with a variety of paint media on various surfaces.

Teaching Strategies

Present an assortment of different color media, such as acrylic paints, pastels, oil paints, watercolors, gouache, designer paints, casein paints, food coloring, dyes, crayons, colored pencils, and so on. Try to obtain each in the same color, if possible. Then, allow the students to experiment with the various media. If that is not possible, use the paints yourself on one surface and let them guess which paint made which mark.

Discuss natural pigments with the class. Have any of the students ever heard about natural sources for colors? Invite them to tell what they know.

One natural pigment source that is easy and safe to demonstrate is onion skin. Ask the produce manager of a grocery store to save onion skins for you the next time the bins are cleaned out. Boil them in water to obtain a golden yellow-orange color. Elaborate formulas have been developed for using natural dyes and making them permanent, but even without a mordant to set the colors, they can be brushed on paper.

If you would like to dye something very simply, do the following. Boil the onion skins in an enamel pot (do not use aluminum) until the water is strongly colored. Strain out the skins. Add about a teaspoon of alum to the mix to set the dye. (Alum can be found in the grocery store; it is used in making pickles and is safe. Add white pure-wool yarn or white natural-cotton fabric to the solution and heat is gently. You cannot dye synthetic fabrics with natural dyes. The longer you leave the fibers in the solution, the stronger the color will be.

Another safe mordant to use is iron. If you boil the skins in an old iron kettle, the iron acts as a mordant. If you do not have an iron kettle, you can buy ferrous sulfate, which is a fetilizer and can be obtained from a garden store. Just add a spoonful to the onion skin liquid. It will make a much darker color, something like a brown, or a very dark, almost black, green. The alum yields a more orange color.

Natural dyes are not as safe to use in school as you might imagine. The dye material is safe, but many of the mordants are poisonous. Check all the directions carefully, and check out the nature of the chemicals before you bring anything into your classroom. Also note that some of the author's experiments with natural coloring materials yielded some horrible aromas, so be careful before you boil them inside the school building.

The directions for making earth pigments are those that have been used by the author for years. The hardest part is separating the clay colors and grinding them up. Findings large chunks of a single color simplifies the process. If you are a city teacher, you might be able to collect some different earth colors on a vacation and bring them back to school to share with your students.

The sky in Figure 7–30 was created by mixing natural beige pigment with some school acrylic paint. All of the other colors are pure earth pigment.

The white glue vehicle suggested in the technique tip is the easiest one to make at school. Some other vehicles that have been successful are polymer medium, gel medium, modeling paste, white school acrylic paint, fingerpaint base, liquid starch, linseed oil, and baby oil. You and your students will probably think of some others that are safe to try.

HOW ARTISTS USE COLOR

Purpose

To explain how artists use color to communicate

Learning Outcomes

After completing this section students will be able to
• identify and illustrate optical color.
• explain how the Impressionists made use of optical color.
• identify and illustrate arbitrary color.
• be able to name at least one artist who used arbitrary colors.
• explain and illustrate how warm and cool colors can be used to create the illusion of depth on a two-dimensional picture plane.

• name at least one artist who used warm and cool colors to create the illusion of depth.
• explain and illustrate two different kinds of movement that can be created using color value.
• name at least one artist who used jumps in color value to create the sensation of dance movement.
• illustrate color tonality.
• explain the difference between tonality and a monochromatic color scheme.
• name at least one artist who used color tonality to create a specific mood.

Teaching Strategies

It is important that the students apply what they have learned about the science of color to the expressive qualities of color.

Ask them to look through the book to find examples of optical color (Figures 7–13, 6–26, 12,–8, 2–4, 6–11, 6–1, 8–14), arbitrary color (5–17, 10–25, 9–2, 2–2, 10–27, 3–17, 3–13, 12–27), special effects with color (2–6, 12–4, 3–12, 1–7c), movement through color value (9–2, 7–20, 7–36, 9–1, 7–3) and color tonality (11–1, 1–7a, 7–27).

Call their attention to 7–18, Hartley's monochrome. Ask them what effect the changes in value have on the work. Ask them to compare that work to the Mondrian in Figure 7–36. Which one has larger jumps in value? Which one is calmer?

IMAGINE AND CREATE

Through the Looking Circle. If you cannot take the class outside for this activity, try an alternative. Ask the students to look through their previous sketches for one they can use. Then move the round viewing frame around the drawing until they find an interesting area. Reproduce that area in a circle at least six inches in diameter and then paint is as instructed in the activity.

Three-dimensional Amusement Park Ride. The student who created the example in Figure 7–41 became so enthusiastic that he hooked up a battery to the wheel. The ride worked for several weeks until the battery ran out. If you and your students get interested in this project, you might divide them into teams. Organize this work so that each team plans and creates a different ride for the park. With a little ingenuity all the rides can be made to work. The entire park might be set up in a display area and be turned on for special performances.

Painting with Expressive Colors. Here's a chance for the students with a love for fantasy to have fun. Let them draw a fantasy scene of their own choosing, filling it with all the monsters and dragons they wish. Then paint it with arbitrary colors to make the scene even wilder.

Painting—One Scene in Two Moods. If the student has created a complicated drawing of a house that is hard to copy, there are several ways to copy the work. The student may trace the original drawing with tracing paper, create a transfer by covering the back of the tracing paper with graphite or chalk, and then place it on a clean piece of white paper to trace over it. The student could also put the original drawing on an opaque projector and project it onto each piece of drawing paper. In that case, just sketch the main lines and add the details afterward. Or the student might hold the second paper over the first drawing and tape them to a window. The light coming through the paper will make the drawing underneath visible so that it can be traced lightly.

ANSWERS

Chapter 7 Review: Talking About Art

USING THE LANGUAGE OF ART

Answers will vary according to the artworks selected. The answers should show, however, that students understand the meanings of the terms as given in Chapter 7 and in the text Glossary. You may wish to require that students include the artist and title for each work cited. If so, titles should be underlined.

LEARNING THE ART ELEMENTS AND PRINCIPLES

1. You see color because light waves are reflected from objects to your eyes. The light hits the retina of the eye where cells receive the color images.
2. Hue, value, intensity.
3. Red, orange, yellow, green, blue, and violet.
4. Monochromatic, analogous, complementary, triad, split-complementary, warm, and cool.
5. A white surface, such as white paper, because only white allows the true color of a medium to show; shiny, dense surfaces because they reflect more light.
6. Optical color to show objects as we perceive them, arbitrary color to express different moods and feelings, warm and cool colors to show the illusion of depth, abrupt, changes in value of colors to create a sense of movement (similar values create calm), tonality to create a unifying effect.

INCREASING YOUR ART AWARENESS

1. Answers will vary, but the warm colors give the feeling of life.
2. Answers will vary, but all should reflect an understanding of color as discussed in Chapter 7.
3. All five ways of using color to achieve different effects can be cited. The work shown in Figure 3–1 seems more vital and lifelike, and color contributes a great deal to this impression.
4. Answers should include line and shape direction, degree of solidity in forms, spatial effects, and color scheme.
5. Answers should include mention of color scheme, intensity, value, and geometric and free-form shapes. The free-form shapes in Figure 3–19 seem to be floating behind the rectangles. The effect is one of happy, organic movement. Figure 7–12 seems much calmer.

UNDERSTANDING ART CULTURE AND HERITAGE

1. *Deer*, Figure 7–29; as part of a hunting ritual, to help hunters capture the animal, to serve as visual prayers that animals would appear during the hunt, or to celebrate a successful hunt.
2. *The Waterfall*, Figure 7–12; *Fatata te Miti (By the Sea)*, Figure 7–33; *Rouen Cathedral*, Figures 7–34 and 7–35. Answers concerning similarities and differences will vary.
3. Figure 7–33, *Fatata te Miti (By the Sea)*; answers will vary as to meaning.
4. Figure 7–21, *Orange and Yellow*.
5. The artist used scientific knowledge about vision to create optical illusions of movement.

JUDGING THE QUALITY OF ART

Answers will vary.

LEARNING MORE ABOUT ART

You may wish to have students research the history of the painting medium and do oral or written reports on their findings.

Study Question Worksheet

1. Light enters the lens of the eye and strikes the retina. The retina is a membrane of nerve tissue at the back of the eye. There, two types of cells react to it—one receives light and dark, the other receives color.
2. Because color is dependent on light.
3. An opposite color image that remains after viewing a shape or object: it is created by the brain in reaction to color stared at originally.
4. Red, orange, yellow, green, blue, and violet.
5. A rainbow.
6. Because a red apple absorbs all colors except for red which is reflected back to the viewer.
7. Finely ground, colored powders that form paint.
8. The material used to carry pigment in art media.
9. Pigments that dissolve in liquid.
10. Paints lie on the surface of a material, whereas dyes sink into a material and color by staining.
11. The surface quality of a car is highly reflective, but the shirt fabric absorbs some of the light.
12. They have been made artificially by scientists. They are brighter and more permanent than their natural counterparts.
13. The name of a spectral color such as red, orange, yellow, etc.
14. Red, yellow, and blue.
15. The secondary colors.
16. (a) Green, orange, and violet.
    (b) Yellow and blue, red and yellow, and blue and red respectively.
17. (a) Red-orange, red-violet, blue-green, blue-violet, yellow-green, and yellow-violet.
    (b) By mixing a primary and secondary color.
18. The spectrum bent into a circle.
19. How much light a color reflects.

20. Black, white, and gray.
21. A light value of a hue.
22. A dark value of a hue.
23. Paintings showing many tints are referred to as *high key*. Paintings that are low-key have dark values.
24. The brightness or dullness of a hue.
25. A high-intensity hue is a pure hue, and a low-intensity hue is a dulled hue.
26. A less intense value of the color.
27. (a) One color.
    (b) A color scheme using tints and shades of only one color.
28. A plan for organizing colors.
29. They sit side by side on the color wheel and they have a common hue.
30. (a) Colors located directly opposite one another on the color wheel.
    (b) When placed side by side they seem to vibrate. They tend to make each other more intense.
31. A color scheme composed of three colors spaced equally distant from each other on the color wheel.
32. The combination of one hue plus the hues on each side of its complement.
33. Warm colors are associated with warm things, cool colors with cool things. Warm colors seem to move toward the viewer, and cool colors tend to move back. Warm colors are red, yellow, and orange. Cool colors are green, blue, and violet.
34. The color of an object is affected by all colors in its environment, such as atmosphere or unusual lighting.
35. When the artist uses color to express feelings and ignores optical color.
36. He painted a cool, blue outline around the shape of a warm, round orange. The fruit seemed to be pushed forward by the surrounding blue.
37. By placing colors with values ranging from very high-key to very low-key next to each other.
38. When one color dominated a work of art. It is not necessarily monochrome since other colors may be present, but the overall effect is an impression of the color.

Chapter Test

1. complement
2. pigments
3. dyes
4. value
5. shade
6. intensity
7. color schemes
8. analogous
9. complementary
10. warm
11. optical
12. tonality
13. monochromatic
14. high-intensity
15. neutral
16. synthetic
17. retina
18. triad
19. afterimage
20. cool
21. monochrome
22. vehicle
23. arbitrary
24. hue
25. split complement
26. high-key
27. tint
28. yellow
29. yellow-orange
30. orange
31. red-orange
32. red
33. red-violet
34. yellow-green
35. green
36. blue-green
37. blue
38. blue-violet
39. violet
40. red and yellow
41. blue and yellow
42. red and blue
43. green
44. blue
45. yellow
46. red-violet
47. blue-green
48. blue; green
49. red-orange; yellow orange
50. red-violet; blue violet

Chapter 8: Texture

INTRODUCING THE CHAPTER

Purpose

To help students understand that texture is the tactile element of art related to the surfaces of things and to make them aware of texture in their environment

Learning Outcomes

After completing this section students will be able to
• classify texture as the element of art related to surface.
• describe the textures of surfaces in the immediate environment.
• name and classify both rough and smooth textures.

Teaching Strategies

This section is designed to make students aware of texture. Get a discussion going about the textures of food and clothing. Or ask them to think about textures that they take for granted, such as smooth chair seats, rough sidewalks that prevent slipping, the texture of hair, the surface of a textbook cover, the top of a desk, the sole of a shoe, and so on.

"Developing Your Skills" 1 and 2 may be done for homework or discussed in class. They have slightly different purposes. Skill 1 is an identification and description problem. Skill 2 is more of a recall problem.

HOW WE PERCEIVE TEXTURE

Purpose

- To make students realize that texture is one element that we perceive with two senses—both sight and touch
- To help students differentiate between real texture and visual texture
- To make them aware of simulated and invented textures

Learning Outcomes

After completing this section students will be able to
- name the two senses that people use to perceive texture.
- explain the difference between real and visual texture.
- describe how values help identify visual textures.
- identify and explain the difference between simulated and invented textures.
- make texture rubbings and use them to create a collage.
- become more aware of tactile experiences usually taken for granted.
- use drawing skills to imitate textured surfaces taken from rubbings.
- create a landscape using visual textures from magazine photographs.

Teaching Strategies

The emphasis in this section should be the differentiation between real and visual textures and between simulated and invented textures.

One interesting way to help students see the relationship between real and visual textures is to show them a collection of interesting surfaces, such as shells, carpeting, burlap, denim, a slice of bread, and so on. At the same time that you are collecting the objects, find photographs of the same textures. Ask the students to match the real and visual surfaces and explain their decisions. The photos do not have to match the real objects in size, shape, or color.

For slower learners you might make a card game in which the real textures are in a box and the visual textures are on cards. The students draw a card and then find the real texture in the box that matches the card.

To help them understand simulated texture, ask them to think of things in the classroom or at home that are made of a manufactured material that imitates a natural material, such as wood. Point out that many synthetic fabrics imitate natural fibers, such as linen and silk. Then look at Figures 8–3 and 8–4 and ask them to determine how the textures in each work were created. Point out that there are similarities between the works. Both stimulate the viewer's sense of touch: the Ingres because the textures are such perfect simulations of satin, skin, hair, and so on, and the Bak because the invented textures make you think of the rough surfaces of rocks and sandy soil.

It may seem unnecessary to include a technique tip on rubbing, but most students do not know how to achieve a clear rubbing. Most of them rub the crayon back and forth across the surface of the paper, and sometimes this succeeds. More often, rubbing back and forth moves the paper and ruins the rubbing. They do not need any special dexterity, so they should not be afraid to change hands during the procedure.

"Developing Your Skills" 3 is different from 1 and 2 in that it concerns the sense of touch and not just textures. Its purpose is to heighten awareness, and it will be equally effective as a discussion or as a written exercise.

Skill 4 involves rubbings and designs. In the student example you can see that a variety of colored crayons were used. This works well with wax crayons, but oil pastels do not make good rubbings. You might want to limit the number of colors used, or you might wish to eliminate color and just use a pencil.

Skill 5 requires drawing skills. It might seem too demanding for some students, but it is not. Ask the students to study the rubbings for repetitions of lines, dots, or small shapes. A magnifying glass can help them analyze the rubbing more easily. When this activity is finished, display the rubbings and the drawings made from them in a random manner, and then ask the students to match the drawings to the rubbings. Of course a student may not choose his/her own to match.

Skill 6 is an interesting challenge to students' creative thinking skills and can be achieved successfully by all students. They must use photographs of visual textures to create a collage of invented textures. If they are not sure what to look for, ask them to look closely at Figure 8-8 to find out what visual textures were used to create the tree trunk, the ground, and so on.

TEXTURE AND VALUE

Purpose

To explain the relationship between value and visual texture

Learning Outcomes

After completing this section students will be able to
- explain how the arrangement of light and dark values on a surface indicate the texture of that surface.
- identify, collect, organize into a design, and draw rough, smooth, matte, and shiny textures.
- identify, design, and create a collage.

Teaching Strategies

In dealing with this section it is important to realize that textures may have more than one characteristic. For example, rough and smooth can be either matte or shiny. Sandpaper and aluminum foil are good examples. Pull a piece of foil out of a box. It is smooth. Crinkle it up. It is still shiny but it is no longer smooth. Figures 8–9 through 8–12 illustrate this concept.

"Developing Your Skills" 7, 8, and 9 require the use of real textures. If you have students who are responsible about bringing things to school when asked, have them start bringing in textured materials about a week before you use these exercises. You might prepare a list of suggested materials, which could include the following: aluminum foil, plastic wrap, wrapping paper, ribbons, wax paper, paper napkins, paper towels, tree bark, sandpaper, screening, styrofoam plates, paper plates, loose sand (in a bag), scrap fabrics, gum wrappers, grasses, pine straw, and so on.

If your students are unreliable about bringing things in, you need to start collecting textured materials yourself well before you get to this unit.

Skill 7 requires students to identify and categorize different textures. Skill 8 requires students to organize textured surfaces into a collage. It is important that students consider the other elements while they arrange the textures. They need shapes that vary in size, and they need to limit colors so that the colors do not detract from the textures. At the same time they must consider lines, shapes, and color as they organize the total design. Skill 7 and 8 can be completed successfully by all students. Skill 9 requires some drawing, but it can be achieved successfully if they have already completed Skill 5. Skill 10 is a perception drawing problem. This skill does not call for composition so that the students can concentrate on rendering various textured surfaces one at a time.

HOW ARTISTS USE TEXTURE

Purpose

To increase student sensitivity regarding the expressive uses of texture

Learning Outcomes

After completing this section students will be able to
- identify and explain *trompe-l'oeil.*
- compare the way Renoir and Albright rendered human skin.

- explain the unique ways that the following artists used texture: Vermeer, Rembrandt, Harnett, Van Gogh, Picasso, Pei, Degas, and Ernst.
- identify and illustrate frottage, grattage, and decalcomania.
- create a design using invented textures.

Teaching Strategies

Start by comparing the Renoir and the Albright works. Ask students to describe the different painting styles and techniques that were used to render the subjects' complexions.

In the 1940s Albright painted the featured portrait for the movie *The Picture of Dorian Gray*. In the story the portrait ages and Dorian Gray, the man, remains young.

All of Albright's paintings have the same quality of age and decay. He renders them using minute details that take a long time to complete. Notice in the credit line that the work took Albright two years to complete. Have students study the work with a magnifying glass to discover all of the details.

Ask students to notice how Rembrandt and Vermeer hint at real textures but use completely different techniques from Albright. A comparison of Rembrandt's *Self Portrait* with Albright's *Ida* would be interesting. What different techniques do the two artists use to render aging skin?

Van Gogh will be studied in detail in Chapter 9.

In looking at the Picasso work, it is important to emphasize what an innovator he was. A collage does not seem very unique today, but he was the first to use collage in fine art. An extra research problem could include having a student find out how many firsts can be attributed to Picasso.

The techniques invented by Ernst always fascinate students, especially the decalcomania. The term *decal* is a derivative of the word.

When looking at the words of deKooning and Van Gogh, remember that photographs and reproductions can never duplicate the experience of seeing the originals. The aesthetic quality of these works is largely dependent on the thick, rich textures of paint that can never be appreciated until seen in the original.

If cost is not a problem, give students some thick acrylic paints to manipulate. There is a joy in working with thick paints that cannot be realized just be looking at two-dimensioanl reproductions.

"Developing Your Skills" 11 should be exciting for all students. One variation that has been tried and tested in the classroom is to use two different surfaces for the decalcomania—one, white drawing paper; the second, small squares of acetate. This is a little expensive, but well worth the result. The students place large lumps of thick, creamy paint on the white paper. Then they place the transparent acetate over the paint. This way they can see the colors as they push them around under the acetate. This gives the student some control over the colors. It is best to have a partner when pulling the two surfaces apart. One person pulls the top surface and the other holds down the bottom surfaces so that the paint textures aren't damaged. Then both people hold all four corners of the work while placing it on a piece of heavy paper or a thick layer of newspapers to dry. When both surfaces are dry, the paint on the acetate may be cut into shapes and added to the white paper. The extra pieces will be useful if the student tries the Textured Fantasy Landscape (see below).

Skill 12 requires imagination and skill to be successful. Words written in cursive and repeated over and over, line after line, make very interesting invented textures.

IMAGINE AND CREATE

Textured Fantasy Landscape. Ideas for creating the textures have been suggested above. In adding cut out objects to the collage, it is important to stress skill in cutting. Also indicate to the students that the shape of the object must fit into the work. The student should not cut out a rough shape and glue it down without considering the area on which it is to be placed. Any details being painted or glued onto the textured background must be planned so that the shapes relate to the background. If needed, students could match background and cutouts by painting over the edges. Then the shape will seem to emerge from the background. In Figure 8–28 notice how the tiger seems to be sitting in the grass. The tiger is a cut out from a magazine. But paint used for the background was applied over the edges of the cutout to make it fit in.

Textured-Clay Wind Chimes. In the photo of the completed wind chimes notice that the impressed designs have been enhanced with a dark glaze. After the tiles were bisque-fired, black glaze was brushed on and the surfaces wiped with a damp cloth. The dark glaze remained in the indentations.

If you do not have rolling pins for the students to roll out the clay, glass jars or large smooth cylinders will do. If nothing suitable is available, students can press out a small amount of clay with the ball of the hand to get a fairly flat slab.

When smoothing the edges of the tiles, it is very important not to use too much water. It will be enough if the student dips just one fingertip in the water and rubs that amount across the remaining fingertips. Too much water makes the tiles muddy and soft. Clay shrinks as it dries. If one surface of the tiles dries faster than the other, that side will shrink faster and cause warping. To prevent warping, dry the tiles slowly and keep turning them.

In Figure 8–30 the chimes are attached to the grapevine wreath. Another support might be made out of clay. Create a shape that matches the shapes of the chimes. Be sure to put holes in it before it dries. Also, consider how the support will be hung.

Texture Stitchery. As indicated in the text, this is not a "girls only" activity. Remind the boys that Rosie Greer (former pro football player) does stitchery to relax. If he can, so can they.

Before they start this activity, help them analyze Figure 8–37 to see how many different stitches they can find. Point out how the artist has used different line directions, as they did in Chapter 5 for their yarn painting. If this is the students' first experience with stitchery, it would be wise to limit the design to abstract shapes, which are less demanding than a representational design. Point out the design of the student work in Figure 8–35. It would also be wise for them to try out each stitch on scrap fabric before working it into the design.

When students are underway on this project, it is best to send it home with them. It will never get finished if they only work on it one hour per day.

Even though the student example is not finished, it was stretched around and taped to a piece of heavy cardboard for the photograph. That is an alternate way to prepare the work for display.

Weaving. The loom suggested in the text is only one of many possibilities for working with fibers without a table loom.

One method that is not very demanding and is easy to control is to turn a branch from a tree into a three-dimensional support for warp threads. Anything that supports warp threads is considered a loom. If the students select this method, be sure that they use a strong set of branches that will not snap when the warp threads are strung.

When weaving on a three-dimensional branch loom, students should not pack the weft threads tightly. Nor do students need to be concerned with removing the weaving from the loom. The branch is an integral part of the weaving. When the weaving is complete, a good way to display it is to drill a large hole in a block of wood and put the bottom of the branch into the hole so that it stands like a flag on a pole.

ANSWERS

Chapter 8 Review: Talking About Art

USING THE LANGUAGE OF ART

Answers will vary according to the artworks selected. The answers should show, however, that students understand the meanings of the terms as given in Chapter 8 and in the text Glossary. You may wish to require that students include the artist and title for each work cited. If so, titles should be underlined.

LEARNING THE ART ELEMENTS AND PRINCIPLES

1. Touch and vision.
2. When you actually touch something, you are experiencing real texture. When you look at a photograph of textures and remember how they feel, you are experiencing visual texture.
3. Simulated textures imitate real textures. Invented textures do not represent any real surface qualities but stimulate memories of real textures.
4. Rough, smooth, matte, shiny.
5. The manner in which it reflects light.
6. The shadows or values.
7. Rough.
8. Smooth.

Increasing Your Art Awareness

1. You may wish to have students read their descriptions aloud to see how many students can guess what is being described.
2. Simulated; for example, the rough surfaces include the woman's face.
3. The armor is shiny and smooth for the most part, the exception being his skirt of chain mail, which is shiny and rough. The horse's body is matte smooth. The armor shows strong highlights, an abrupt jump in value from light to dark. The horse's body shows very gradual changes in value and no highlights.
4. Students should list as many textures as they can see. All are simulated.
5. Answers should reflect an understanding of texture as it is discussed in Chapter 8.
6. Both artists used heavy applications of paint to create real texture in their paintings. Each work communicates the feeling of living things or subject matter that is alive and growing.

Understanding Art Culture and Heritage

1. *Women Holding a Balance*, Figure 8–1.
2. 1845, *Comtesse d' Haussanville* Figure 8–3; 1876, *Young Woman Braiding Her Hair*, Figure 8–15; 1880, *Little Fourteen-Year-Old Dancer*, Figure 8–21; 1889, *Cypresses*, Figure 8–17. Answers concerning similarities and differences will vary.
3. Figure 8–3 is an example of the Neoclassic style, and Figure 8–15 is an example of Impressionism. Students should refer to Chapter 3 to support their answers.
4. Cubism.

Judging the Quality of Art

Answers will vary.

Learning More About Art

Answers will vary.

Study Question Worksheet

1. (a) Texture - the element of art that refers to how things feel, or how they look as if they might feel.
   (b) Visual texture - illusion of a three-dimensional surface.
   (c) Simulated texture - textures that imitate real textures.
   (d) Invented texture - a texture created by making two-dimensional patterns by repeating lines or shapes.
   (e) Rubbing - a technqiue for transferring a three-dimensional (real) texture to a smooth two-dimensional surface.
   (f) Matte surface - a surface that reflects a soft, dull light.
   (g) Shiny surface - a surface that reflects so much light, so brightly, that it seems to glow with light.
   (h) Frottage - the transfer of texture through the process of rubbing.
   (i) Grattage - a process of grating or scratching into wet paint with a variety of tools.
   (j) Decalcomania - a technique for producing random patterns; canvases between which blobs of paint have been squeezed are pulled apart.
2. Sight and touch.
3. The purpose of simulated texture is imitation.
4. Rough surfaces reflect light unevenly. Smooth surfaces reflect light very evenly.
5. A matte surface absorbs some light and reflects a soft, dull light. Shiny surfaces reflect so much light that they seem to glow.
6. He was concerned with the wrinkles of old age.
7. "Fool the eye;" so many details, the paintings look real.
8. Used thick paint and swirling brush strokes.
9. (a) To create interesting surfaces (b) stucco, brick, wood, stone, cement, metal, glass.
10. Through the use of fibers and weaving techniques.
11. By pressing objects into clay, scratching into the clay, or by the application of glazes (either matte or gloss).
12. Frottage, grattage and decalcomania.
13. Rococo; he revealed personality, used hard edges, strong lights, and dark backgrounds.
14. Colonial America.

Chapter Test

1. collage
2. shiny
3. invented
4. decalcomania
5. texture
6. simulated
7. matte
8. smooth
9. grattage
10. assemblage
11. rough
12. frottage
13. simulated
14. van Gogh or de Kooning
15. Renoir
16. tromp-l' oeil
17. Ernst
18. simulated
19. architects
20. imitate

Chapter 9: Rhythm and Movement

INTRODUCING THE CHAPTER

Purpose

To make the students aware of rhythms all around them

Learning Outcomes

After completing this section students will be able to
- give at least five examples of rhythmic events.
- name six examples that are a part of their own daily rhythms.
- record five non-musical rhythms from the environment.

Teaching Strategies

During the introduction you want to make the students aware of as many different rhythmic events in their lives as you can. Brainstorm with them to see how many they can think of.

If you have a student who plays a musical instrument that can be brought to class, you might ask him/her to demonstrate various musical rhythms. If you have a music lover, ask her/him to tape a collection of different musical rhythms and bring them to class.

Challenge one student to clap out a complex repetitive rhythm until the other students can catch the beat and clap along.

Discuss the concept of rhythm as a comforting feeling. Take a vote to see which students like to do the same things at the same times every day and which ones like to keep changing their daily routines.

"Developing Your Skills" 1 can be discussed in class or done as written homework. Skill 2 can be an interesting challenge if some of the students who make recordings bring in their tapes and let the others guess what activities the rhythms belong to.

HOW WE PERCEIVE VISUAL RHYTHM

Purpose

- To help students develop a sensitivity to the visual rhythms in their environment
- To help them understand how visual rhythms create a sensation of movement in works of art

Learning Outcomes

After completing this section students will be able to
- identify visual rhythms in their environment and describe them in terms of positive beats and negative rests.
- explain the difference between real and visual movement and cite specific examples of each.
- select two advertisements that use rhythm to create visual movement and indicate the positive beats.

Teaching Strategies

It is important that students grasp the concept of visual movement as something we perceive with our eyes. It is also important that they understand how visual movement is different from real movement.

A painting of flowers may have more visual movement than a stop-action photograph of a football player. The painting may cause your eyes to jump from one flower shape to the next, while the stop-action photograph may have frozen the movement in such a way that your eyes hardly move.

Bring in some natural objects such as leaves, acorns, small round pebbles, or shells. Demonstrate the feeling of movement by asking students to arrange them in a row across a table top. Give different groups of students different groups of objects and ask them to make patterns that move the viewers' eyes across the table. Some students may see that these regular rhythms are implied lines. This would be a good time for you to make the point that the elements and principles of art are all interwoven, and in real life it is hard to separate them. As you go through the remaining chapters, encourage the students to look for interrelationships among all of the concepts and to notice how they affect each other. This type of thinking is one you want to encourage at all times.

Ask the students to look for the repetition of all elements in Figures 9–3 and 9–4. Both of the paintings are visually very active.

Ask the students to think of implied lines when they look at *The Horse Fair*. Where do they see an implied line? Once again, you may bring up the relationship between implied lines and visual rhythm. How does Bonheur control the movement of the viewer's eyes in this work?

After the students study the visual movement in *The Horse Fair*, you might ask them if they have ever heard of the artist. They probably have not. However, her life spanned most of the 19th century, and she was very popular and successful painter. By the time she was nineteen her work was being exhibited. This painting was donated to the Metropolitan Museum of Art in 1887.

As students can guess from this painting, her favorite subject was animals. Ask them to note the size of this work. Does its size seem to be what they might expect from a 19th century woman? Another of her paintings depicted ten life-size horses. But, because she was a woman, her name has not been in art history books until the present day.

To prepare the students for "Developing Your Skills" 3, have them go over the description of the lily pad photograph, pointing out positive beats and negative rests. Show them how they are building upon information learned in the chapters about the elements of art. Ask them to recall the discussions about positive shapes and negative spaces.

Skill 6 requires the visual perception of positive beats. If the students have trouble finding advertisements that show rhythms, refer them to fashion magazines such as *Vogue*. If they have to go to the library and can't cut out the ads, suggest that they photocopy the ad and then mark it to indicate the beats.

REPETITION

Purpose

- To help the student understand the relationship between rhythm and repetition
- To make them aware of motif as the unit of repetition
- To explain the decorative qualities of pattern

Learning Outcomes

After completing this section students will be able to
- explain the relationship between rhythm and repetition.
- identify and illustrate motif and module.
- explain the difference between pattern and rhythm.
- make a collection of patterns and identify the motif in each pattern.
- make a drawing of a local house and indicate the rhythms on the house.
- make a design illustrating the difference between 3/4-time and 4/4-time in music.

Teaching Strategies

Study the *Basket of Flowers Quilt* with the students. After they discover that the motif in the design is the basket of flowers, ask them to notice how the craftsperson made small changes in the motif to make it more interesting.

In some complex patterns, finding motif is hard to do, but if they study each other's clothes it will be easy. Ask them to find the exact areas that are being repeated. It would be also helpful if you wore clothes with obvious motifs and brought fabric samples that showed the motif clearly.

It is important that they understand that the motif is the unit of repetition. It can be as complex as one marcher in a marching band and as simple as a single red stripe repeated over and over on a shirt.

In explaining module, ask if any of the students have heard of modular furniture. Explain that it is composed of repeated units that fit together.

The difference between pattern and rhythm can be difficult to see clearly. Many artists cannot agree, and many use the terms interchangeably. Pattern is flat and decorative, like the design on fabric and wall paper. Rhythm is a repetition that causes a viewer's eyes to move around a composition.

"Developing Your Skills" 5 requires perception. Skill 6 requires drawing skills and may be too difficult for some

students. Skill 7 is fairly abstract and requires higher levels of cognitive thinking. It also requires some understanding of music.

One simple variation of Skill 7 would be as follows. Play music: rock, waltzes, marches, music from other cultures, etc. After each listening session ask the students to create designs using lines that visually match the beat of the music.

To help students who attempt skill 6, show them some photographs of houses similar to those they might find in their neighborhoods and point out the types of rhythms they might expect to find. Students need to be shown what to look for. This doesn't mean you should spoon-feed them, but if they have never done this before, verbal instructions are not always enough. Very often, if you show them something similar to what you expect them to find, they have little difficulty.

If you have some students who are interested in architecture, you might suggest that they find out more about Louis Sullivan.

TYPES OF RHYTHM

Purpose

- To help the students recognize and use five different types of rhythms
- To help them understand the expressive qualities of each of these rhythms

Learning Outcomes

After completing this section students will be able to
- use a grid to organize motifs into regular rhythms.
- identify and illustrate random, regular, alternating, flowing, and progressive rhythms.
- explain the expressive qualities of each of the five types of rhythm.
- discuss the expressive effects of the visual rhythms used by artists in Figures 9–8, 9–13, 9–14, 9–15, 9–17, 9–18, 9–21, 9–22, and 9–24.
- make a stamp motif and use it in several skill activities.

Teaching Strategies

All of your students may seem to grasp the concepts and types of rhythm easily. The difficult part is getting them to understand that different rhythms have different effects on the viewer. Look at the various works of art reproduced in this chapter and ask them to notice how rhythm affects the "feel" of the work. Ask them to imagine how the work would look if a different rhythm were used. For example, look at the Currasco work. How would the work be different if the artist had used regular rhythm? Then they would see only glads, or only watermelons. Each motif would have to be arranged in a regular order with even spaces between it and the next. How would that change the mood of the work? Would it still be funny? What if the artist had used alternating rhythm? She might have used both watermelons and glads, for example, but how would they have been arranged? Would they look the same as the original? Ask the students to consider other works in the same way. What conclusions can they reach about the rhythms?

Go over the technique tip directions with the students. Figure 9–9 shows some potato stamps. After discussing this with the students, ask each one to bring in something with which to make a stamp. There are several suggestions in the box, but if you brainstorm with the students, they can come up with some pretty unusual stamp materials.

You do not need to make stamp prints to complete the "Developing Your Skills" activities. There are alternatives, such as rubbings, suggested. The stamp directions may be used for the "Imagine and Create" *Fabric Stamp Print*. The brown print on the white pillow, Figure 9–35, was made with a potato print.

If you would like to try some variations, bring to class some locking block toys and let students create three-dimensional rhythms with the blocks and modules. Or you could bring in packages of styrofoam cups and let groups create a different rhythm using cups as modules. Of course those doing progressive rhythm would have the greatest challenge, but it can be done without changing sizes. They could change colors, cut chunks from the cups, or add something in each step.

All of the skills in this section are fairly easy to understand. The student need do only one under each heading, and if you do not have enough time for that, you might let different groups create different types of rhythms. The only ones that will require your help will be those featuring progressive rhythm. Skills 17 and 18 have illustrations that should explain them, but you might need to go over the directions with anyone who attempts Skill 19, which is more complex.

A very easy stamp print that you can use as an alternate is a thumb print. All you need is a stamp pad that the office can supply. The students press their thumbs on the pad and then print different rhythms. Several prints can be made after each inking.

Another variation would be to bring in a variety of leaves and have all of the students make rubbings. They may form teams at different tables, cut out all of their leaves, and arrange them into a specific kind of rhythm on a large sheet of colored banner paper (the kind purchased in large rolls for the halls).

You could also let students use their old glue prints from Chapter 5. Two or more students could create large rhythmic patterns on banner paper by repeating their glue prints in a preplanned design.

For slower students, give each group a collection of natural objects and ask them to organize these into various rhythms on a table top. Then, to evaluate, the class may tour the tables and discuss the results with you.

Once again, it is important to remember that all of the students do not need to be doing the same activity using the same media. One group may work with natural objects, another may print glue prints, a third may use thumb prints, etc. How you choose to use the activities is up to you.

HOW ARTISTS USE RHYTHM

Purpose

To help students understand the expressive effects of rhythm

Learning Outcomes

After completing this section students will be able to
- explain how the Futurists used visual rhythms to capture the idea of movement.
- explain the meaning of Duchamp's *Nude Descending a Staircase*.
- explain the relationship between Duchamp's *Nude* and Boccioni's sculpture.
- explain the similarities and differences between the works of the Futurists and the works of Calder.
- use their knowledge of the elements of art and the principle of rhythm to create designs that express contrasting moods.

Teaching Strategies

Although the Futurist movement lasted only a short time, the artists were important because they tried to express movement on nonmoving surfaces using rhythmic effects. They took the philosophy of Cubism a step farther. Figures 9–28, 9–29, and 9–30 are examples of visual rhythm used to create the effect of movement. Ask students to analyze how these artists created their illusions.

Calder was an innovator. His mobiles seem to float on the air like dancing forms. Most students have made imitations of mobiles by tying strings to rods. Ask them to study the engineered joints of *Lobster Trap and Fish Tail* closely to see how Calder made them move so gracefully.

"Developing Your Skills" 20 is a review activity. First the student must use knowledge about the elements of art to create two different motifs. Then the motifs must be arranged in repetitions that enhance their expressive effect.

IMAGINE AND CREATE

Painting with a Rhythmic Theme. The purpose of this activity is to apply an understanding of rhythmic concepts to create a painting that expresses the sensation of visual movement. Encourage students to select an activity they like. Then think about the movements inherent in that activity. Are they movements light and bouncy as in soccer, or are they the heavy, thudding movements of football. Take time to discuss the different movements and how they can be expressed in rhythms.

Modular Sculpture. The purpose of this activity is to express a strong sense of rhythm through repetition. The subject may be the repetition of abstract form or a specific mood created in three dimensions. Modules that are similar in size and position seem calmer than those that vary in size and position. Modules that are rounded and smooth seem calmer than angular modules that seem to pierce the negative space.

One variation is to have the class do this as a group sculpture. Collect rectangular boxes. The size should be limited only by the plan for the final size of the work. Join the boxes by stapling, gluing, or taping. As students work, remember that this is a relief sculpture and that they must consider depth as well as length and width during construction. Some boxes may have no lids so that they create negative spaces. Some may project toward the viewer. Some spaces may be left empty. Encourage the students to think of positive and negative areas as they join. Then, when the structure is completely joined, it can be covered with a few layers of papier-mache. Paper towels are better than newspaper for the top layer. The work may be left the beige color of the towels or painted to enhance the rhythmic quality of the work.

Printing a Rhythmic Fabric Design. The purpose of this activity is to create a practical, functional object. Skill is important. Even if the primary function is not expressive, the object can carry some expressive weight. Is this fabric for a formal living area? Must it match a specific color scheme? Is it for a child's room, for a teenager, or for someone's office? The purpose should control the end product.

Clay Coil Pot. The purpose of this project is function. The function of the end product should determine its look. For whom is the student designing this pot? Where will it stay? What will it contain?

ANSWERS

Chapter 9 Review: Talking About Art

USING THE LANGUAGE OF ART

Answers will vary according to the artworks selected. The answers should show, however, that students understand the meanings of the terms as given in Chapter 9 and in the text Glossary. You may wish to require that students include the artist and title for each work cited. If so, titles should be underlined.

LEARNING THE ART ELEMENTS AND PRINCIPLES

1. By the measure of time between musical sounds.
2. By repeated positive areas separated by negative spaces.
3. The viewer's eyes follow the visual beats through the work of art.
4. Rhythm is repetition intended to create the feeling of movement. Pattern is intended to be flat and decorative.
5. With different arrangements of motif and space.
6. A motif is repeated in no apparent order, with no regular spaces.
7. Identical motifs and equal amounts of space between are used.
8. A second motif is used, the placement or content of the original motif is changed, or the spaces between the motifs are changed.

9. Repeating wavy lines are used.
10. A steady change is made in the motif each time it is repeated.

INCREASING YOUR ART AWARENESS

1. Answers will vary according to the photograph selected. Discussions should reveal an understanding of rhythm as described in Chapter 9.
2. Answers will vary.
3. Answers will vary.
4. Answers will vary according to the artworks selected.
5. Regular; answers will vary, but one example is feeling of calm.

UNDERSTANDING ART CULTURE AND HERITAGE

1. *The Horse Fair*, Figure 9–5, 1853–55; *Basket of Flowers* Quilt, Figure 9–6, 1850; *Elevator Grille*, Figure 9–7, 1893; *Child's Sidesaddle*, Figure 9–17, C 1820; *Bench*, Figure 9–18, C 1860–1900; *The Starry Night*, 1889, Figure 9–48.
2. They were a group of artists who wanted to capture the idea of movement through the use of rhythm. The Futurist artist Giacomo Balla is represented by three works in this chapter: *Swifts: Paths of Movement + Dynamic Sequences*, 1913 (Figure 9–22); *Street Light*, 1909 (Figure 9–24); and *Dynamism of a Dog on a Leash, in Motion*, 1912 (Figure 9–28). Other Futurist artists represented in Chapter 9 are Gino Severini (Figure 9–1) and Umberto Boccioni (Figure 9–30). One of the last artists to work in the Futurist style was Joseph Stella, an Italian-American, whose work appears at the beginning of Part Three (page 208)
3. Severini and Duchamp. Answers will vary as to similarities and differences.
4. This show introduced Americans to the new art being created by Europeans. Many artists were challenged and took the first steps toward making modern art in America.
5. Andy Warhol, like other Pop artists, turned to mass media for subject matter. He, in typical Pop art fashion, made people take a new look at everyday objects. In repeating Marilyn Monroe's lips many times, Warhol makes us take a new and somewhat negative look at a familiar image from the film medium and popular magazines.

JUDGING THE QUALITY OF ART

Answers will vary.

LEARNING MORE ABOUT ART

Answers will vary.

Study Question Worksheet

1. Rhythm
2. Visual
3. The unit of repetition in visual rhythm.

4. A three-dimensional motif in sculpture and architecture.
5. A two-dimensional, decorative surface quality that is repeated.
6. Rhythm has movement; pattern doesn't.
7. A motif repeated in no apparent order with no regular spaces.
8. Identical motifs and equal amounts of space between.
9. A regular arrangement of parallel lines.
10. Occurs when a second motif is introduced, some change is made in the placement or content of the original motif, or changes are made in the spaces between the motifs.
11. A change is made in the motif every time it is repeated.
12. Rhythm created by the repetition of wavy lines.
13. A group of artists who used rhythm to capture the idea of movement.
14. The forces of movement.
15. Abstract shapes put into real motion.
16. Alexander Calder.
17. 1600.
18. That of the Impressionists and Japan.

Chapter Test

1. random rhythm
2. grid
3. flowing rhythm
4. module
5. motif
6. regular
7. progressive
8. pattern
9. alternating
10. rhythm
11. kinetic sculpture
12. patterns
13. D
14. A
15. D
16. E
17. B
18. C
19. A
20. B

Chapter 10: Balance

INTRODUCING THE CHAPTER

Purpose

To introduce the students to the idea that balance is a principle of life

Learning Outcomes

After completing this section students will be able to give examples of balance in the natural environment, in other school subjects, and in the events of daily living.

Teaching Strategies

During the introduction students should expand their thinking about balance in general.

While they look at Figure 10–2, ask the students if they know about the concern for the Leaning Tower of Pisa. Are they aware of how soon it is expected to fall? Do they know why it is leaning? Why do so many people care about this one building?

Borrow a balance beam from the physical education teacher. Invite the students to walk the beam, and then ask them to describe how they felt trying to maintain their balance. Relate this to how a young child feels when learning to walk.

If you have ballet dancers in the class who can dance on point ask them to discuss the training. Ask for a demonstration.

Ask the students to think about balance in athletics. Ask them to talk about specific events in specific sports that require good balance. If possible, have them demonstrate.

"Developing Your Skills" 1 and 2 may be done for homework or as class discussions. Since they are both planned to help the student think of balance in terms of the immediate environment, you may wish to assign one or the other for homework.

VISUAL BALANCE

Purpose

- To make students aware of visual balance as a principle of design
- To help students understand the different types of balance

Learning Outcomes

After completing this section students will be able to

- explain balance, visual balance, visual weight, central axis, vertical axis, and horizontal axis.
- identify and illustrate formal balance, symmetry, approximate symmetry, radial balance, and informal balance.
- explain how the following factors affect visual weight: size, contour, color, value, texture and position.

Teaching Strategies

To help the students understand the concept of the axis that divides a work, first show them how the axis works in Figures 10–3 and 10–4. Ask them to look through other chapters to find works where the axis is obvious and works where the axis can only be sensed. The following are works in which a central vertical axis is obvious: 3–9, 6–26, 6–11, 7–3, 7–37, 7–1, 9–7. In the following works the vertical axis is sensed and off-center: 4–1, 7–13, 12–28. A horizontal axis is usually found in landscapes like those in Figures 1–4, 5–22, 9–5 or in radial designs where both vertical and horizontal axis can be found, as in Figure 7–20, 9–6, and 10–11.

Borrow a balance scale with weights from the science department to help students grasp the concepts of formal and informal balance.

Bring in an assortment of objects of varying densities, such as paperclips, styrofoam forms, a baseball, a leather football, a foam football, a large feather, an acorn, a live plant in a pot of soil, an arrangement of silk flowers in a basket, pebbles, corks, a plastic cup, a stoneware mug, and so on. Try to find more objects that are the same size but different weights, such as the leather and foam balls. Allow the students time to experiment with scales to discover that size and weight are not always equal.

Use the scales to demonstrate the difference between formal and informal balance. With formal balance both size and weight must be equal. With informal balance the weights must remain equal, but the sizes may change. A few small paperclips may balance a stryofoam ball.

All types of formal balance, symmetry, approximate symmetry, and radial balance, are concrete arrangements of elements and can be easily defined and understood. But informal balance is elusive, vague, and difficult to comprehend, since it must be felt and cannot be measured. This means that for slower students experimenting with an assortment of objects of various densities on the balance scales will make the concept easier to grasp. When they understand how objects that are different in size can have the same real weight, the concept of different visual weights seems less foreign. Arranging sets of objects that have the same weight but vary greatly in size can also be helpful.

The following is an interesting group activity that will help students remember the different types of balance. Divide the class into small groups of from three to five. Write the following terms on cards: *symmetry, approximate symmetry, radial balance,* and *informal balance.* Turn the cards over so the words are hidden; then have one student from each group choose a card. Each group is to pose in a tableau to illustrate the type of balance on the card. Give the groups about five minutes to plan their design. They may use props found in the classroom if they wish. For example, each member of one group may hold a book, but the way that the book is held may add to the pose. One student in the center may hold the book over his/her head, while one student on each side holds a book at his/her side. Students may use chairs to sit upon, to lean against, etc. While they are planning, circulate around the room and ask about the poses. If the students have trouble, there is no reason why you can't drop a few hints to start them thinking. The purpose of this exercise is not to win, but to remember types of balance.

When they are ready, have them act out the scenes. Ask the viewers to guess which type of balance the group is acting out.

"Developing Your Skills" 3 offers the students a choice of drawing or writing. But either choice requires perception of the student's own features.

Skill 4 is a verbal perception exercise.

Skill 5 is a collage activity. If the students are going to be accurate, it is important that they understand the difference between ordinary formal balance and symmetry. In skill 5 it is important that the shapes on either side of the vertical axis are mirror images of each other. That means that you should explain that the shapes reverse. Figure 10–3 illustrates this.

Skill 6 requires some time and perception. This might be a good homework assignment. It will be impossible for you to set up one still life in the classroom for all of the students. If each student is to view a symmetrical arrangement properly, each one must set up his/her own arrangement. Of course, if you wish to do this in school, you might ask each student to use a few small objects, such as erasers, scissors, pencils, thumbtacks, paperclips, etc.

Skill 7 is a perception drawing activity that may be done at school if students have the freedom to leave the room and move about. But if you must keep your eyes on the students at all times, this might better be done for homework.

Skill 8 is a discussion activity that may be done in class or written for homework.

Skill 9 is a perception activity that can be achieved successfully by all students.

Skill 10 is similar to 9, but it requires perception drawing. You might wish to assign Skill 9 to less skilled students and 10 to those who are able to draw easily.

Skills 11 and 12 both involve the same concepts of visaul weight, but 11 is perceptive and 12 requires drawing. Before the students try these activities, be sure that they review the factors that influence visual weight and discuss Figures 10–16 through 10–23 with you. If you have a collection of reproductions, you might ask the students to look through them to find examples of each of the factors that influence visual weight before they try to do skills 11 and 12.

Additional Activities

Bring in live flowers so that everyone in the room can hold one (do not use plastic or silk flowers for this activity). Any kind of flower will do, but the simpler the better. Choose blossoms from a fruit tree, wild violets, clover, daffadils, wild roses, dogwood blossoms, etc. Avoid flowers with multiple layers of petals.

Have each student imagine that he/she is studying the blossom analytically so that it can be reconstructed artificially. Have them look at it from every angle, make rough pencil sketches of the blossom from different points of view, analyze the radial structure, and draw it. Also have them carefully analyze the patterns of the seeds or miniature blossoms in the center of the flower. Does the center have a definite structure?

The blossom may not display perfect symmetry, but even if the blossom has five petals, it is still organized so that the petals radiate out from the center.

Finally, have the student draw the blossom with chalk. The drawing should be large enough to fill an 18-inch square. The drawing should be done from a point of view that emphasizes the radial structure of the petals.

This work may be colored with paints, oil pastels, or pastels.

THE EXPRESSIVE QUALITIES OF BALANCE

Purpose

- To help the students expand their understandings of the expressive qualities of balance

Learning Outcomes

After completing this section students will be able to
- explain the expressive effects of symmetry, approximate symmetry, radial balance, and informal balance found in various art forms.
- find examples of the various types of balance in works of art and describe how the balance used affects the feelings expressed.
- find a local building that illustrates one type of balance, sketch the building, and write a description of the feelings expressed.

Teaching Strategies

In this section it is important that you discuss the reproductions and their expressive effects with the students. In Figure 10–25 the calm and order of formal balance turn the horror of the attacking terrorists into comedy because there is nothing calm or orderly about battle. The use of incongruities creates comedy.

Figure 10–26 is an excellent example of the dignity and regal quality of formal balance. The people in the portrait seem to be frozen in their rigid poses.

Figure 10–27 is an example of the minimalist use of formal balance for simplicity.

Figure 10–28 is typical of the dignified calm that formal balance gives to architecture.

Figure 10–29 needs to be studied closely so that the students can find the tiny variations that make the balance approximate rather than pure symmetry. Notice how the right side is slightly lighter than the left side. You can see the horizontal slits of light in the right shutter. Notice how the siding at the bottom slants up ever so slightly so that the shadow on the bottom right is wider than that at the bottom left. Have them look back to Figure 10–8 and compare it with this one. Ask them to look for similarities and differences. Notice that the O'Keeffe has very subtle variations and the Wood has very strong variations.

"Developing Your Skills" 13 requires perception and writing ability, while skill 14 requires both perception and drawing abilities.

IMAGINE AND CREATE

Formal and Informal Group Portraits. An alternate to drawing portraits is to cut out figures from magazines or newspapers, organize them in formal and informal arrangements, glue them on to a background, and then paint over the original clothes with school acrylics or oil pastels to dress the figures as fits the pose. Finally, appropriate furniture and scenery should be added to the paintings.

Fabric Medallion. Before any students begin this activity, look at the student example and discuss it. Notice how both the student's name and symbols of the student's life have been organized in a radial pattern.

An alternate to the applique project would be to have the students create a radial design for a tempera batik painting. First the design must be planned. Then, after it is drawn on strong white paper, the student should paint in all the shapes with thick, creamy, liquid tempera. (For some reason, this technique does not work if you mix powdered tempera). When the paint is thoroughly dry, paint over the design with waterproof black ink. The ink will stick to the paper only where there is no paint. Let the ink dry for one day. Then place the paper on a tray and let water run over it gently. The ink will remain on the unpainted spots and wash off the others. But there will be streaks of black left, and they should not be washed off until the paint fades away. Overwashing will ruin a tempera batik. After the painting is washed, move it from the tray to a heavy layer of newspaper until it dries. When it is thoroughly dry, the areas of faded color can be enhanced using oil pastels. Then the work can be protected with a coat of polymer medium.

Round Plaster Relief. Before the students start this project, go over the directions in the technique tip carefully with them. Be sure that they understand how the positive and negative areas reverse. Even though this may be very obvious to you, it is difficult for students to understand. Give each team a different kind of material to press into the mold. Have teams compare their finished samples so that they can give each other ideas before they start working on their own individual relief projects.

ANSWERS

Chapter 10 Review: Talking About Art

USING THE LANGUAGE OF ART

Answers will vary according to the artworks selected. The answers should show, however, that students understand the meanings of the terms as given in Chapter 10 and in the text Glossary. You may wish to require the students to include the artist and title for each work cited. If so, titles should be underlined.

LEARNING THE ART ELEMENTS AND PRINCIPLES

1. Artists use this feeling to communicate with us. An unbalanced work gives us an uneasy feeling.
2. Art elements.
3. In bilateral symmetry the two halves of a composition are identical. In approximate symmetry, the two halves are *almost* identical (in other words, *almost* symmetrical).
4. Size and contour, color, value, texture, and position.
5. Warm.
6. The stronger the contrast in value between an object and the background, the more visual weight the object has. Also, dark values are heavier than light values.
7. Dignity, stability, calm.

INCREASING YOUR ART AWARENESS

1. Formal.
2. Informal.
3. Possible answers: size and contour, color, value, texture, and position—all the weight factors are found in this work.
4. Approximate.
5. Answers will vary according to the artworks selected. Works should illustrate the visual weight factors of size and contour, color, value, texture, and position. Some examples of artworks illustrating these weight factors are as follows: size and contour—*Christina's World* by Andrew Wyeth (Figure 2–10), color—*Sortie Made by the Garrison of Gibraltar* by John Trumbull (Figure 1–6), value—*The Skater* by Gilbert Stuart (Figure 12–1), texture—*Paul Revere* by John Singleton Copley (Figure 8–45), and position—*Breezing Up* by Winslow Homer (Figure 2–4).

UNDERSTANDING ART CULTURE AND HERITAGE

1. 15th—*Mary, Queen of Heaven* (10–1).
   16th—*The Adoration of the Shepherds* (10–20).
   17th—*The Family Group* (10–26).
   18th—*A Game of Hot Cockles* (10–19).
   19th—Answers will vary. Possible answers are 10–5, 10–23, 10–31.
   20th—Answers will vary. There are many 20th century pieces in Chapter 10.
2. Religious beliefs and musical instruments typical of that time.
3. *Great Wave Off Kanagawa* (Figure 10–23) and *Family Portrait*, (Figure 10–26).
4. The painting is delicate, graceful, and depicts the lives of the eighteenth-century French aristocracy.
5. Answers will vary. Possible answers are *American Gothic* by Grant Wood (Figure 10–8), which expresses "the good old days;" *Long May Our Land Be Bright* by Elizabeth Garrison (Figure 10–11), which expresses the celebration of liberty; and the Federal Reserve Building by Cram, Goodhue, and Ferguson (10–7), which expresses the security and stability of the U.S. government.

JUDGING THE QUALITY OF ART

Complete answers will vary. However, all students should include in their answers the fact that the painting contains a loose arrangement of radiating lines (a loose, radial balance), which draws attention to the main figure, Mary, at the center of the painting. This type of balance helps the artist express the importance of *Mary, Queen of Heaven*.

LEARNING MORE ABOUT ART

Answers will vary.

Study Question Worksheet

1. (a) Balance - the principle of design concerned with equalization of forces.
   (b) Visual balance - when all parts of a design appear to work together.
   (c) Formal balance - when equal, or very similar, elements are placed on opposite sides of a central axis.
   (d) Symmetry - formal balance in which both halves of a composition are identical.
   (e) Bilateral - another name for symmetry.
   (f) Approximate symmetry - almost symmetrical.
   (g) Radial balance - occurs when the visual elements radiate out from a central point. The axis is the center point.
   (h) Informal balance - balancing unlike objects in a design.
   (i) Asymmetrical - another name for informal balance.
   (j) Visual weight - the attraction something has for the viewer's eyes.

2. In the center of the design; no.
3. With bilateral symmetry.
4. Dignity, endurance, and solid stability.
5. Because it varies slightly from one side to the other.
6. In the center.
7. Because four or more matching units are used instead of only two.
8. Because unequal elements must be balanced through the use of visual weights.
9. Size, contour, color, value, texture, position.
10. To imply that the institution housed in the building is stable and dignified.
11. Because they want their home to look as if it were dignified and away from the "hustle and bustle."
12. A balance of unlike objects.
13. To focus attention on a part of the work.
14. The American West.
15. Flowers larger than life.

Chapter 11: Proportion

INTRODUCING THE CHAPTER

Purpose

- To make the students aware of the principle of proportion as it relates to everyday living.
- To help students realize that proportion is a matter of comparisons.

Learning Outcomes

After completing this section students will be able to
- cite examples of proportions in daily living.
- compare the proportions of furniture used in kindergarten, third grade, and the student's classroom.
- consider the measurements necessary to design a closet, a kitchen cooking space, or a lunch-counter.

Teaching Strategies

Ask the students to look closely at Figure 11–2. The photograph may look like a picture of cliffs, but it is really a pile of sand. Using an unusual angle, Nix has created an illusion. Notice the large grains of sand. They look like pebbles. Without a reference for proportion many of your students might mistake these sand "cliffs" for real ones.

Students are too self-conscious to discuss their own body proportions, but there's probably not one person in the class who doesn't wish that some of those proportions were different. Although this subject is too touchy for a class discussion, you might get them to talk about the popularity of cosmetic plastic surgery.

One subject that the students might be able to handle without embarrassment is orthodontics. Many have had to wear braces on their teeth. For most it was a matter of health; for others it was cosmetic.

Discuss how industrial designers must consider human proportions. Look around the classroom at tables, counters, sinks, scissors, pencils, brushes, paper sizes, windows. Think about steps, doors, busses, driveways, sports equipment. Then think about things at home, in factories, and examples farther from the local environment, such as space vehicles and space stations. Each time the student mentions an object, make sure that he/she explains how proportion affects the size and shape of the final product.

One proportional problem that every student can relate to is the proportion of ingredients used in cooking. Ask what would happen to a chocolate cake if the baker added one teaspoon of sugar instead of one cup. What would happen to a pot of homemade vegetable soup if the cook added one cup of salt instead of one spoonful?

"Developing Your Skills" 1 requires access to different classrooms. If a student has a younger sibling in nursery school, a comparison between the nursery school furniture and your classroom furniture will be interesting.

Skill 2 requires a high level of thinking because the student must develop a plan for designing a specific area for people. You want students to come up with their own plan for making measurements to design the area. Actual measurements may or may not be made. If a student is interested in interior design, you might suggest that he or she make a model of the finished area to scale.

THE GOLDEN MEAN

Purpose

- To present the relationship between mathematics and visual art
- To introduce the concept of the Golden Mean

Learning Outcomes

After completing this section students will be able to identify works of art in the text that illustrate the Golden Mean and make simple diagrams showing how the artist has used it.

Teaching Strategies

In the past, aesthetics was the philosophy of beauty. Until the twentieth century the purpose of Western art was the pursuit of beauty. The Greeks though they had found it in the Golden Mean, which they considered the perfect ratio.

Vitruvius, a Roman who lived in the first century B.C., wrote about how the Greeks used human proportions as the basis for architectural construction: the inch came from one joint of a finger, the palm of the hand and the foot were measures, and the cubit was the length of the forearm from the tip of the middle finger to the elbow.

Vitruvius noted that the height of a person from the soles of the feet to the top of the head equals the width of the outstretched arms from finger tip to finger tip. He also recorded that if a person lies flat and extends the arms above the head, the navel becomes the center of the body's total length. If the navel is used as a center, both the tips of the fingers and the toes will touch the circumference of a circle drawn around the person. Leonardo's famous drawing of the human male within a circle and a square is based on the Vitruvian figure. Le Corbusier based his modular figure on the Vitruvian norm and in 1948 wrote a book dealing with Vitruvian proportions.

Until the present, the relationship between human proportions and architectural forms has been studied purely for aesthetic reasons. Today there is a discipline of science called *ergonomics* that is concerned with the relationship between people and the environment. It had its start during World War II in the design of efficient aircraft cockpits, and it is now concerned with all areas of interface between a user and a designed interior environment. This applies equally to space travel and to ensuring that people are comfortable and safe in the everyday environment. Such things as kitchen counters, classroom desks, auditorium seats, shelves in stores, automobiles, and many other everyday things are designed for comfort and maximum efficiency.

The answer to the question about Figure 11-8 can be seen if you measure the height of the reproduction and then use that measure to make a square from the right. The left side of the square will line up with the vertical side of the engineer's booth.

"Developing Your Skills" 3 and 4 require perception and measurement. In Skill 3 the student should be looking for the interior measurements of the rectangle and square as illustrated in Figure 11–6, not just the exterior measurements of the rectangle. While there are many possible answers to skill 3, the following are a few examples of works that have measurements close to those of the Golden Rectangle.

Figure 11–19. Measure the square from the top. Uncle Sam fills the square; the lettering fills the remaining rectangle.

Figure 6–24. Measure the square from the top. The bottom line of the square lines up with the bottom of the table.

Figure 3–10. Measure the square from the top. The bottom line of the square is the top line of the marble table.

Figure 3–11. Measure the square from the right. The left line of the square matches a strong vertical line in the composition.

Figure 7–13. Measure the square from the right. The left edge of the square lines up with the outside of the white boxer's leg.

Challenge students who like math to look for other interesting proportional ratios in paintings and three-dimensional works.

In skill 4 students should be looking for objects that have the exterior proportions of the Golden Rectangle. Some rectangular objects might include toasters, table tops, the front or top of a desk or dresser, windows, and doors.

Additional Activities

Have students take a survey to learn if people really prefer the Golden Rectangle over other rectangles. They could make up a chart showing about five rectangles, one of which would have the proportions of the Golden Rectangle. This chart could be drawn on a sheet of notebook paper and the rectangles numbered. Then all the survey-taker needs to do is show the chart of shapes to different people and ask each person which shape he or she prefers.

One student could not gather enough samples to make an accurate survey, but if everyone in the class talks to about ten people, the sample will be large enough from which to draw some conclusions. Encourage students to ask people outside of school, people they work with, and friends and neighbors.

SCALE

Purpose

To help the student understand how scale can affect a work of art

Learning Outcomes

After completing this section, students will be able to
- differentiate between scale and proportion.
- identify and explain the two kinds of scale used in art.
- explain why the scale of reproductions in books must be judged from the real measurements of the work.
- identify and list works of art in *ArtTalk* that use scale to create special effects.
- create collages that illustrate both normal and unrealistic scale.
- study the proportions of a variety of chairs and prepare a chart to illustrate the findings.
- study the proportions of various cars.

Teaching Strategies

Find a photograph of the pyramids that has people in it so that the students can comprehend the immensity of the pyramids. Then ask the students if they have heard of someone creating a work of art on the head of a pin, or at least in miniature.

Oldenburg has created other works that are much larger in scale than normal, including a clothespin sculpture that stands ten stories high, and a soft-sculpture hamburger taller than a person. Ask the students why they think Oldenburg takes ordinary objects and makes them larger than life. Help them understand that he is trying to get viewers to notice and become aware of the unusual characteristics of everyday objects usually taken for granted.

The mention of works that seem monumental, but are not, was included because of the Rembrandts included in the text. Due to their monumental look, people always imagine that Rembrandt's paintings are very large. Then, when someone who has only seen reproductions of Rembrandt's paintings confronts an original, he or she is always shocked. Of course there are some large Rembrandts, such as *The Night Watch*. Leonardo's works also surprise viewers because of their small dimensions.

"Developing Your Skills" 5 requires the perception of scale used to create special effects. The following use unusual scale: Figures 3–3, 3–25, 3–26, 10–5, 10–15, 3–8, 12–11, and 7–1.

Skill 6 can be achieved successfully by all students. Figures 11–12 and 11–13 will help them understand what to do.

Skill 7 requires measuring and critical thinking. The study of chairs is suggested because almost everyone has had problems with chairs that are either uncomfortable or so comfortable that no one wants to get out of them.

Some students might wish to study the proportions of other everyday objects, such as stairs, doors, doorknobs (including vehicle doors and door handles), and hand tools, such as eating utensils, pencils and pens, erasers, and scissors. Challenge students to think of a unique item encountered frequently during the day.

Skill 8 is limited to students who have access to antique cars. But you may modify the assignment to (a) comparing cars that have been manufactured ten years apart or (b) comparing the proportions of two different types of vehicles, such as pick-up trucks and family cars, sports cars and family sedans, etc. The vehicles to be studied depend upon what is available.

Another important topic involving scale is the misrepresentation of scale in advertisements, such as those for jewlery. If you can, bring in jewelry shown in local ads and let students see how small the objects really are. Warn them to read ads carefully to see if things are photographed life-size or are made to seem larger than life. Students also need to be conscious of scale during grocery shopping. Some manufacturers package things in larger boxes to make it look as if there is more product. Labels should always be studied for weights and sizes. If students help with grocery shopping, ask them to look at sizes of boxes and the weights of the contents to see if they can find examples of packaging designed to fool the purchaser. Point out that bigger is not always the best buy. They need to check to see how much they are paying per ounce or per liter. Very often the largest package is not the most economical based on weight. Perception of scale is important in all areas of life.

DRAWING HUMAN PROPORTIONS

Purpose

- To help students understand that different cultures have different ideas about ideal proportions and that within cultures proportions vary depending on their purpose
- To help them perceive figure and face proportions and draw them accurately

Learning Outcomes

After completing this section students will be able to
- use the length of the head as a unit to describe the proportions of the human figure at different stages of development.
- measure, record, and chart their own proportions using the length of the head as the unit of measure.

- measure the proportions of people in photographs using the head as a unit of measure.
- compare the proportions of fashion models with those of average people.
- use sighting to make accurate figure drawings.
- identify and illustrate foreshortening.
- observe and draw both the front and the profile view of a face.
- observe the differences between the proportions of adults and infants.

Teaching Strategies

Find out if any students have considered a modeling career. What do they know about the size of today's fashion models? Bring in a high fashion magazine, such as *Vogue*, and a catalog from Sears or Penney's and point out the different proportions emphasized in the fashion photos.

Have students observe the proportions in Figure 11–16 and then measure the proportions of the infant in Figure 11–17. An example of an infant who has the proportions of a little adult can be seen in Figure 3–6. Bring in some *Sports Illustrated* magazines and ask the students to check to see if college and pro basketball players really have the same proportions as average people. Be sure that they look at photos showing the whole figure.

It depends upon the mood of your class as to how to carry out "Developing Your Skills" 9. You might team the students up in groups of two or three to record measurements. Of course you must team girls with girls and boys with boys to avoid embarrassing moments. You might assign this activity as homework, but if you think you will have problems, you might also ask for a few volunteers to do the measuring for the entire class. The important point is for students to understand that proportions are not just numbers created out of thin air—they are accurate.

Skills 10 and 11 can be achieved successfully by all students.

Read over with the class the technique tip directions about sighting and observe students as they sight specific objects in the room. You can tell by watching their eyes and hands whether or not they understand the process.

Skill 12 might be done best in class with volunteer models. Be sure that if you place the model upon a raised surface that you do not select a girl wearing a short skirt. If the model stands on the floor, this will not matter. Once again, it is wise to givel the model a prop or some kind of costume to make both students and model feel at ease. For some reason it is easier to look at a friend who is dressed up in a silly outfit than to study one dressed in everyday attire. The costume acts like a mask behind which the real person can hide. Before the students start to draw, you might want to give them a pep talk, reassuring them that they are beginners, not cameras or professional artists. They should try to capture the position and proportions of the model but not worry about facial features.

When drawing heads and faces, people tend to pay attention to the parts that identify the model: the distinctive features. The features are often drawn acurately, but the areas we do not use for identification, such as the top of the head and the back of the skull, are often drawn too small. Make the students measure the different lengths in Figure 11–21 to be sure that they understand how much width they must allow from the eyes to the back of the skull.

Skill 13 requires perception drawing. It might help if you emphasize again that it is not necessary to obtain a true likeness at this point; they are drawing to understand correct proportions. It is likely that some students achieve a vague likeness, but it will not satisfy them because it won't be perfect. So if you can convince them that accurate representation is not important, they will be less likely to "freeze up."

Skill 14 requires perception, but it is not as demanding as skill 13.

Additional Activities

Have the students find a magazine photograph of a face. Ask them to cut it in half and glue one half to a piece of drawing paper. When the glue is dry, students should draw the missing side of the face to complete the head. This activity is less demanding than drawing from life. You might assign it first. Then, when they have been successful with this, they may not be as afraid to try drawing from life.

HOW ARTISTS USE PROPORTION AND DISTORTION

Purpose

To help students understand the strong expressive quality of proportion and distortion

Learning Outcomes

After completing this section students will be able to
- identify and illustrate exaggeration and distortion.
- identify specific works of art that are examples of the use of accurate proportion.
- explain how proportion affects the expressive quality of a work.
- identify specific works of art that are examples of the use of exaggeration and distortion.
- explain how exaggeration and distortion affect the expressive quality of a work.
- locate caricatures of contemporary people that illustrate exaggeration and compare them with realistic photographs of the same people.

Teaching Strategies

It is important for students to understand that artists who use distortion do so for specific purposes, not because they can't draw accurately. For example, Picasso was a master of realism at the age of fourteen. At that point he began advanced art training. By the time he was in his twenties he was bored with doing things that had been done before and was looking for new ways to express feeling. Both Figure 11–29 and 7–37 are from what is now called Picasso's "Blue Period." At this time he lived in poverty in Paris. It was at the turn of the century, and he was not yet famous. He later tried many different innovative styles. This didn't mean that he was unable to draw using realistic proportions. The most emotional work he created, *Guernica*, was painted for the Spanish exhibit at the 1937 World's Fair. Guernica was a town in Spain chosen by the Germans to test the ability of their air force to destroy towns and cities. The test was successful. The painting is a timeless expression of anguish and pain.

If any of your students can perform as mimes, invite them to give a demonstration. Acting without words requires the same kind of exaggeration as expressive abstract visual art.

Caricature is another powerfully expressive technique. Artists have used it since the days of ancient Egypt and Babylon, and it is still a powerful political weapon. Editorial cartoonists can sway public opinion. If you have students who are interested in this field, suggest that they research Honore Daumier or Thomas Nast. both of these artists were successful with caricature. Nast was able to turn people against the infamous Tammany political machine in New York City. Nast was an illustrator. His work appeared in newspapers and magazines.

"Developing Your Skills" 15, 16, and 17 can be achieved successfully by all students.

IMAGINE AND CREATE

Modern Spirit Mask. Before you get involved in making anything with papier-mâché with the students, be sure that you understand the process. If you have never tried it, please do so before you undertake a project. It is messy, complex, and can be frustrating if you do not know how to deal with the many little problems that may come up, such as how to get the surface smooth enough to paint. You have to try it yourself so that you will know how to help students.

Do not ignore the safety warning about commercial wallpaper paste.

An alternative way to deal with masks is to make them out of clay. Start with a slab of clay about ½ inch thick. Drape it over some crumpled newspaper to form a raised oval. Then build up the surface using the clay joining techniques explained in the technique tip in Chapter 9. Of course the clay mask is not meant to be worn, but it will look good hung on a wall. After it is fired, it may be painted with school acrylics or glazed.

Life-size Papier-Mâché Figure Environment. This is a project that is better done in teams than by individuals because it takes so long. With a team of three or four working, it goes much faster.

This might be very effective for a homecoming event or for prom decorations.

Expressive Painting. Be sure that the students study the reproductions in the book to understand the many possibilities that can be achieved by distortion and exaggeration, not only pain and sorrow, but joy, monumentality, and religious ecstasy.

ART CRITICISM

After completing the critical study of Marisol's *The Family*, try the following extra activity with your students.

Ask them to imagine that they have just turned on the TV set and Marisol's people fill the screen, just as they appear in the reproduction in the book.

What kind of program have they turned on: documentary, a comedy, a drama, or a commercial?

Imagine that the figures are real. They are about to move and speak. What kind of conversation will they have with one another? Ask the students to write a brief script for a scene that includes all of the characters in the sculpture. Each character should be given a name.

ANSWERS

Chapter 11 Review: Talking About Art

USING THE LANGUAGE OF ART

Answers will vary according to the artworks selected. The answers should show, however, that students understand the meanings of the terms as given in Chapter 11 and in the text Glossary. You may wish to require that students include the artist and title for each work cited. If so, titles should be underlined.

LEARNING THE ART ELEMENTS AND PRINCIPLES

1. 1 to 1.6 (or 1:1.6).
2. Proportion is the relationship of one part to another; scale refers to size as measured against a standard reference.
3. Golden Rectangle.
4. The scale of the work itself and the scale of objects or elements within the design.
5. Length of the head from the chin to the top of the skull.

INCREASING YOUR ART AWARENESS

1. Answers will vary.

2. Both Figures 11–4 and 7–13 use exaggeration, but for very different effects. Exaggerated color plays a key role in Figure 7–13. Exaggeration of human body proportions contributes to the effect of Figure 11–4.
3. It expresses loneliness and lack of warmth.
4. Grünewald distorts his figures. Dürer does not use distortion. He uses realistic proportions.
5. No; realism.

UNDERSTANDING ART CULTURE AND HERITAGE

1. 50 B.C.—*Dancing Lady* (11–9), Greece.
   1st-3rd century—*Ornamental Mask* (11–32A), Peru.
   1460—*Portrait of a Lady* (11–4), Flanders (now parts of Belgium, Netherlands, and France).
2. *The White Girl (Symphony in White, No. 1)*, 1862, Figure 11–1; *Flax Scutching Bee*, 1885, Figure 11–24; *See-non-ty-a, an Iowa Medicine Man*, 1845, Figure 11–25; *The Shriek*, 1895, Figure 11–28; *False Face Mask*, 1860, Figure 11–32C.
3. Figure 11–22 is more closely tied to Renaissance ideas. It shows the solid, realistic appearance of people and things that was important to the artists of the Renaissance. Figure 11–26, on the other hand, distorts the figures to emphasize the agony of the event.
4. Mannerism featured highly emotional scenes and distorted figures such as those in the works of El Greco.
5. The forms and figures of Baroque art turn, twist, and spiral in space. The Baroque artists also added dramatic lighting effects, using dark mysterious shadows and brightly lighted areas. Rubens' art contains these features.

JUDGING THE QUALITY OF ART

Answers will vary.

LEARNING MORE ABOUT ART

Answers will vary.

Study Question Worksheet

1. (a) Proportion - a principle of art concerned with the size relationships of one part of a work with another.
   (b) Golden Mean - a ratio (1 to 1.6) developed by Euclid that compares part of a line to the whole line: this ratio was considered to be the perfect proportion by the Greeks.
   (c) Sighting - a technique used to determine proportions; your arm and a pencil are used as the measuring device.
   (d) Scale - the size of an object as measured against a standard reference.
   (e) Exaggeration - changes in the real proportions in which the normal is enlarged.
   (f) Monumental - a term used to describe the large, imposing quality of an artwork

(g) Papier-Mâché - sculpture involving newspapers and liquid paste; French for "mashed paper."
2. The things around them.
3. The furniture must fit the human form in order to be functional and comfortable.
4. (a) An ancient Greek philosopher.
   (b) That it could be explained in mathematical terms.
5. To control the relationship of the parts in sculptures, architecture, and pottery.
6. The Golden Rectangle.
7. The human body.
8. As ideal figures.
9. A Roman writer who set down ratios or human proportions.
10. The human form.
11. (a) The length of the head from the chin to the top of the skull.
    (b) 7 ½ heads, 5 or 6 heads, 3 heads.
12. (a) George Catlin-American Indians.
    (b) Reginald Marsh - N.Y. City people.
    (c) Isabel Bishop - N.Y. City people
13. (a) Scale of the work itself.
    (b) Scale of objects or elements within a design.
14. To give some idea of its scale.
15. Silent movies and mimes.
16. (a) Edvard Munch - horror radiates from the figure.
    (b) Pablo Picasso - elongated hands and arms of the lovers weave the bodies into expression of tenderness.
    (c) Alberto Giacometti - elongation of form to show impersonal, lonely isolation.
17. (a) Pulp method—Newspaper, paper toweling, or tissue is shredded into tiny pieces, soaked in water, strained, and then wrung dry. The paper is then mixed with prepared wheat paste or white glue until it is of the consistency of soft clay. Small shapes and/or forms can then be modeled from the mixture.
    (b) Strip method—Newspaper torn into strips is dipped into a creamy mixture of wheat paste and applied to a form made from wadded newspaper, balloons, or wire.
    (c) Sheet method—Wheat paste is spread on sheets of paper until several layers are made.

Chapter Test

1. sighting	11. Golden Mean
2. proportion	12. 7-½
3. exaggeration	13. 3
4. papier-mâché	14. Golden Rectangle
5. ratio	15. Pop
6. Golden Mean or Section	16. oval
7. monumental	17. beauty
8. scale	18. Pythagoras
9. Vitruvius	19. scale
10. head	20. ideal

Chapter 12: Variety, Emphasis, and Unity

INTRODUCING THE CHAPTER

Purpose

- To introduce the students to the principles of variety, emphasis, and unity
- To point out that unity is the ultimate principle of design and that when all of the elements and principles work properly, a unified work of art results

Learning Outcomes

After completing this section students will be able to
- identify variety, emphasis, and unity as principles of art.
- explain the complementary relationship between unity and variety.
- write several paragraphs describing variety in some area of their lives.
- give three examples of emphasis that are found in their daily experiences.

Teaching Strategies

During this introductory section students should first become aware of the principles in their own environment. It is important that they understand that variety adds interest to life and art, while emphasis dominates or directs your attention to one focal point.

"Developing Your Skills" 1 requires the student to write complete paragraphs, while skill 2 just asks for a list. If you do not want to make these written assignments, both could be discussed in class. One way to organize the discussions would be to form small groups of five or six. Assign skill 1 to half of the groups and skill 2 to the other half. Ask each group to appoint a secretary to keep notes as they talk. Give the groups about ten minutes for discussion. While they are talking, circulate around the room to check that each group is on task. Then gather them together and let one student from each group report to the whole class using the secretary's notes.

VARIETY

Purpose

- To help students understand the importance of variety in daily life and in visual art
- To introduce students to the concept of contrast as a means to create variety

Learning Outcomes

After completing this section students will be able to
- identify variety and contrast.

- explain why variety is important in daily living and in the visual environment.
- explain how to add variety to a work of art.
- make a series of designs to illustrate strong contrast using each of the elements of art.
- explain and illustrate the difference between bold and subtle contrast.
- select a work made during this class that seems dull and write a description of how variety could be introduced without destroying unity.
- list reproductions in *ArtTalk* that show bold contrast of each element of art and explain how the artist created the contrast in each work.

Teaching Strategies

To get the students thinking about variety, ask them to discuss what they do to relieve boredom. Help them to see that they are introducing variety or contrast into a given situation.

Ask if anyone has a family member or friend who uses shopping sprees to relieve depression. Try to get them to see how the shopping spree is an attempt to introduce change or variety.

The MTV logos illustrate how one television station uses variety to keep station breaks interesting. Ask them to think of other network logos. Can they recall them vividly? Can they describe them? Do the students pay attention to them as much as they do to logos that introduce variety as does MTV's? Ask them to pay attention to the logos on other stations and report back to class. They may be surprised to find out that they have seen those logos but do not remember them because they are not as interesting.

This would be a good time to talk about logos in general. A *logo* is a symbol that represents a company or a product. You might bring in examples of some familiar logos and ask the students to identify the products. Or you might ask each student to make a sketch of one logo seen at home and bring it to school the next day. Which logos are remembered by most students? Ask the students to guess why they are remembered. Does remembering have something to do with quality of design? With organization? Ask them to decide if the logos have unity. When they see these logos in the environment, are they always the same, or is some variety introduced? Of course there is always variety of size, since the logo on a soft drink bottle will be much smaller than the same logo on a billboard.

"Developing Your Skills" 3 requires some design ability and media control, but all students should be able to complete this assignment with some degree of success. To save time and give each student a chance to produce a quality design, you might assign only one element to each student. Then each student can place the finished work on display on a bulletin board. All students can then see how the others used contrast.

To insure that all the elements are covered and assigned randomly, you might make folded slips of paper with one element written on each slip. Then each student could draw one slip from a container. Or you might ask students to volunteer for each element. You know your students best. In any case, use a new method of selection, for variety can add interest even to a classroom procedure. While there is security in repetition, variety will spark student interest.

If you have asked each student to do one design, he or she might choose someone else's design for skill 4. It might be wise for you to make a visual example illustrating the difference between strong and subtle contrast. A very easy one is to show a design of black lines on a white ground and then make it more subtle by changing the ground to light gray and the lines to a slightly darker gray.

Skill 5 may seem simple, but it requires the highest levels of thinking. This assignment asks the students to write a description of how they would change a completed work. This requires the use of verbal symbols to describe changes in visual symbols. If there is time, you might want to have them actually re-do the work after they have thought through the changes.

Skill 6 requires perception of the bold contrast of elements in this text. Some examples are Figures 1–2 (line), 5–1 (line and value) 6–43 (form), 3–14 (line direction), 3–9 (value), 7–6 (color), 12–3 (texture), 8–23 (texture), 11–45 (value and form), 12–11 (shape), 2–6 (space), 7–20 (color).

EMPHASIS

Purpose

- To make students aware of the principle of emphasis as it relates to everyday living and to visual art

Learning Outcomes

After completing this section students will be able to
- discuss emphasis as it relates to everyday life.
- identify emphasis and explain its function in visual art.
- identify, describe, and illustrate the two major types of visual emphasis.
- identify and illustrate focal point.
- identify, explain, and illustrate how contrast, isolation, location, convergence, and the unusual are used to create a focal point.

Teaching Strategies

To help the students understand emphasis or dominance, ask them if one thought or event has ever occupied their minds to the point that they ignored everything else. For example, if one student has just had a falling out with a best friend, he or she may not be able to think of anything but the argument. The words keep running through the person's throughts, blocking out what other people are saying. Another example might be getting a driver's li-

cense. The driving test may dominate the student's thoughts so that everything else takes second place. Ask students to give other examples of emphasis in their own lives.

It is important that students see the difference between the dominance of one element, as in Figure 12–4, and the dominance of an area, or focal point, as in Figures 12–5, 12–7, 12–8, 12–9, 12–10, and 12–11.

It is also important to point out that every work of art does not need to have one focal point. Some have several with different degrees of importance, as in Figure 12–27, and some, as in Figures 12–4 and 12–6, have no focal point at all.

"Developing Your Skills" 7 is a perception problem. Some possible answers are Figures 7–3 (color), 6–40 (form), 5–44 A, B, C, D, (line), 9–29 (shape), 7–27 (color), 8–22 (texture), 5–28 (line), 11–22 (form), 7–45 (color), 7–21 (color).

Skill 8 is a design problem and can be achieved successfully to some degree by all students. Allow the students to choose the medium they prefer if you can. Some students may wish to use paint, some a collage of magazine pictures, others a collage using found materials. Any medium is acceptable for this problem.

If you have some students who need challenging, let them make clay relief tiles to illustrate the types of focal point. If you don't have colored glazes, the tiles can be painted with acrylics after they have been bisque-fired.

Skill 9 is a perception problem using advertisements. This activity will help the students to expand their developing understandings of advertising "propaganda." As they look for focal points, you can ask them to try to understand how the advertisers are using certain images to sell all kinds of products. If some students have to look in the library for advertisements, suggest that they photocopy the ads and then mark the points with a colored marker.

Answers to Figure 12.11 caption: Besides the unusual, Siqueiros has used the following devices to emphasize the screaming head: (a) Contrast between the free-form human shape and the scrap metal pieces. (b) Contrast of color. The red drape is the only bright color in the work. The child's skin is a metallic bronze color surrounded by silver gray colors. (c) Location. The figure of the child is to the right of center, and his knee is almost dead center.

UNITY

Purpose

- To explain the abstract concept of unity in terms of the real world

Learning Outcomes

After completing this section students will be able to
- identify unity and explain how it occurs in both natural and man-made objects.
- name the five different, unified objects that might be found in the everyday environment.

Teaching Strategies

Study Figure 12–12 with the class. Ask them to read the credit line to find out when the work was drawn. In terms of the date, the students should be able to deduce that the snake stands for the United States. Franklin's message is very clear: if the states don't unify, they will be conquered. In unity there is strength. The whole is greater than the sum of its parts.

"Developing Your Skills" 10 may be written or discussed in class. Again, it is suggested that small discussion groups be set up so that every student has some input into the discussion. The small groups should report back to the class before the end of the class period. You can usually get a greater variety of response from several small groups than from one large group. To make the small groups meet a greater challenge, you might prepare several slips of paper on which the term "natural" or "manufactured" is written. Each discussion group must draw one slip from a bowl and then think of unities on that topic.

If students have trouble coming up wtih ideas, suggest the following: natural unities, such as animals, people, fish, living cells, birds, flowers, the ocean, the world, a covey of quail, a pack of wolves, an atom, a molecule, the universe; manufactured unities, such as buildings, cities, countries, tribes, clans, families, an automobile, an airplane, a computer, a book, a clock, a television set, a newspaper, a telephone system, the army, a battleship, a flag, a movie, or a musical composition.

CREATING VISUAL UNITY

Purpose

- To help students understand the complex concept of visual unity
- To explain several techniques that can be used to create visual unity: harmony, simplicity, proximity, repetition, and continuation

Learning Outcomes

After completing this section students will be able to
- identify unity, explain how it functions, and tell how it can be recognized in a work of art.
- identify, illustrate, and explain how the following concepts can be used by artists to create unity: harmony, simplicity, proximity, repetition, and continuation.

Teaching Strategies

Answer to Figure 12–8 caption. Malevich has simplified this work by limiting the elements of shape, color, and value. The elements that vary are value and texture; however, they vary only slightly.

Answer to Figure 12–19 caption. Singing Man was much easier to unify than *The Burghers of Calais* because it only has one figure, while the other has six.

If you have students who play musical instruments, ask them to demonstrate the difference between harmony and sounds that lack harmony.

To illustrate how space can help create harmony, gather together ten totally unrelated objects. Using tape, mark off ten rectangular shapes of equal size on the top of a table or on the floor. Be sure the shapes are large enough to contain the objects. Place one object directly in the center of each rectangle. Such an organization has more unity than if the objects were arranged haphazardly. Another way to demonstrate unity is to use the stamps that were made in Chapter 9. Print them on a large sheet of paper, being sure to keep each stamp equally distant from all the other stamps.

"Developing Your Skills" 11 requires perception. It may be assigned as written homework, or it may be done in class in groups. You might divide the class into six groups, and assign each concept to one group. Give them about fifteen minutes of class time to search for examples and list them. Then gather the class together and have each small group report its findings. The following are some possible answers.

Simplicity: Figures 8–23 (limited color), 8–22 (limited color), 6–16 (sculpture of a single figure), 11–31 (single figure sculpture), 3–4 (single figure sculpture), 6–37 (single figure sculpture), 2–3 (single cat in a painting).

Harmony of color: Figures 7–12, 10–27, 4–1, 9–29, 7–27, 7–26, 7–37, 9–32. Harmony of Shape: Figures 10–27, 9–5, 6–40, 2–8, 9–18, 9–31, 9–8, 9–29, 5–21, 7–22, 5–22, 10–1, 7–36, 1–9, 11–11, 7–6, 6–43, 1–8. Repetition: Figures 6–35, 2–6, 9–48, 10–26, 3–25, 5–25, 7–3, 9–22, 9–24, 9–18, 10–25, 9–2, 9–29, 6–13.

Proximity: Figures 10–13, 2–7, 2–1, 10–16, 11–29, 2–6.

Continuation: Figures 2–10, 10–31, 9–48, 11–15, 9–1, 6–43, 3–14, 5–50, 11–26 and 10–1.

Skill 12 requires design skills. You may wish to divide the topics and have each student do one quality design rather than have each student do all six problems. You might allow each student to select a preferred medium in which to work.

Skill 13 involves collage and drawing or painting. Point out Figure 12–26. Have them notice how carefully each item is cut out.

HOW ARTISTS USE VARIETY AND EMPHASIS TO ENHANCE UNITY

Purpose

- To expand students' comprehension of the expressive qualities of variety, emphasis, and unity

Learning Outcomes

After completing this section students will be able to
- explain how Lichtenstein and Bishop create unity in their work.

- select a work of art done during the course that seems to lack unity, study it, and write a brief statement describing how the devices studied might improve the work's unity.

Teaching Strategies

Have the students select some work that was done early in the course. It would be good to put these works on the bulletin board and let classmates offer positive suggestions on how the work might be improved. Do not allow any negative remarks. They are not helpful and might destroy the morale of the student whose work is being discussed.

IMAGINE AND CREATE

Tissue and Found-Paper Collage. Be sure that the students experiment with the tissue after reading the directions in the technique tip before they work on their finished composition. They need to understand how the materials behave before they use them in a finished work.

Mixed Media Collage Combining Visual and Verbal Symbols. Study Figure 12–32 with the class. Discuss the different materials that they notice in the work. Be sure that they select words for their compositions that they feel comfortable with. It might be best if you approve the verbal part of the work before they begin.

Special-Occasion Calendar. Point out the vastly different media used in Figures 12–33 and 12–34. Look closely at the details in Figure 12–34. Since this is near the end of the course, the students have probably had experiences with a variety of materials. Challenge them to select something unique to create.

Group Project Mural. This is one project that must involve the teacher. Based on the experience of many teachers, it is suggested that, although the mural can be planned during class time, it is almost impossible to find the energy to complete one during the school day or after school. It is best to plan a few long weekend sessions rather than daily short sessions. Otherwise, students will tire of the project before it is half completed.

ANSWERS

Chapter 12 Review: Talking About Art

USING THE LANGUAGE OF ART

Answers will vary according to the artworks selected but should show that students understand the meanings of the terms as given in Chapter 12 and in the text Glossary. You may wish to require that students include the artist and title for each work cited. If so, titles should be underlined.

LEARNING THE ART ELEMENTS AND PRINCIPLES

1. (a) The type in which a certain element of art dominates the entire work and (b) the type in which one area of the work is dominant over all of the other areas.
2. Dominant.
3. The degree of emphasis needed to create the focal point.
4. Contrast, isolation, location, convergence, and the unusual.
5. Harmony, simplicity, repetition, proximity, and continuation.

INCREASING YOUR ART AWARENESS

1. Answers will vary.
2. Students should try to use as many of the art elements and principles as possible in their answers. Vermeer creates variety, for example, with the geometric shape behind the free-form shape of the woman. The lifelike quality of the free-form shape contrasts with the static quality of the painting of the Last Judgment—further emphasizing the difference between life and death. Emphasis is created by the light shapes on the woman's body that contrast with the dark background. The viewer's eye is led by these light shapes to the woman's hand holding the balance.
3. Please see "Learning More About Art," page 45 of the text, for a comment on the allegorical, or symbolic, content of painting.
4. In Figure 6–11, *contrast* creates emphasis in the detailed treatment of the girl's jewelry, dress, and hair, which stands out against the plain, dark background. The girl's hands, dress lace, necklaces, and hair framing her face create an oval shape at the center *location* in the painting. This light-colored shape *contrasts* with the dark background, drawing the viewer's eyes to the girl's face and helping to unify the work. In Figure 11–4, the headdress is made of a thin, almost smooth material with no decoration to distract the viewer's eyes from the woman's face. *Contrast* is used to create emphasis and unity in this painting. The light area of the headdress dominates in the dark design. The angular lines of the headdress carry the viewer's eyes up to the woman's face at the center *location* in the painting. This emphasis unifies the work by drawing attention to the face.
5. Both sculptures are unified. The sculpture in Figure 12–13 is more complex than the one in Figure 6–16, but Rodin has unified the many parts of his work by placing (or locating) them in a close-knit group so the viewer's eyes travel easily from one figure to another through the entire work.

UNDERSTANDING ART CULTURE AND HERITAGE

1. *Self-Portrait* by Rembrandt van Rijn, Figure 12–5.
2. Answers will vary according to the artworks selected.

3. Answer will vary.
4. Possible answers include (a) the invention of oil painting (any example of oil painting would be correct, but one of the earliest examples is Figure 11–4), (b) the invention of perspective (Figure 6–26), and (c) the discovery by scientists that matter is made up of atoms that are constantly in motion (Figure 3–14).
5. Answers will vary, but several examples of ways religious beliefs have influenced the art of Western and non-Western cultures are: (a) in the depiction of important figures, events, or symbols of the religion (Figure 3–6, *Madonna and Child*, Byzantine; Figure 3–22, *Figure of Vishnu*, Medieval Indian; and Figure 3–8, *Pietà* by Michelangelo, Italian Renaissance), (b) in the style used for Egyptian tomb and coffin paintings, which were meant to remind the deceased's spirit of its life on earth (Figure 3–3, *Deir el Bersheh* coffin painting detail, Ancient Egyptian), and (c) in the architectural style in which churches seem to soar toward heaven with their many-pointed arches (Figure 3–7, Cathedral of Reims, Gothic).

JUDGING THE QUALITY OF ART

Answers will vary.

LEARNING MORE ABOUT ART

Answers will vary. As an example, a number of chair styles through the ages are pictured on pages 104–109 of the *Ladies' Home Journal*, February 1987 issue.

Study Question Worksheet

1. (a) The art principle concerned with difference.
   (b) The art principle that makes one part of a work dominant over the other parts.
   (c) The art principle that allows you to see a complex combination of elements, principles, and media as a complete whole.
   (d) An area in a work of art that is emphasized.
   (e) Agreement among the elements of a work.
   (f) Less important.

2. Contrast, isolation, location, convergence, and the unusual. Examples will vary.
3. It's the one the viewer's eyes are drawn toward first.
4. It can cause confusion.
5. When many elements point to one item. Radial lines or many figures pointing to one point.
6. Harmony, simplicity, repetition, proximity, continuation. Examples will vary.
7. Helps you concentrate on the whole image; keeps the parts working together.
8. Variety—the different shapes of the flowers. Unity—the color family of reds or repetition of flowers.
9. The reality of America, the outdoors, the sea.
10. Five.
11. Scenes of troops.

Chapter Test

1. variety
2. emphasis
3. subordinate
4. dominant
5. focal point
6. contrast
7. isolation
8. location   } Order may vary
9. convergence
10. the unusual
11. unity
12. harmony
13. simplicity
14. harmony
15. simplicity
16. repetition   } Order may vary
17. proximity
18. continuation
19. the sea
20. the use of the paper for areas of white

Part Three

Reproducible Worksheets and Tests

The following pages contain reproducible study sheets and tests for each of the twelve chapters in *ArtTalk*. The publisher grants you permission to photocopy these pages for use in your classroom.

Chapter 1: The Language of Art

Activity 1: Study Question Worksheet

DIRECTIONS: Using a separate sheet of paper, write the answers to the following questions.

1. Define symbol.

2. As a group, what are the basic visual symbols in the language of art called?

3. As a group, what are the "rules" of the language of art called?

4. Define medium.

5. What is the plural of medium?

6. List the three major parts of a work of art.

7. How does art cross language barriers?

8. List the seven elements of art.

9. List the six principles of design.

10. An artist makes a statue out of marble. What is the art form used? What is the medium?

11. In a painting about the horrors of war an artist shows the ruins of a house. What is the subject of the painting?

12. If an artist paints a series of squares to express a dislike of conformity, what art form has been used?

13. What is the most important part of an art-work?

14. How might the study of art affect your everyday life?

15. If an artist makes a sculpture of a metal wire to express a dislike of technology, what is the content of the work?

Chapter 2: Art Criticism and Aesthetic Judgment

Activity 1: Study Question Worksheet

DIRECTIONS: Using a separate sheet of paper, write answers to the following questions.

1. Define art criticism.

2. Define aesthetic judgment.

3. Define emotionalism.

4. List the four steps in art criticism and tell what question each answers.

5. How can studying art criticism give you confidence?

6. Why are many different interpretations of a work of art possible?

7. On what parts of a work does formalism focus?

8. Define imitationalism.

9. How is art criticism like playing detective?

10. Define interpretation.

11. Why is it usually not a good idea to stick to one theory when judging a work of art?

12. How does judging functional objects differ from judging fine art?

13. During which critical steps is objectivity most important?

14. What subjects does Andrew Wyeth like to paint?

15. With what media does Andrew Wyeth like to work?

Chapter 3: Art History

Activity 1: Study Question Worksheet

DIRECTIONS: Using a separate sheet of paper, write answers to the following questions.

1. Define culture.

2. Define artistic style.

3. What art objects were left by prehistoric artists?

4. What was the strongest influence on Egyptian painting?

5. What country was the birthplace of Western civilization?

6. Where did early Christians put their first paintings?

7. Of which three types of art was Byzantine art a blend?

8. How long did the Middle Ages last?

9. What is another name for the Middle Ages?

10. Increased size; solid, heavy walls; and the use of the Roman arch distinguished which art style?

11. The pointed arch and stained glass windows belong to which style?

12. Define Renaissance.

13. How did social and power structures change during the Renaissance?

14. Define perspective.

15. What artistic medium was invented during the Renaissance?

16. What are some features of Mannerism?

17. How did Baroque artists portray space?

18. How did Baroque artists use light?

19. On what other styles was Neoclassic art based?

20. What did Romantic artists rebel against in Neoclassic art?

21. What subjects did the Realists choose to paint?

22. What features characterize Impressionist paintings?

(Continued on next page)

23. Name three important Post-Impressionist painters.

24. Define Abstract art.

25. The sculpture of what culture helped influence Cubism?

26. Which artist developed De Stijl?

27. What scientific discovery influenced Cubism?

28. What characterizes Dadaist art?

29. How does Surrealism resemble Realism?

30. What subjects were painted by the Ashcan School?

31. What art form did Alexander Calder create?

32. What subjects did the Regionalists paint?

33. What type of artist was Frank Lloyd Wright and what did he believe?

34. Which group of artists came into being during the Mexican Revolution?

35. What minor arts were taken more seriously after 1950?

36. What characterizes Abstract Expressionism?

37. What subjects did Pop artists paint?

38. How does Op Art use science?

39. In which style did Mark Rothko work?

40. What are two other names for Photo-realism?

41. Which religions influence Indian art?

42. Define meditation.

43. What is forbidden in Islamic art?

44. What purpose does African art have?

Chapter 3: Art History

Activity 2: Artist Profile

DIRECTIONS: Using the text and an encyclopedia or other resources, fill in the blanks for an artist of your choice.

1. Name of artist: _____

2. Dates of birth and death: _____

3. What important events took place during the artist's lifetime: _____

_____

4. Factors that affected artist's style: _____

_____

_____

5. Outstanding characteristics of the artist and his or her style: _____

_____

_____

6. Influences on (other artists or events, etc.): _____

_____

_____

7. List of five most outstanding works: _____

_____

_____

_____

_____

8. Media this artist prefers: _____

_____

9. Style or period to which this artist belongs (Baroque, Impressionist, etc).: _____

_____

_____

Chapter 3: Art History

Activity 3: Period Analysis

DIRECTIONS: Using the text and other sources, fill in the blanks for a style of your choice.

1. Name of style: _____

2. Dates of occurrence _____

3. Important world events that occurred during this time: _____

_____

_____

4. Major factors that brought about the style: _____

_____

_____

_____

_____

5. Features of the style: _____

_____

_____

DIRECTIONS: For each art form listed below, name five major artists and an example of their work.

Architecture

Name	Work
1. _____	_____
2. _____	_____
3. _____	_____
4. _____	_____
5. _____	_____

(Continued on next page)

Sculpture

	Name	Work
1.		
2.		
3.		
4.		
5.		

Painting

	Name	Work
1.		
2.		
3.		
4.		
5.		

Others

	Name	Work
1.		
2.		
3.		
4.		
5.		

Chapter 3: Art History

Activity 4: Using the Credit Line

DIRECTIONS: Decode the credit line for Figure 3.3 in the text by filling in the blanks below with the proper information.

1. What is the artist's full name? _____

   _____

2. What is the full title of the work? _____

   _____

3. When was the work completed? _____

   _____

4. What medium was used? _____

5. What is the size of the work? (label as to height, etc.) _____

   _____

6. Where is this work exhibited? _____

7. Names of doners? _____

   _____

8. In the space below, write a credit line for one of your own works. Assume you are the doner. Follow the sequence

   used in Figure 3.3. Include all the information asked for in question 1–10. _____

   _____

Chapter 3: Art History

Activity 5: Time Line

		A.D.
_____	1986	
_____		
_____		
_____		
_____	1984	Pioneer 10 leaves the solar system
_____		
_____	1983	*Time* magazine names the microcomputer as its "man of the year"
_____		
_____	1982	
_____		
_____	1981	First reusable space vehicle-shuttle launched
_____	1980	Beginning of the Information Age
_____		
_____		
_____	1978	
_____		
_____		
_____	1977	
_____	1976	
_____		
_____	1975	Microcomputers for home use
	1973	Britain becomes member of Common Market

(Continued on next page)

———————————————— 1970

————————————————

———————————————— 1969   Neil Armstrong first man on the moon

————————————————

————————————————

————————————————

———————————————— 1966   Indira Ghandi first woman prime minister of India

————————————————

———————————————— 1965   USA enters into Vietnam conflict

————————————————

————————————————

———————————————— 1963

————————————————

————————————————

———————————————— 1962   Silicon chips mass-produced

————————————————

————————————————

————————————————

————————————————

————————————————

———————————————— 1961   Berlin Wall erected
                               Alan B. Shepherd first American astronaut in space
                               Yuri A. Gagarin first person to orbit earth

———————————————— 1960   Laser light developed

————————————————

————————————————

———————————————— 1959   Silicon chip developed

———————————————— 1958
                                       (Continued on next page)

_____	**1957**	Kornberg grew DNA in a test tube
		Sputnik I launched by Soviets
_____		
_____		
_____		
_____	**1956**	
_____	**1955**	Martin Luther King leads civil rights movement
_____	**1953**	Jonas Salk's polio vaccine
_____	**1952**	
_____		
_____	**1951**	
_____		
_____	**1950**	Television era begins
		Korean conflict (1950–53)
_____	**1949**	Communists establish People's Republic of China
		Germany divided into East and West
_____		
_____		
_____		
_____	**1948**	Cold war begins between Russia and U.S.
_____		
_____		
_____		
	1947	Transistor developed
	1946	ENIAC - first electronic computer
		Republic of Italy established
_____	**1945**	Hiroshima - end of WW II
		UN Charter goes into effect
_____	**1943**	Italy surrenders to Allies
_____	**1942**	Atomic reactor developed
	1941	U.S. enters World War II (1941-45)
_____	**1940**	Italy sides with Germany in WW II
_____		(Continued on next page)

127

1939   World War II begins (1939-45)

1938

1937   Photocopying invented

1936   Spanish Civil War begins (1936-39)

1935   Fluorescent light
The "Great Purge" in Russia

1933   Adolph Hitler comes to power

1931

1930

1929   Stock Market crash

(Continued on next page)

_____ 1928

_____

_____

_____

_____ 1926

_____ 1924

_____

_____ 1923

_____ 1922   Stalin comes to power in Russia

_____ 1920   First radio station (KDKA Pittsburgh)
                            Mahatma Ghandi begins non-violent disobedience against British rule in India
                            TV camera and receiver invented

_____ 1919

_____ 1918   Leonard Bernstein, music composer, born in USA

_____

_____ 1917   Communist Revolution in Russia - Lenin becomes dictator

_____ 1915

                    1914   World War I begins (1914-18)

                    1913   Assembly line production

_____

_____

_____

_____ 1912   Republic of China established

_____

_____

_____

(Continued on next page)

_____	1911 Rutherford's theory of atomic structure
_____	1910
_____	
_____	1909
_____	
_____	1908
	1906 San Francisco earthquake
	1905 Albert Einstein's theory of relativity
_____	1904
_____	1903 Wright Brothers' first flight at Kittyhawk, NC
	1902 Airconditioning
_____	1900 Aaron Copeland, American music composer
_____	
_____	
_____	
_____	1899
	1898 Spanish American War
	George Gershwin, American music composer (1898–1937)
_____	1895 Marconi sent first radio waves through air
_____	1894
_____	
_____	1893
_____	
_____	1892
_____	
_____	1891
_____	
_____	1890
_____	

(Continued on next page)

_____	1889	
_____		
_____		
_____	1888	
_____	1886	
_____		
_____	1885	Gasoline automobile
	1884	Skyscraper
	1883	Brooklyn Bridge, New York
	1882	Igor Stravinsky, Russian music composer (1881–1945)
	1881	
_____	1880	
_____		
_____	1879	Incandescent light invented
	1878	Carl Sandburg, American poet
_____	1877	Phonograph invented
_____	1876	Telephone invented
_____		
	1875	Maurice Ravel, French music composer (1875–1937)
	1874	Robert Frost, American poet (1874–1963)
	1873	Sergi Rachmaninov, Russian music composer (1873–1943)
	1871	Rome becomes capitol of unified Italy
	1867	Typewriter invented
	1865	Rudyard Kipling, English author (1865–1936)
	1863	Emancipation Proclamation, United States
_____	1862	Gregor Mendel developed laws of heredity Claude Debussy, French music composer (1862–1918)
_____	1861	American Civil War (1861–65)

(Continued on next page)

_____	1860	Internal combustion engine developed Gustav Mahler, Austrian music composer (1860–1911) Maxwell's electromagnetic theory
_____		
_____		
_____	1858	Darwin's theory of evolution (England) Great Britain takes control of India Giacomo Puccini, Italian music composer (1858–1924)
	1856	George Bernard Shaw, English author (1856–1950) Bessemer (steel) process Synthetic dye from coal tar
_____	1853	
_____	1850	Robert Louis Stevenson, American author (1850–94)
_____		
_____		
	1848	California "Gold Rush"
	1846	Sewing machine invented Mexican-American War (1846–48)
_____	1845	
_____		
	1841	Anton Dvorak, Bohemian music composer (1841–1904)
	1840	Peter Iliach Tchaikovsky, Russian music composer (1840–93)
	1838	George Bizet, French music composer (1838–75)
	1836	Texas wins independence from Mexico
	1835	Samuel Clements (Mark Twain), American author (1835–1910)
	1833	Johannas Brahm, German music composer (1833–97)
	1830	Emily Dickenson, American poet (1830–86)
	1826	Beginning of photography
_____	1825	Johann Strauss, Austrian music composer (1825–99)
_____		
_____	1823	
_____	1820	
	1819	Herman Melville (1819–97)

(Continued on next page)

_____	1813	Guiseppe Verdi, Italian music composer (1813–1901) Richard Wagner, German music composer (1813–88)
	1812	Charles Dickens, English author (1812–70) War of 1812 (1812–14) - England invades U.S.
	1811	Franz Liszt, Hungarian music composer (1811–86)
	1810	Frederick Chopin, Polish music composer (1810–49)
	1809	Edgar Allen Poe, American author (1809–49)
	1804	Nathaniel Hawthorne, American author (1804–64)
	1803	John Dalton proposes theory of atoms
_____	1800	Washington, D.C. becomes capitol of U.S.
_____		
	1799	Napoleon seizes control of France
	1797	Franz Schubert, Austrian music composer (1797–1828)
	1796	Jenner's smallpox vaccine (England)
_____	1795	
	1793	Cotton gin invented by Eli Whitney (U.S.)
_____	1789	French Revolution (1789-99) James Fenimore Cooper, American author (1789-1851)
_____	1787	Constitution of United States written
_____	1782	
_____	1776	United States' Declaration of Independence
	1775	American Revolutionary War (1775-83)
	1774	
	1773	Boston Tea Party
	1770	Ludwig von Beethovan, German music composer (1770-1827)
_____	1768	
_____	1767	
	1764	
	1763	French and Indian War, North America
_____	1762	

(Continued on next page)

———————————	1759	
	1756	Wolfgang Mozart, Austrian music composer (1756-91)
	1746	
	1743	Thomas Jefferson, American (1743-1826)
	1733	
	1732	George Washington (1732-99) Joseph Haydn, Austrian music composer (1732-1809)
———————————	1718	
———————————	1716	
	1707	United Kingdom formed
	1706	Benjamin Franklin (1706-90)
	1690	Steam engine
	1687	Sir Isaac Newton, scientist, developed law of gravity and spectral light theory
	1685	J. S. Bach, German music composer (1685-1750) George Frederick Handel, German music composer (1685-1759)
	1675	Antonio Vivaldi, Italian music composer (1675-1741)
———————————	1664	
———————————	1660	
———————————	1659	
———————————	1650	
	1642	Montreal, Canada founded
	1640	
———————————	1635	
Taj Mahal, India (Islamic)	1630	
———————————	1626	
	1620	Plymouth, Massachusetts established

(Continued on next page)

_____ 1615	
1608	Quebec, Canada founded
1607	First English settlement in North America (Jamestown, Virginia) established
1600	
_____ 1597	
_____ 1590	Cortez conquers Aztec Empire for Spain Microscope invented
1585	Sir Francis Drake of England defeats Spanish Armada fleet
1567	Monteverdi (music) - Italy
1565	St. Augustine founded in Florida by Spaniards
1564	William Shakespeare, English poet (1564-1616)
1556	Height of Spanish Empire under Phillip II (1556-1598)
1534	Henry VIII broke with Catholic Church to create the Church of England
_____ 1524	
_____ 1521	
_____ 1519	
_____ 1517	
1513	Ponce de Leon explored Florida and Georgia in North America
_____ 1510	
_____ 1506	
_____ 1505	
_____ 1500	Protestant Reformation
_____	
1498	Vasco de Gama found sea route to India
1497	John Cabot, English explorer
_____ 1495	
1492	Columbus discovered America
_____ 1485	

(Continued on next page)

_____	1480	
_____		
_____	1474	
	1473	Nicholas Copernicus, astronomer, developed theory of earth as a moving planet (1473-1543)
_____	1460	
	1455	
	1440	Gutenberg printing press invented in Germany
	1412	Joan of Arc rallies France to fight England
	1400	
	1368	Ming Dynasty (1368-1644)
	1350	Aztecs founded Mexico City
	1348	Black Death (plague) kills 50% of Europeans
	1337	Hundred Years War between France and England (1337-1453)
	1325	
_____	1320	
	1300	Renaissance begins in Italy
	1275	Marco Polo visits China (1275-1292)
_____	1250	
	1231	Spanish Inquisition
	1225	
	1215	King John (England) signs Magna Carta
_____	1174	
	1096	Crusades start
	1066	William the Conqueror, Duke of Normandy, invades England
	960	Sung Dynasty, China (960-1279) - magnetic compass, gun powder, movable type for printing
_____	900	Toltec Empire in Mexico (900-1200)
	800	First Russian city-state, Kiev

(Continued on next page)

	768	Emperor Charlemagne, Holy Roman Empire (768-884)
	618	T'ang Dynasty, Golden Age of China (618-909) - printing invented
	610	Mohammed preaching of Islam
Sant' Apollinaire in Classe, Ravenna	549	
	500	Rise and fall of Buddism (500-800); replaced by Hinduism in India
	478	Western Roman Empire ceases to exist
	400	Fall of Western Roman Empire (400-500)
	395	East and West Roman Empire split; beginning of Byzantine era
	387	Rome is sacked by the Gauls
	325	Constantine recognizes Christianity
	324	Constantine emperor of Roman Empire (324-337)
	200	
Pantheon (118-125)	118	
	105	Paper invented during Han Dynasty, China
_____	100	
	79	Vesuvius eruption destroys Pompeii
Roman Colosseum (70-82)	70	
	B.C. 36	Anthony and Cleopatra married
	44	Caesar assassinated
_____	50	
_____		
	55	Caesar invades Britain (54-55)
Nike of Samothraco (Winged Victory) - Greek sculpture	190	
	207	Han Dynasty (207-220 B.C.) - beginning of Chinese empire
Great Wall of China, Chin Dynasty (221-206 B.C.)	221	

(Continued on next page)

	280	Archimedes (280-212 B.C.)
	300	Euclid
	310	
Roman Aqueduct	312	
	331	Alexander the Great conquers the Persian Empire
————————	400	
Parthenon (448-432 B.C.)	448	
————————	450	
	510	
	550	
————————	600	
	750	Homer writes *The Iliad* and *The Oddysey*
	753	Romulus and Remus founded Rome (legend)
	900	
————————	1000	Phoenician writing developed
	1006	King David's rule in Israel (1006-966 B.C.)
	1027	Chou Dynasty in China (1027-256 B.C.)
Temple of Karnak, Egypt	1280	
	1348	Tutankhamen is pharoh of Egypt (1348-1339 B.C.)
	1400	Shang Dynasty (1400-1027 B.C.) - first dynasty recorded in China
	1500	Tribes of Israel go to Palestine Village life develops in Mexico
	1570	New kingdom of Egypt (1570-715 B.C.)
	1600	
————————	1850	
	1890	
	1900	
Stonehenge, England	2000	

(Continued on next page)

_____	**2050**	
	2052	Middle Kingdom of Egypt (2052-1570 B.C.)
Ziggurat at Ur (Mesopotamian)	**2100**	
Egyptian pyramids at Gizeh	**2500**	
	2850	Old Kingdom of Egypt (2850-2052 B.C.) - hieroglyphics developed
	3000	Cuneiform writing developed in Middle East Indus Valley civilization in India Upper and lower kingdoms of Egypt united
	3500	Wheel invented
	4000	Mesopotamia Copper smelting
	5000	Plow invented
	6000	First cities
	7000	Agriculture established
	7500	Jericho wall
_____	**15,000**	
_____	**15,000**	
	30,000	

Chapter 4: Careers in Art

Activity 1: Study Question Worksheet

DIRECTIONS: Using a separate sheet of paper, write answers to the following questions.

1. How did aspiring artists of the past receive training?

2. Name five art-related jobs available in the publishing business.

3. Name three areas that an illustrator could specialize in.

4. List two aims of the political cartoonist.

5. What is the primary aim of the comic strip artist?

6. What do industrial designers design? (Give examples.)

7. List three requirements of a good industrial design.

8. How does the package designer use shape and color?

9. Who is Raymond Loewy, and why is he important?

10. Name three items that fashion designers design.

11. What does the high-fashion designer do?

12. List three things an architect must keep in mind when designing a building.

13. List four things an architect must be able to do to be successful.

14. In general, what is a city planner concerned with?

15. What are some of the responsibilities of a city planner?

16. What does a landscape architect design?

17. What material does a landscape architect use?

18. What does an interior designer decorate?

19. List five places where an exhibit and display designer might find a job.

20. Why would a department store need a display designer?

21. What equipment must the graphic designer be able to use today?

22. List ten jobs in a graphic design team.

(Continued on next page)

23. What are photojournalists, and who do they work for?

24. List six careers in photography?

25. What sort of background does a computer artist need?

26. What are the advantages of doing graphics with a computer?

27. What is the role of the director in the theater?

28. Name the visual artists involved in a professional theater performance.

29. List six steps in the production of an animated film.

30. What is a storyboard?

31. How many drawings must be done for every second of movement in an animated film?

32. Where do special effects artists get their start?

33. Name five places you could work if you were interested in art education.

34. What do art therapists do?

Chapter 4: Careers in Art

Activity 2: Art Career Checklist

DIRECTIONS: Choose an art career that interests you. Using library sources, research the career. Then fill out this page with the information required.

Career choice: _____

Related careers: _____

_____

Job responsibilities: _____

_____

_____

_____

Traits necessary to be successful in this field: _____

_____

_____

_____

Education required: _____

_____

_____

Job possibilities: _____

_____

_____

Job availability: _____

_____

_____

_____

(Continued on next page)

Average yearly salary: _____

List of colleges and universities offering programs in this field and average costs: _____

_____

_____

_____

_____

Chapter 5: Line

Activity 1: Study Question Worksheet

DIRECTION: Using a separate sheet of paper, write answers to the following questions.

1. List ten examples (other than those in the text) of line in objects created by people.

2. List ten examples (other than those in the text) of line that may be found in nature.

3. Define line in terms of (a) drawing and (b) geometry.

4. What happens to your eyes when you view a drawn line?

5. Define dimension.

6. Why is line thought of as having one dimension?

7. Define implied line.

8. Identify the following as implied or real lines:
   (a) the path a baseball takes when you throw it
   (b) the mark you make with a pencil
   (c) the lines of words on this page
   (d) a row of stones
   (e) the yellow line down the center of the highway

9. Describe what the following lines can express:
   (a) horizontal
   (b) vertical
   (c) diagonal
   (d) curved
   (e) zigzag

10. Define active line.

11. Define static line.

12. Which types of lines are considered active? Static?

13. Define the following:
    (a) contour lines
    (b) gestures
    (c) calligraphy
    (d) value
    (e) crosshatching

(Continued on next page)

14. What does value depend on?

15. Tell five ways that line can vary in appearance.

16. What do contour drawings capture?

17. What do gesture drawings capture?

Chapter 6: Shape, Form, and Space

Activity 1: Study Question Worksheet

DIRECTIONS: Using a separate sheet of paper, write answers to the following questions.

1. Define shape.

2. Define form.

3. What is the difference between natural and manufactured shapes and forms?

4. What is a silhouette?

5. Define geometric shape. List the geometric shapes mentioned in the text.

6. Define free-form shapes. Draw five free-form shapes.

7. What forms are three dimensional projections of the following shapes?
   (a) circle
   (b) square
   (c) triangle

8. Give an example of a naturally occurring geometric form.

9. What is scoring paper? When would you use this technique?

10. What is chiaroscuro? Who introduced this technique? What is its purpose?

11. Define highlights.

12. List and define four techniques for shading an object with different values.

13. What does hard-edge mean? What aspect of a form would hard-edge lines emphasize?

14. What three dimensions do we see in?

15. Compare and contrast open and closed shapes.

16. Give examples of shapes and forms that are active. Give examples that are static.

17. Explain how the eyes and brain enable us to see in three dimensions.

18. Define the following: (a) relief sculpture, (b) bas-relief, and (c) high relief.

19. Define hologram.

20. List and define the three parts of the picture plane.

(Continued on next page)

21. List and explain the six ways artists suggest three-dimensions on a two-dimensional surface.

22. What is the vanishing point?

23. What is atmospheric perspective?

24. Define space.

25. Explain what is meant by positive area and negative space.

26. Define point of view.

27. What ideas or feelings do the following express:
    (a) geometric shapes and forms
    (b) very dense forms
    (c) free-form shapes and forms

28. Define assemblage.

29. In what country was Louise Nevelson born?

Chapter 6: Shape, Form, and Space

TECHNIQUE TIP: MOUNTING A TWO-DIMENSIONAL WORK OF ART

Materials

A two-dimensional work of art
Mat board or poster board
Pencil and yardstick (meterstick)
Knife with a fine, precision blade
Heavy cardboard
Rubber cement

SAFETY NOTE

Be very careful to use rubber cement in a well-ventilated area. It contains solvents which should not be inhaled.

Procedures

1. Measure the height and width of the work to be mounted. In this example the work is 9″ high and 12″ wide.

2. Since you want a 3″ border around the work, you must add 6″ to its height and width measurements.

$$9'' + 6'' = 15''$$
$$12'' + 6'' = 18''$$

The outer measurements of the mounting board will thus be 15″ high and 18″ wide.

3. Using the yardstick, carefully measure off the mounting board on the backside and mark it with light pencil marks.

4. Place the board on the heavy cardboard to protect the surface of the table as you cut.

5. Do not try to cut all the way through the mounting board on the first cut. Hold the yardstick firmly in place and lightly score the mounting board along the measured lines. Score it several times until you cut through the board easily.

6. Using the yardstick, center the work of art on the board and mark the corners with a dot.

7. If you want to create a permanent mount, both surfaces must be covered with rubber cement. If you want a temporary mount, cover only one surface with rubber cement. Place the work of art, face down, on a piece of newspaper and coat it with the rubber cement. If you are making a permanent mount, coat the mounting board too within the measured area.

8. If you are making a permanent mount you need a partner to help you place the work. Once the two surfaces touch, their placement cannot be changed. Ask your partner to hold the work of art by two corners in the air above the mounting board. Carefully place the remaining two corners on the marked dots. Gradually lower the rest of the work in place and press it smooth.

9. Remove any excess cement by rubbing it with an eraser or a small ball of the cement that has dried. It will lift off cleanly.

Chapter 6: Shape, Form, and Space

TECHNIQUE TIP: MAKING A SIMPLE MAT

Materials

A two-dimensional work of art
Mat board or poster board
Pencil and yardstick (meterstick)
Knife with a fine, precision blade
Heavy cardboard
Tape

Procedures

1. Measure the height and width of the work to be matted. In this example the work is 9″ (22.9 cm) high and 12″ (30.5 cm) wide.

2. The mat must overlap the edges of the work by 1/4″ (0.6 cm) on all sides. Therefore you must subtract 1/2″ (1.3 cm) from each measurement.

$$9'' - 1/2'' = 8\ 1/2''$$
$$12'' - 1/2'' = 11\ 1/2''$$

Thus the inside "window" cut in the mat will be 8 1/2″ high and 11 1/2″ wide.

3. If you want a 3″ border around the work, you must add 6″ to the inside measurements of the mat.

$$8\ 1/2'' + 6'' = 14\ 1/2''$$
$$11\ 1/2'' + 6'' = 17\ 1/2''$$

Thus the outer measurements of the mat will be 14 1/2″ high and 17 1/2″ wide.

4. Using your yardstick, carefully measure and mark the mat on the backside with light pencil marks.

5. Place a thick piece of cardboard under the mat before you cut to protect the table surface.

6. Do not try to cut through the mat board on the first cut! Hold the yardstick firmly in place and lightly score the mat along the measured lines. Score along the line several times until you cut through the board easily.

7. Be careful to cut up to the corners on the inside window marks. If you have not cut through properly the corners will tear when you press out the window.

8. Remove the inner window.

9. Place the art work on the back of the mat, face down, and center it carefully.

10. Attach the work to the mat with a few small pieces of tape, and turn the mat over to be sure you have centered the work correctly.

11. If it is centered correctly, tape the work in place.

Chapter 7: Color

Activity 1: Study Question Worksheet

DIRECTIONS: Using a separate sheet of paper, write answers to the following questions.

1. Explain how our eyes enable us to see colors.

2. Why do we see colors as dull or as grays in dim light?

3. What is an afterimage? Why is it always a weak color?

4. What are the colors of the spectrum?

5. Which natural phenomenon breaks white light into the spectrum of colors?

6. Why do we perceive a red apple as being red?

7. What are pigments?

8. What is a vehicle?

9. What is a dye?

10. How are paints and dyes different?

11. Why do an apple-red car and an apple-red shirt look different in color?

12. What is synthetic pigment? How is it different from natural pigment?

13. Define hue.

14. What are the primary colors?

15. What colors can be made by mixing the primary colors?

16. Name the secondary colors? What primary colors combine to make each secondary color?

17. Name the intermediate colors. How are they made?

18. What is a color wheel?

19. What is color value?

20. Name the three neutral colors.

21. What is a tint?

22. What is a shade?

(Continued on next page)

23. What is the difference between high-key and low-key paintings?

24. Define intensity.

25. What is the difference between a high-intensity and a low-intensity hue?

26. What type of color results when you mix a color with its complement?

27. What does monochrome mean? What is a monochromatic color scheme?

29. What is a color scheme? How are analogous colors related?

30. What are complementary colors? How do complementary colors affect each other?

31. What is a color triad?

32. What is a split-complement: Why would this color scheme be easier to work with than a complementary color scheme?

33. Explain what is meant by warm or cool colors.

34. What is optical color?

35. What is arbitrary color?

36. Explain how Cezanne created the illusion of space using color.

37. How can you create movement using color?

38. What is tonality?

Chapter 8: Texture

Activity 1: Study Question Worksheet

DIRECTIONS: Using a separate sheet of paper, write answers to the following questions.

1. Define the following:
   (a) texture
   (b) visual texture
   (c) simulated texture
   (d) invented texture
   (e) rubbing
   (f) matte surface
   (g) shiny surface
   (h) frottage
   (i) grattage
   (j) decalcomania

2. Which two senses are involved in the perception of texture?

3. What is the purpose of simulated texture? Invented texture?

4. How does a rough surface reflect light? A smooth surface?

5. How do we perceive matte and shiny properties of surfaces?

6. How did Ivan Albright portray people in his work?

7. Define *tromp-l' oeil*.

8. How did Van Gogh create real textures in his work?

9. (a) Why do architects use a variety of materials when designing buildings?
   (b) List seven materials used by architects to create textures.

10. How do weavers control texture?

11. List two ways potters change the texture of clay.

12. Name three techniques Max Ernst used to create unusual textures.

13. What painting style was popular in Europe when John Singleton Copley worked there? How did his own style differ?

14. In what country was Copley born?

Chapter 9: Rhythm and Movement

Activity 1: Study Question Worksheet

DIRECTIONS: Using a separate sheet of paper, write answers to the following questions.

1. _____ is the repetition of elements to indicate movement.

2. _____ rhythms are created by repeating positive shapes separated by negative spaces.

3. What is a motif?

4. Define module.

5. Define pattern.

6. How do pattern and rhythm differ?

7. Define random rhythm.

8. Define regular rhythm.

9. Define grid.

10. Explain alternating rhythm.

11. Define progressive rhythm.

12. Define flowing rhythm.

13. Who were the Futurists and what did they contribute?

14. What is dynamism?

15. Define kinetic sculpture.

16. Who invented kinetic sculpture?

17. How many paintings did Van Gogh create?

18. Which art styles influenced Van Gogh?

Chapter 10: Balance

Activity 1: Study Question Worksheet

DIRECTIONS: Using a separate sheet of paper, write answers to the following questions.

1. Define the following:
   (a) balance
   (b) visual balance
   (c) formal balance
   (d) symmetry
   (e) bilateral symmetry
   (f) approximate symmetry
   (g) radial balance
   (h) informal balance
   (i) asymmetrical
   (j) visual weight

2. In formal balance, where is the axis located? Does it have to be part of the design?

3. How is the human body arranged in terms of balance?

4. What do artists express with symmetry?

5. Why is approximate symmetry usually more interesting than symmetry?

6. Where is the axis in radial balance?

7. Why is radial balance more complicated than symmetry?

8. Why is informal balance more complicated to produce than formal?

9. List six factors that can influence visual weight.

10. What purpose does formal balance serve in buildings such as city halls and courthouses?

11. Why do people like to live in formally arranged dwellings?

12. Define informal balance.

13. For what expressive purpose do artists use radial balance?

14. What was Georgia O'Keeffe's favorite subject to paint?

15. What did O'Keeffe paint that shocked the art world?

Chapter 11: Proportion

Activity 1: Study Question Worksheet

DIRECTIONS: Using a separate sheet of paper, write answers to the following questions.

1. Define the following:
   (a) proportion
   (b) Golden Mean
   (c) sighting
   (d) scale
   (e) exaggeration
   (f) monumental
   (g) papier-mâché

2. What must be taken into consideration when judging the proportion of an object?

3. Why is proportion important in furniture design?

4. Who was Pythagoras? What did he believe about the universe?

5. How did the Greeks use the Golden Mean?

6. What did the Greeks consider to be the most pleasing geometric shape?

7. To the Greeks, what was the true expression of order?

8. How did Greek sculptors show the human figure in their works?

9. Who was Vitruvius and what did he do?

10. What measurements did Le Corbusier base his building designs on?

11. (a) What is the unit used to define body proportion when drawing?
    (b) Based on this unit, what would be the height of the average adult? Young child? Infant?

12. Name one American Realist painter mentioned in the chapter and the subjects he or she painted.

13. Name two kinds of scale to consider in art.

14. Why are the dimensions of an artwork always listed beside reproductions in an art book?

15. Name two art forms other than drawing, painting, or sculpture that make use of exaggeration as an expressive device.

16. Name the three artists mentioned in the chapter who use exaggeration and distortion to convey feelings. Tell what feelings they convey.

17. List three methods of using papier-mâché, and tell in general how each is done.

Chapter 12: Variety, Emphasis, and Unity

Activity 1: Study Question Worksheet

DIRECTIONS: Using a separate sheet of paper, write answers to the following questions.

1. Define the following:
   (a) variety
   (b) emphasis
   (c) unity
   (d) focal point
   (e) harmony
   (f) subordinate

2. Name the five ways emphasis can be added to a work and give an example of each.

3. How can a viewer identify the dominant element in a work?

4. What is the danger in having more than one focal point in a work?

5. What is convergence and how can it be created in a work?

6. Name the five ways visual unity can be created in a work and give an example of each.

7. What does unity add to a work of art?

8. An artist wants to paint a bowl of flowers. Some of the flowers are red roses, some are pink carnations, and some are purple iris. What could give this painting variety? What could give it unity?

9. What subjects did Winslow Homer like to paint?

10. How many art lessons did Winslow Homer take?

11. What did Winslow Homer illustrate during the Civil War?

Chapter 1: The Language of Art

Chapter Test

Part I. Matching

DIRECTIONS: Match the term in the left-hand column with the group it belongs to in the right-hand column. Write the letter of the correct answer in the blanks at the left. Each letter will be used more than once.

Terms

_____ 1. Line

_____ 2. Movement

_____ 3. Rhythm

_____ 4. Shape and form

_____ 5. Balance

_____ 6. Form (as in how materials are used)

_____ 7. Proportion

_____ 8. Space

_____ 9. Subject

_____ 10. Variety

_____ 11. Sculpture

_____ 12. Color

_____ 13. Content

_____ 14. Copper

_____ 15. Texture

_____ 16. Unity

_____ 17. Emphasis

_____ 18. Paint

_____ 19. Architecture

_____ 20. Value

Group

A. Principles of design
B. Elements of art
C. Parts of a work of art
D. Media
E. A type of art

(Continued on next page)

Part II. Completion

DIRECTIONS: Write the word that completes the sentence in the blank at the left.

_____ 21. The _____ is what can be recognized in a work.

_____ 22. A raw material used for artistic purposes is called the _____.

_____ 23. A _____ is a visual image that stands for something else.

_____ 24. The message the artist is trying to communicate is the work's _____.

_____ 25. The way the artist uses the material chosen to create the work makes up its _____.

Chapter 2: Art Criticism and Aesthetic Judgment

Chapter Test

DIRECTIONS: Write the word that completes each sentence in the blank at the left.

_____ 1. The judgment you use in evaluating a work of art is called _____ judgment.

_____ 2. (2–5) List in order the steps in art criticism.

_____ 3.

_____ 4.

_____ 5.

_____ 6. During which critical step do you answer the question, "What is the artist trying to say?"

_____ 7. During which critical step do you offer your personal evaluation?

_____ 8. The critical theory that focuses on the elements of art and principles of design is called _____.

_____ 9. Critics who prefer that art copy real life believe in the theory of _____.

_____ 10. If you prefer a painting with horses in it because you like horses, you are using the theory of _____.

_____ 11. When judging your own work, which critical step may prove the most useful to you?

_____ 12. When judging _____ objects, attention must be paid to their usefulness.

_____ 13. The skill of judging a work of art is called _____. (Two words)

_____ 14. During which critical step do you ask the question, "What do I see?"

_____ 15. During which critical step do you ask the question, "How is the work organized?"

_____ 16. When you give only the facts, you are being _____.

_____ 17. A realistic portrait conforms to which theory of art?

_____ 18. What is the last name of the artist who painted *Christina's World*?

_____ 19. To which theory of art does *Christina's World* conform?

_____ 20. What is the subject of *Christina's World*?

Chapter 3: Art History

Chapter Test

DIRECTIONS: Below are three sets of matching questions. Match the clues in the left-hand column with the terms in the right-hand column. Do not mix terms and clues from different sets. Some terms in set I may be used more than once.

Set I

Clues

_____ 1. Cave paintings

_____ 2. Paintings found in tombs

_____ 3. Statues representing the ideal of a perfect body

_____ 4. Blend of Roman, Greek, and Oriental art

_____ 5. Huge cathedrals

_____ 6. Roman arch and sculptural decorations

_____ 7. Stained glass in church windows

_____ 8. Use of perspective

_____ 9. Leonardo da Vinci

_____ 10. Invention of telescope and microscope changed the way people saw the universe

Terms

A. Egyptian
B. Byzantine
C. Gothic
D. Prehistoric
E. Greek
F. Renaissance
G. Baroque
H. Romanesque

(Continued on next page)

Set II

Clues

_____ 11. Based on the art of Greece and Rome

_____ 12. Reaction against "coolness" and rules

_____ 13. Peasants and factory workers shown accurately

_____ 14. Melted solid forms and blurred edges

_____ 15. Vincent van Gogh

_____ 16. "Wild beasts"

_____ 17. Scientific discovery that matter is made up of whirling atoms

_____ 18. Angular forms suggesting motion

_____ 19. Black lines and the three primary colors

_____ 20. Realistic images in strange, dreamlike situations

Terms

A. Romanticism
B. Impressionism
C. Fauves
D. Cubism
E. Neoclassic
F. Realism
G. Post-Impressionism
H. Futurists
I. De Stijl
J. Surrealism

Set III

Clues

_____ 21. Tenement buildings and poor people

_____ 22. Showed Americans as happy and hardworking

_____ 23. Alexander Calder

_____ 24. Painted on walls and ceilings

_____ 25. Emphasized the elements and principles of art; stressed emotions

_____ 26. Giant hamburgers

_____ 27. Flat fields of color

_____ 28. Optical illusion

_____ 29. Images of many gods

_____ 30. North American Indians

Terms

A. Ashcan School
B. Mobiles
C. Abstract Expressionism
D. Regionalists
E. Color Field Painting
F. Op Art
G. Pop Art
H. Mexican Muralists
I. Pre-Columbian Art
J. Indian Art

Chapter 4: Careers in Art

Chapter Test

Part I. Matching.

DIRECTIONS: Match the clues in the left-hand column with the careers in the right-hand column. Write the correct letters in the blanks at the left.

Clues

_____ 1. Decorates homes and offices

_____ 2. Designs outdoor areas

_____ 3. Designs book pages

_____ 4. Arranges art gallery exhibits

_____ 5. Works with electronic equipment

_____ 6. Plans the looks of a chair

_____ 7. Draws cartoons for films

_____ 8. Creates fantasy scenes and creatures

_____ 9. Works with weavers and tailors

_____ 10. Designs TV weather maps

_____ 11. Must know about building materials and heating systems

_____ 12. Helps control the growth and development of a city

_____ 13. Helps others develop their artistic skills

_____ 14. Designs costumes

_____ 15. Goes where the news is happening

Careers

A. Editorial designer
B. Computer artist
C. Television graphics artist
D. Industrial designer
E. Fashion designer
F. Architect
G. City planner
H. Lanscape architect
I. Interior designer
J. Display designer
K. Photojournalist
L. Animator
M. Theatre art director
N. Special effects artist
O. Art teacher

(Continued on next page)

Part II. Completion

DIRECTIONS: Complete the sentences by writing the missing word in the blank at the left.

_____ 16. The art of moving cartoons is called _____.

_____ 17. A collection of still drawings that shows a cartoon's progress are called a(n) _____.

_____ 18. Someone who learns by assisting a master artist is called a(n) _____.

_____ 19. The way items are arranged on a page is called a(n) _____.

_____ 20. Editorial cartoonists must be interested in _____.

Chapter 5: Line

Chapter Test

DIRECTIONS: Complete the sentences by writing the correct words in the blanks at the left.

_____ 1. A ____ drawing captures body movement.

_____ 2. A ____ line changes direction gradually.

_____ 3. In art, a ____ is a mark drawn with a pointed, moving tool.

_____ 4. A ____ line stands straight up at a right angle with the horizon.

_____ 5. ____ lines are made from a combination of diagonal lines that form angles and change direction suddenly.

_____ 6. ____ means to be at rest.

_____ 7. ____ lines define the edges and surface ridges of objects.

_____ 8. ____ in Chinese means "beautiful handwriting."

_____ 9. ____ is a technique in which lines cross each other to create shading.

_____ 10. ____ is the art element that refers to darkness and light.

_____ 11. When you make a ____ drawing, you do not look at your drawing until it is finished. (Two words)

_____ 12. ____ means moving or not at rest.

_____ 13. ____ is defined as an infinite series of dots.

_____ 14. ____ lines go from side to side and are parallel to the horizon.

_____ 15. ____ lines are a series of points that the viewer's eyes automatically connect.

_____ 16. ____ lines slant and look as if they are rising or falling.

_____ 17. Artists like to think of a ____ as the path of a dot through space.

_____ 18. Artists use line to control the viewer's ____ movement.

_____ 19. ____ is a type of opaque watercolor.

_____ 20. ____ is a paint containing a binder made from milk.

Chapter 6: Shape, Form, and Space

Chapter Test

Part I. Completion

DIRECTIONS: Complete the sentences by writing the correct word in the blank to the left.

——————————————— 1. A ——— is a small area of white in a drawing or painting that shows the very brightest spot.

——————————————— 2. A ——— is a two-dimensional shadow-like shape.

——————————————— 3. ——— shapes or forms are those created by the forces of nature.

——————————————— 4. A drawing technique in which shading is done by intersecting two or more sets of parallel lines is known as ———.

——————————————— 5. ——— is a technique for making neat, sharp folds in paper.

——————————————— 6. ——— shapes and forms are those made by people.

——————————————— 7. Shading through the smooth, gradual application of dark value is known as ———.

——————————————— 8. ——— is a drawing technique in which shading is done with dots of varying values.

——————————————— 9. ——— is shading with a series of parallel lines.

——————————————— 10. ——— shapes include the circle, square, and triangle.

——————————————— 11. The ——— of an object tells how much space it takes up in a given direction.

——————————————— 12. ——— shapes are irregular and uneven and may be silhouettes of living things.

——————————————— 13. The arrangement of light and shadow developed during the Renaissance is known as ———.

——————————————— 14. An ——— shape or form is inviting and can be seen into or through.

——————————————— 15. A form has ——— dimensions.

——————————————— 16. ——— sculpture projects out from a flat plane into negative space.

——————————————— 17. ——— shapes appear to be fixed in one place.

——————————————— 18. ——— perspective is a way of using lines to show distance and depth.

(Continued on next page)

_____ 19. When positive areas of relief sculpture project far out into negative space, it is called _____. (Two words)

_____ 20. The part of a picture farthest from the viewer is known as the _____.

_____ 21. In two- and three-dimensional art, the areas between and around shapes and forms are called _____ space.

_____ 22. The _____ is the spot on the horizon where parallel lines seem to meet. (Two words)

_____ 23. The part of a picture between the background and the foreground is known as the _____.

_____ 24. The technique for creating the illusion of depth on a two-dimensional picture plane is called _____.

_____ 25. A _____ is a three-dimensional image created with a laser beam.

_____ 26. In both two- and three-dimensional art, the shapes or forms are the _____ areas.

_____ 27. The part of a picture closest to the picture plane and to the viewer is called the _____.

_____ 28. The surface of any drawing is called the picture _____.

Part II. Matching

DIRECTIONS: Match the terms in the left-hand column with the clues in the right-hand column. Write the correct letters in the blanks at the left.

Terms	Clues
_____ 29. Overlapping	A. A circle above the horizon appears closer than a circle on the horizon.
_____ 30. Size	B. The angle from which an object is seen.
_____ 31. Placement	C. What perspective drawing is based on.
_____ 32. Detail	D. When one shape covers part of another shape and appears to be closer.
_____ 33. Color	E. Bright seems closer, dull seems further away.
_____ 34. Converging lines	F. When one shape is larger than another and appears closer.
_____ 35. Point of view	G. Shapes with sharp edges and visible detail appear closer.

Chapter 7: Color

Chapter Test

Part I. Completion

DIRECTIONS: Complete the sentences by writing the correct words in the blanks at the left.

_____   1. A color's _____ is located directly opposite it on the color wheel.

_____   2. _____ are finely ground colored powders.

_____   3. _____ are colored powders that dissolve in liquid and color by staining.

_____   4. _____ is the property of color concerned with the amount of light a surface reflects.

_____   5. A _____ is a color with black added to it.

_____   6. The property concerned with the brightness or dullness of a hue is _____.

_____   7. Plans for organizing colors are called _____. (Two words)

_____   8. _____ colors sit side by side on the color wheel and have a common hue.

_____   9. The strongest contrast of hue is produced by atmospheric conditions or unusual lighting.

_____   10. _____ colors tend to move toward the viewer and include red, orange, and yellow.

_____   11. _____ color is a true color changed by atmospheric conditions or unusual lighting.

_____   12. _____ refers to letting one color dominate a work even though other colors may be present.

_____   13. A _____ color scheme is one in which tints and shades of only one color are used.

_____   14. A pure hue is called a _____ color in terms of brightness or dullness.

_____   15. Black, white, and gray reflect only a certain amount of light. They are called _____ colors.

_____   16. _____ pigments are brighter and more permanent than their natural counterparts.

_____   17. The _____ is the membrane of nerve tissue at the back of the eye that receives light waves.

(Continued on next page)

_____ 18. A color _____ is made up of three colors spaced equally distant from each other on the color wheel.

_____ 19. An opposite image caused by your eyes after viewing an object is called an _____.

_____ 20. Colors such as blue, green, and violet that seem to move away from you are known as _____ colors.

_____ 21. _____ means one color.

_____ 22. The material used to carry pigment in art media is called a _____.

_____ 23. An _____ color is used to express meaning and is not a realistic color.

_____ 24. _____ is the name of a spectral color.

_____ 25. A _____ is the combination of one hue and the hues on each side of its complement. (Two words)

_____ 26. A painting with many light values is considered _____.

_____ 27. A _____ is any color with white added.

Part II. Color Wheel

DIRECTIONS: Write the names of the primary, secondary, and intermediate colors in their proper places on the color wheel.

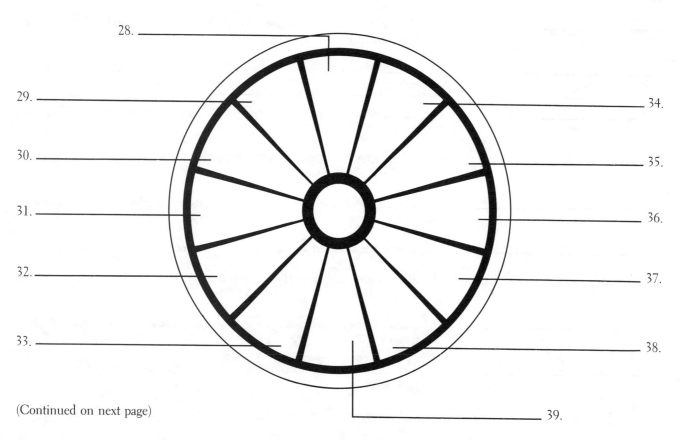

28. _____
29. _____
30. _____
31. _____
32. _____
33. _____
34. _____
35. _____
36. _____
37. _____
38. _____
39. _____

(Continued on next page)

Name _____

Date _____

DIRECTIONS: Below are the three secondary colors. List the two primary colors that make them up in the spaces provided.

40. Orange
_____
_____

41. Green
_____
_____

42. Violet
_____
_____

Part III. Color Schemes

DIRECTIONS: Write the complement for each color in the blanks below.

43. red _____

44. orange _____

45. violet _____

46. yellow-green_____

47. red-orange _____

DIRECTIONS: Which colors would combine with those given below to form split-complements?

48. red-orange _____ + _____

49. blue _____ + _____

50. yellow _____ + _____

Chapter 8: Texture

Chapter Test

DIRECTIONS: Complete the sentences by writing the correct words in the blanks at the left.

_____ 1. A ____ is a work made by pasting various two-dimensional materials onto a surface.

_____ 2. A ____ surface reflects so much bright light that it seems to glow.

_____ 3. ____ texture is the illusion of a three-dimensional surface by repeating lines or shapes.

_____ 4. ____ is a technique for producing random textures in paint.

_____ 5. ____ is the element of art that refers to how things feel or how they look as if they would feel.

_____ 6. ____ textures imitate real textures.

_____ 7. A ____ surface reflects a soft, dull light.

_____ 8. A ____ texture reflects light evenly.

_____ 9. ____ means scratching into wet paint with a variety of tools.

_____ 10. An ____ is a three-dimensional collage.

_____ 11. A ____ surface reflects light unevenly.

_____ 12. If you lay a paint-covered canvas over a texture and rub across it, the technique is called ____.

_____ 13. ____ textures imitate real textures.

_____ 14. ____ used thick applications of paint to create actual textures in his paintings.

_____ 15. ____ painted young people with healthy, glowing complexions.

_____ 16. ____ is French for "fool the eye."

_____ 17. ____ used frottage, grattage, and decalcomania to create fantasy paintings.

_____ 18. John Singleton Copley, Rembrandt, and Jan Vermeer were experts in the use of ____ texture.

(Continued on next page)

_____   19. Stucco, brick, wood, stone, cement, metal, and glass are materials used by ____ to create interesting surfaces for buildings.

_____   20. In the days when realism was the goal of art, texture was used to ____ reality.

Chapter 9: Rhythm and Movement

Chapter Test

Part I. Completion

DIRECTIONS: Complete the sentences by writing the correct words in the blanks at the left.

_____ 1. A motif repeated in no apparent order with no regular spaces creates ____ rhythm.

_____ 2. A ____ is a regular arrangement of parallel lines.

_____ 3. A ____ rhythm is created by the repetition of wavy lines.

_____ 4. A three-dimensional motif is called a ____ in sculpture and architecture.

_____ 5. The unit repeated in visual rhythm is called a ____.

_____ 6. ____ rhythm has identical motifs and equal amounts of space.

_____ 7. To create a ____ rhythm, the motif must be changed every time it is repeated.

_____ 8. ____ is a two-dimensional, decorative surface quality that is repeated.

_____ 9. ____ rhythm occurs when a second motif is introduced, some change is made in the placement or content of the original motif, or changes are made in the spaces between the motifs.

_____ 10. ____ is the indication of movement by the repetition of elements.

_____ 11. Works of art that move in currents of air are called ____. (Two words)

_____ 12. All rhythms have a pattern; not all ____ have rhythm.

(Continued on next page)

Part II. Matching

DIRECTIONS: Match the clues in the left-hand column with the types of rhythm in the right-hand column. Write the correct letters in the blanks at the left. Some letters may be used more than once.

	Clues	Types of Rhythm
_____	13. A row of cans in a grocery store.	A. Random
_____	14. Rush-hour commuters.	B. Flowing
_____	15. A checkerboard.	C. Progressive
_____	16. Bricks in a house.	D. Regular
_____	17. Surface of a river.	E. Alternating
_____	18. The gradual change of a circle into an octogon.	
_____	19. Members of a baseball team in uniform.	
_____	20. A flag blowing in the wind.	

Chapter 10: Balance

Chapter Test

Part I. Completion

DIRECTIONS: Complete the following sentences by writing the correct words in the blanks to the left.

_____   1. _____ balance involves balancing unlike objects.

_____   2. _____ is concerned with equalizing forces.

_____   3. Symmetry is a type of _____ balance.

_____   4. If something has _____, this means it attracts the eye. (Two words)

_____   5. _____ has the stability of symmetry but is usually more interesting because of slight variations. (Two words)

_____   6. _____ balance occurs when items with equal weight are placed on opposite sides of a central axis.

_____   7. _____ balance occurs when the visual elements move out from a central point.

_____   8. _____ is a special type of formal balance in which one side of a design is a mirror image of the other.

_____   9. _____ symmetry is used to describe the arrangement of the human body.

_____   10. A central _____ is a dividing line that works like the point of balance on a scale.

(Continued on next page)

Part II. Matching

DIRECTIONS: Match the arrangements in the left-hand column with the type of balance in the right-hand column. Write the correct letters in the blanks at the left. Letters may be used more than once.

Arrangements

Types of Balance

A. Symmetry
B. Formal balance
C. Radial balance
D. Informal balance
E. Approximate symmetry

_____ 11. Petals on a dandelion

_____ 12. A teapot next to several cups

_____ 13. Rays of light from a star

_____ 14. A basket of flowers with a candlestick on each side

_____ 15. A red cube next to two blue cubes

_____ 16. The body of a snake

_____ 17. A large, plain box next to a tangle of yarn

_____ 18. The face of a clock

_____ 19. Two identical chairs on either side of a chest of drawers

_____ 20. A pine tree

Chapter 11: Proportion

Chapter Test

Part I. Completion

DIRECTIONS: Complete the sentences by writing the correct answers in the blanks at the left.

_____ 1. _____ is a technique used to determine proportions in which you use your arm and a pencil as a measuring device.

_____ 2. _____ is a principle of art concerned with the relationship of one part of a work to the others.

_____ 3. _____ and distortion are two devices used to change real proportions to create expression in an artwork.

_____ 4. _____ refers to several sculptural methods involving the use of newspaper and liquid paste. (Two words)

_____ 5. A _____ is a mathematical way to show a comparison of sizes.

_____ 6. The _____ was a ratio developed by Euclid. (Two words)

_____ 7. _____ is a term used to describe a large and imposing artwork.

_____ 8. _____ refers to the size of an object as measured against a standard reference.

_____ 9. The Roman writer who set down ratios for human proportion was _____.

_____ 10. The length of the _____ is the unit used to define proportion when drawing people.

_____ 11. During the Renaissance the _____ was called the Divine Proportion. (Two words)

_____ 12. The adult figure is _____ heads tall.

_____ 13. An infant is _____ heads long.

_____ 14. To the Greeks the most pleasing shape was thought to be the _____. (Two words)

_____ 15. Marisol was supposed to belong to the _____ art style.

_____ 16. The shape of the human head in front is an _____.

_____ 17. In art, proportion is concerned less with function than with an ideal of _____.

(Continued on next page)

_____ 18. The first Greek philosopher to use mathematics to describe the universe was ____.

_____ 19. ____ can be used to emphasize rank in a painting.

_____ 20. Greek artists portrayed ____ forms rather than reality.

Chapter 12: Variety, Emphasis, and Unity

Chapter Test

DIRECTIONS: Complete the sentences by writing the correct word in the blank at the left.

_____   1. When you relieve the sameness or monotony in a work, you use ____.

_____   2. When you make one part of a work dominant over other parts, you add ____.

_____   3. Elements that are less important than others in a work are called ____.

_____   4. The most important element in a work is called the ____ one.

_____   5. When one area in a work is emphasized, this area is called the ____. (Two words)

_____   6-10. Name the five ways that emphasis can be created in a work.

_____   7.

_____   8.

_____   9.

_____   10.

_____   11. ____ is the principle of design that allows you to see a complex combination of things as a complete whole.

_____   12. Agreement among the elements of a work is called ____.

_____   13. ____ in a work is achieved by limiting the number of variations.

_____   14-18. Name the five ways in which unity can be accomplished in a work.

_____   15.

_____   16.

_____   17.

_____   18.

_____   19. What was Winslow Homer's favorite subject to paint?

_____   20. What new watercolor technique did Winslow Homer develop?